DISCOVERING
SANDS POINT
ITS HISTORY,
ITS PEOPLE, ITS PLACES

by Joan Gay Kent

Front Cover Picture: This painting of the Old Mott House (c. 1715), rendered in 1869, is by W. R. Miller of New York City. Both steam and sail boats cruise the Hempstead Harbor below the homestead. The painting is owned by Richard Fraser, a direct descendent of the original builder, and his wife Fay. *(Photo by Will Wright)*

Inside Front Cover Map: This illustrated historic sites map was created by professional artist Donald Ross in 1975. A Port Washington native, he was living with his wife Marie (nee Dodge) at the time in her old family home—the 1721 Thomas Dodge House—on the Mill Pond. *(Courtesy, Cow Neck Historical Society)*

Many people and institutions helped make this book possible, from the present mayor and trustees—Leonard Wurzel and Edward A. K. Adler, Eugene Luntey, Daniel Scheyer and Katharine Ullman—to Mary Backus Rankin and Harriet Backus Todd, granddaughters of James Lees Laidlaw, the first mayor of Sands Point.

Residents and former residents (see bibliography) shared their memories in personal interviews. George Bergman and others shared their Sands Point pasts in earlier memoirs for the Port Washington Public Library's Oral History Project. Peter Fraser produced a treasure trove of family photos and historical vignettes, as did Marcia and Jay Forman and Katharine Ullman. Fay and Richard Fraser of Flower Hill helped us untangle complicated family relationships. Ann and Vincent Mai graciously let us take extensive photos both inside and outside their historic home, the oldest in Sands Point. Mina Weiner made sure that the dedicated people from Sands Point who served as trustees for Union Free School District Number 4 were enumerated. Marian and Ed Goodman shared memories of their friend and neighbor Averill Harriman.

Village Clerk Linda Mitchell and her staff (Colleen O'Neill, Mary Ellen Bromberg, Bonnie Trinchitella, Joanne Peterson and Randy Bond Ginsberg) cheerfully acceded to my every request for information and saw to it that copies of the manuscript were delivered to board members and other volunteers. Manuscript readers included Village Historian Irmgard Carras, whose field of study is Colonial history; my sister Janet Gay Hawkins, the family proofreader; and Jay Forman, writer of historical novels. Former resident Bruce Shroyer provided expertise on the formation of the Civic Association. Harvey Levine shared the joy of coming of age in Sands Point during the '40s and his knowledge of Sands Point today, plus his skill with a red pencil as a proofreader.

Archival material was found in many places. The Port Washington Public Library's Local History Collection, the Bryant Library (Roslyn), the Cow Neck Peninsula Historical Society, the Long Island Studies Institute at Hofstra University and Nassau County's Garvies Point Museum in Glen Cove were all sources of valuable information. The Historical Society's Witmer collection provided some splendid views of turn-of-the-century Sands Point. The Village Club office had extensive photo files of recent events. The Methodist Church and Community Synagogue both dipped into their photo files at our behest. Eleanor Kurz had saved all of the Civic Association newsletters for the 1980s and Elaine Wurzel had the Community Synagogue's 25th Anniversary Journal. Ed Adler supplied the locally famous photo of the Dorsey Brothers at the Sands Point Bath Club.

The Sands Point Village records were an important source for the later chapters. Especially helpful was "The Study of Historic Resources," done for the Landmarks Commission in 1996, and copies of the Sands Point Civic Association and official Village newsletters for the 1990s. Sands Point Police Chief John Montalto had a rare Village book, the meticulously hand-written log book of the police department for 1929.

Copy Editor Joan Wheeler and Indexer Lee Sender provided efficient, professional services and many useful suggestions. Will Wright took many of the contemporary photos.

In addition to the people mentioned above, many others who heard of this work-in-progress stepped forward with anecdotes and information. Their names appear in the text as the source of quotations or on photo credits. My thanks to all who provided information, encouragement or assistance, especially Mayor Leonard Wurzel and the Village trustees, who were supportive from the very beginning of this project.

Though only 4.2 square miles in area, Sands Point has a colorful and varied history. During its evolution from Indian hunting ground to a prosperous farm community, through the great estates era to the affluent family-centered residential community of today, the Village has reflected the growth and development of the country as a whole. Unlike most local histories, *Discovering Sands Point* recognizes this and touches upon the highlights of national and world history that particularly affected this Gold Coast enclave.

This year, 2000, marks the 90th anniversary of the incorporation of the Village of Sands Point and perhaps (because no one knows for certain) the 360th year since the first white settler pulled a boat ashore on one of its sandy beaches. So this seemed an appropriate time to make the fascinating history of Sands Point, as well as the Cow Neck Peninsula of which it is a part, readily available to Sands Point families and interested students and historians.

Our author has gone back to original documents wherever possible, dipped into a number of local and regional published sources, and interviewed numerous longtime residents. Some of the illustrations in the book are photographs taken a century ago; others were taken expressly for this book during the past 18 months. Many came from family albums and private collections. All tell the story of our Village.

Sands Point has been home to heroes and villains, thinkers and doers, politicians and performers, people of accomplishment and mettle. The Sands Point Village Board is proud of the Village it serves, as its residents are too, we believe. We are also proud of the people who served the Village in the past and helped to make it the kind of place it is. We hope that *Discovering Sands Point* will give you a better understanding of why we feel that way.

Leonard Wurzel, Mayor
Incorporated Village of Sands Point
July 2000

NOTES FROM THE AUTHOR

INCLUDING AN EXPLANATION OF CREATIVE SPELLING AND POLITICAL CORRECTNESS

If you find that a favorite Sands Point historical figure, celebrity or community leader has been left out, please bear with me. I have tried to include as many people as possible, choosing Sands Pointers who were, or are, representative of their era, occupation or avocation. I selected others for the impact they had on the Village. However, I am sure that some worthy persons were inadvertently omitted.

I was equally frustrated trying to cover every significant event as well as adhering to a self-imposed cut-off date of December 31, 1999. Whether I satisfied the first goal is doubtful—and I know I did not achieve the second, as I continued to work into early 2000, adding new information to the narrative.

If you think that my computer lacks a spellchecker, rest assured, it is there and fully functioning. However, during the Colonial era there were few schools and most of the population was either illiterate or just barely literate. Hence, creative spelling was the order of the day. I have quoted the old records exactly as they were written, overriding the objections of my high-tech machine. Also, when more than one version of a family name has been used—i.e., Cornwall, Cornwell, Cornell—I selected the one that seemed to be most commonly employed.

As to the name of the first people to live in North America, I have settled on "American Indian" or "Indian," which seems to be preferred by most modern scholars as well as the population thus designated.

I am most grateful to the Board of Trustees of the Village of Sands for giving me the opportunity to have a fascinating time exploring Sands Point's past and present, and I hope that readers enjoy *Discovering Sands Point* as much I enjoyed writing it. I came away with a better understanding of Sands Point—its history, its people and its places, and hope that you will, too.

Joan Gay Kent
Port Washington, NY
July 2000

TABLE OF CONTENTS

Maps

    Mayors, Incorporated Village of Sands Point, 1910-2000
    Police Chiefs, 1928-2000
    Village Clerks, 1963-2000
    Presidents, Sands Point Civic Association, 1971-2000
    Presidents, Sands Point Garden Club, 1950-2000
    Presidents, Harbor Acres Property Owners Association, 1952-2000

CHAPTER 1

BEFORE 1650
FIRST FOOTPRINTS ON LONG ISLAND:
THE INDIANS AND THE DUTCH

We don't know the identity of the first European to set foot on Cow Neck or even catch a glimpse when sailing by, but historians are fairly certain that the first white person to set foot on what later became Long Island was either Captain Henry Hudson or one of his 18-man crew. The Dutch ship *Half Moon* dropped anchor off the "sands of Coney Island" on September 3, 1609, and a crew member wrote in his journal that the natives welcomed the voyagers: "They seemed very glad of our coming and brought green tobacco and gave us of it for knives and beads."

Nobody has definitive evidence as to when the first Indians arrived. Most authorities agree that the people who occupied North America before the Europeans came to the Western Hemisphere from Asia via the Bering Strait in a series of migrations, starting around 12,000 years ago. (Some experts think it might have been earlier—perhaps between 15,000 and 40,000 years ago.) From Alaska, the nomads spread to the east and south. Successive migrations brought a variety of native languages, with Algonquian dialects prevailing along the northeast coast of North America. Genetics produced common physical attributes among the many tribes — Mongol features, coarse straight black hair, dark eyes, sparse body hair.

THE FORMATION OF LONG ISLAND: GLACIAL ORIGINS

Ten thousand years before the arrival of the first Paleo-Indians, the great glacier that covered most of North America retreated from Long Island.

The signing of the Treaty of August 29, 1645, which ended the Indian wars in New Amsterdam. (Steel engraving, probably late 19th century. Courtesy, Cow Neck Historical Society)

It left behind an elevated central spine, North and South forks in a fishtail shape, rocks and sand that had been scooped up as the glacier advanced, and "kettle hole" lakes (Lakes Ronkonkoma and Success are the largest examples).

It took a long time for Long Island to become a true island. It was finally accomplished some 11,000 years ago, as warming temperatures accelerated glacial melt and rising seas separated the island from the mainland. The warming trend also brought about a change in vegetation; the Arctic tundra disappeared and was replaced by pine trees and, later, hardwoods. Unfortunately, there are few plant and animal fossils— the damp Long Island climate does not lend itself to preservation. The geological history of the land enjoyed by the Indian visitors is revealed in the strata of the sand pits on West Shore Road in Port Washington. Years of digging up fine sand, used in making concrete for Manhattan's skyscrapers and sidewalks, has revealed many clues to the geological upheavals of the past. The bottom layers are of bedrock from a series of continental collisions that began 450 million years ago. This was covered by sandy sediment deposited by streams running from the eroding Appalachians. The final layer of sand, sometimes mixed with large boulders, was deposited by the retreat of the last glacier.

17TH CENTURY ENVIRONMENT

The attractions of the Cow Neck Peninsula, which those very early Americans called Sint Sink (place of large stones), were numerous in the early 17th century. Rolling hills covered with tall oak trees and other hardwoods sloped to the sandy shores. Streams ran down to the bays where unpolluted waters teemed with fish. Clams, oysters, mussels, lobsters and scallops thrived. Deer lived in the woods, as did a number of wolves.

The wolves proved a problem for the early European settlers. A 1640's entry in the Town of Hempstead Records stated, "Thomas Langdon haveing killed ten wolves shall be paid by rate to be levyed against the towne...if anyman kill wolves accidentally and if he kill not ye number of ten he is to have noe pay...." Muskrat, fox and raccoon scouted the edges of the wetlands. Waterfowl floated offshore or settled down on the many small fresh water ponds that dotted the landscape. Gulls soared overhead. Song birds nested in trees at the edges of woodlands.

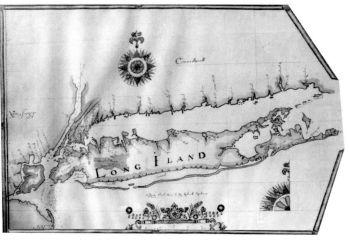

Map of Long Island drawn in 1675 by Robert Ryder. The familiar fishtail shape is apparent. The original is at Brown University. (Reproduction courtesy, Cow Neck Historical Society)

WHAT THE INDIANS FOUND

There is little doubt that members of the Algonquian Nation lived on Cow Neck. Bits and pieces of the Indians' lives, literally buried in the sands of time, have been found in excavations throughout the peninsula.

Though definite evidence, from caches of pottery shards and tools to written 17th century records, show that Indians lived along the north shore of Long Island, there is sparse evidence that Indians lived on the Cow Neck peninsula in any number. However, substantial evidence indicates that they spent time nearby; pottery fragments and stone implements were discovered in a 1946 archeological dig at Shelter Rock in Manhasset and in exploratory studies of the wooded areas of the Sands Point Village Club. (The late Otto Buerger, organizer of the Half Moon Beach Nature Conservancy, told of unearthing arrowheads when planting shrubs around his Sands Point Road home.) Most historians believe the Indians used the attractive Cow Neck area as summer hunting and fishing

grounds, retreating in the blustery winter months to the interior and its straight trails, such as the one that grew to become Jericho Turnpike.

The recent "Draft Environmental Impact Statement, Village Club of Sands Point Proposed Master Plan" offers some fascinating glimpses into the past. Many of the 208 acres that comprise The Village Club were never cultivated extensively. The acreage, which for generations was Mott and Dodge family fields and orchards, later served as the country estate of tycoon Solomon Guggenheim and then as a conference center for the IBM Corporation. About 80 acres were heavily wooded at the time the Village purchased the property and may never have felt the cut of a plow. At one site, not far from Motts Point, "prehistoric pottery shards, a Fishtail projectile point, a gorge and two hearths" were recovered, the Impact statement says. A nearby site "embraced several shell heaps and a burial place." Another may have been the last dwelling spot of the Sachem Tackapausha, who, back in the mid-1640s, sold a big chunk of what is now Nassau County to the early English settlers.

The men and women who made the pottery, fish hooks and arrowheads weren't "red men." That erroneous designation probably stemmed from the early Dutch and English settlers' first sight of the natives' faces painted with ocher for a ceremonial occasion. The color of their skins was actually in the brown family, ranging from tan to dark brown. A seventeenth-century document found in the Royal Library at the

Photo above: Fragments of a clay vessel, found in the Port Washington area, that would have been used for carrying water or storing food. On display at the Gravies Point Museum in Glen Cove, Long Island. (Photo by Will Wright at Garvies Point Museum)

Arrowheads like these, called Wading River Points, have been found in Sands Point. (Photo by Will Wright at Garvies Point Museum)

Hague described the Natives as, "of ordinary stature, strong, broad shouldered and olive color." Yet, the use of "red" as a descriptive adjective for Native Americans continued well into the 20th century. A scholarly piece, *History of the Sachem Tackapausha*, published by the Town of North Hempstead in 1977, refers to the "life styles of the Redmen and Whites of Colonial North Hempstead."

A PEEK AT THE DISTANT PAST

One way to get a good idea of what the Indians and early Europeans saw when they first viewed the delights of Cow Neck is to walk the nature trails at Sands Point Preserve (formerly the Howard Gould, then the Daniel Guggenheim, estate) or stroll the wooded areas at the Village Club. Herbert Mills, Bureau Head, Nassau County Museums and Preserves, and Martin Garille, Museum Supervisor, Sands Point Preserve, reported on a Village Club walk in the woods in 1994: "The entire parcel is dominated by large, mature trees with a dense under story of smaller trees, shrubs, vines and herbaceous plants....The species composition in the valley is unusual, if not unique, on Long Island, with over 80 large specimens of Black Walnut trees dominating the woodland." Moving to the west, "the species composition of the large trees changes to an assemblage more typical of the North Shore. Tulip Tree, Red Maple, Oaks (Black, Northern, Red and White), Bitternut Hickory, Black Birch, Black Cherry, Black Locust and Sassafras are most common with scattered examples of Sugar Maple, Norway Maple and Pignut Hickory, Cherry and White Ash." The undergrowth included such native plants as poison ivy, blackberry, wild grape, wild lettuce and the non-native but ubiquitous multiflora rose. Opossum, red and gray squirrels, woodchuck, gray and red fox, raccoon, striped skunk, long and short tail weasel are among the "mammals whose range may encompass the area of the Village Club of Sands Point," and according to studies, woodcock, wild turkey, grouse and quail might have lurked at the edge of the woods. If you want to see what the north shore bluffs looked like before they retreated in front of the 19th-century sand miners' shovels, just sail by Hempstead House, which sits tall on a 100-foot bluff overlooking Hempstead Harbor.

Collecting "Indian Paint Pots" has been a Cow Neck hobby since the first Native Americans arrived. These iron oxide concretions of stone and clay are often found along the shores of Hempstead Harbor and Long Island Sound. These hollow hemispheres may have been used as ready-made pots for mixing ceremonial face paint. Largest pot shown is 3-1/2" long. (Collection of Katharine Ullman, Photo by John Schaub)

THE FIRST LONG ISLANDERS

Little but place names remains to remind us of the 6,500 Indians who are said to have lived on Long Island at the time of the first European settlement. Descendants of the once-important Matinecock group, which dominated the north shore of western Long Island, are scattered throughout Queens, Nassau and Suffolk. About 300 Indians, some of mixed race, live on the Shinnecock reservation near Southampton.

What were these early Long Islanders like? Journals of the time describe them as peaceful,

Illustration by Myrna Turtletaub.

trusting, and untutored in the ways of caucasians who appeared almost magically on their shores. They certainly weren't natives of the Indian sub-continent, despite the misnomer established—seemingly for all time—by the explorer Christopher Columbus, who thought he had arrived at the outer reaches of the Indies when he landed at a small island in the Bahamas on October 10, 1492.

LOOSE TRIBAL SYSTEM

Silos Wood, an early Long Island historian, identified 13 tribes in 1824, and this 13-tribe myth, taught as fact to generations of Long Island school children, gained credence through constant repetition. The basis for Wood's statement is a little vague, but it seems that he accepted place names such as Masapeqgue and Manhasset as "tribal" names. Other writers relying on secondary sources picked up and embellished on Wood's conclusions.

According to the most recent investigators, such as John A. Strong, author of *The Algonquian Peoples of Long Island from Earliest Times to 1700*, there was no tribal system on Long Island when the whites first arrived. He writes: "The tribal systems which developed later did so in response to the pressures from the expanding European communities." When we do count tribes (actually loose affiliations of villages), four is the most likely number, says Stone, who summarizes:

The primary documents make it quite clear that there were no tribal systems on Long Island prior to the sporadic series of raids known as

Wigwams of the Long Island Indians were conical in shape, made by bending branches or saplings and covering the structure with layers of bark or thatch. (Photo by Will Wright at Garvies Point Museum)

Algonquian Indians of Long Island did not build light and graceful birch bark canoes, as their northern relatives did, simply because there were no birch trees available this far south. Instead, they fashioned dugouts from tulip trees, laboriously hollowing out the trunks using controlled burning and primitive stone tools. (Photo by Will Wright at Garvies Point Museum)

Governor Kieft's War (1640-1645), which resulted in the deaths of more than one thousand Native Americans and a few dozen whites. After 1650, tribal systems emerged among the Montauketts, Shinnecocks, and Matinecocks. A similar structure developed at Poospatuck after the reservation was established in 1700 for the Unkechaugs and the remnants of several western Long Island groups. These social adoptions, imposed to manipulate and control, were later turned into mechanisms for group survival by the Algonquians themselves.

However, the 17th-century Dutch document casts doubts over Strong's theory. It says of the Indians, "they dwell together mostly of friendship, in tribes over which commands a chief who is generally called Sackema possessing not much authority and little advantage, unless in their dances and other ceremonies."

Though the Cow Neck Peninsula was largely the province of the Matinecocks, the generally friendly relations between Long Island's Indian villages meant that members of other groups visited the area frequently, paddling along the shore from the east or followed twisting paths through the woods. They all spoke the parent Algonquian language.

PROBLEMS OF COMMUNICATION

The transfer by Indians of large holdings for very little money—the legendary purchase of Manhattan for $24

The arrival of a Dutch trader at a Long Island Indian village. A wigwam is on the left. (Museum diorama photo by Will Wright at Garvies Point Museum)

being the best known example—was basically the result of ignorance on the part of the Native Americans, who really didn't understand the concept of land ownership, and greed and deception on the part of the newcomers. Long Island historian Dr. Myron Luke points out that, "in virtually all land sales, peace treaties and other agreements, Indian leaders, such as Tackapausha, who could neither read nor write English, signed with their marks." A civilization that had no written language could not comprehend contracts, deeds and treaties. And, unfortunately, recording the terms of those transactions was in the hands of white officials who had a vested interest in such matters as terms of purchase, boundaries and locations. Spoken language presented a problem, too; the Long Island Indians spoke only Algonquian. (Further north, the Indians spoke Iroquois.) The Dutch and the English spoke only Dutch and English with very few exceptions. However, things improved when the Rev. John Eliot, who arrived in Connecticut in the early 17th century, decided to learn the Indian language. Fortunately, Eliot met a Montauk youth named Cockenoe, who had been captured by raiding mainland warriors and bound out to a farmer in Connecticut. Cockenoe's master taught him English and the boy, in turn, helped Eliot learn the Indians' language. Returning to Long Island, Cockenoe served as interpreter and helped arrange land deals and settle boundary disputes. Many of his fellow Indians also learned to speak English, and some to read it. But by then, despite their new skills, they had little land left to protect.

THE DUTCH TRADERS

The first white men to arrive in Cow Neck were Dutch hunters and trappers bent on amassing wealth and then returning to live in style in the prosperous and progressive Netherlands. Although Hudson failed to find the "Northwest Passage" to the Orient, the Dutch viewed the lands he did find as rich sources of fur and other trade goods such as lumber and pitch. The Dutch government organized the Dutch West India Company in 1621 and gave it a 24-year monopoly on trade along the shores of the Americas as well as in the Atlantic Ocean south of the Tropic of Cancer.

The major Dutch settlements were New Amsterdam (on Manhattan Island) and Fort Orange (now Albany), about 150 miles north on the Hudson. Buildings in New Amsterdam followed the brick and stucco styles of the homeland, with stone from upstate sometimes used. Timber, which was plentiful, was the preferred building material for Long Island houses, which were built long and low. The front door was always divided, its upper half lighted by two round glasses called bulls-eyes. (Two-fold "Dutch" doors can be seen on Cow Neck today at the c. 1721 Thomas Dodge House, 58 Harbor Road, Port Washington.) The trade of fur—especially mink and beaver—rather than homesteading was the company's primary concern. Farming developed slowly; along the Hudson, fear of hostile natives kept settlers close to the

Thomas Dodge House (c. 1721) at the head of the Mill Pond in Port Washington, taken in 1870 when it looked much the same as the day it was completed. Though the builders were of English stock, the house is typical of the homes built by Dutch families in Cow Neck. (Courtesy, Nassau County Museum Collection, Institute for Long Island Studies at Hofstra)

The old Thomas Dodge House has many of its original details intact, including two Dutch-style divided doors. The simple design was ingenious; it kept children in and livestock out while letting fresh air and light reach the interior. (Photo by John Meehan. Courtesy, Town of North Hempstead)

forts. But the more peaceful attitude of the Long Island Indians allowed the Dutch to spread out to Brooklyn, Queens and further into Long Island. Tobacco and cotton were among the crops grown here.

DUTCH SETTLERS: THEIR EARLY INFLUENCE

Although not one of Sands Point's historic Landmark Houses is said to have been built by a Dutch family, the Dutch nevertheless played an important role in the early days of Cow Neck, intermarrying with such families as the Sands and the Dodges and producing grandchildren who were active in the cause of independence. The names Luyster and Monfort (Monfoort), Onderdonk, Bogart, Schenck, Nostrand and Remsen are threaded repeatedly throughout the history of Long Island, especially in regard to the Town of North Hempstead. Cow Neck attendees at the Provincial Convention, called in 1775, included Adrian and Peter Onderdonck and Martin Schenck. Adrian later became the first supervisor of the Town of North Hempstead (1783-1785) after it separated from Hempstead. Adrian was probably born in his father's Flower Hill home, near the small cemetery (extant) at the junction of Port Washington Boulevard and Country Club Drive. He is buried in Monfort Cemetery in Port Washington, along with other early Dutch landowners. Peter was one of the first teachers in the community. Another brother, Hendrick, lived in Roslyn, where he built a paper mill.

THE DUTCH MAKE THEIR MARK

As time passed, the Dutch and English families living in and around Cow Neck intermarried. Thomas Dodge II, for instance, married Sarah Onderdonck in 1749. His grandson was Henry Onderdonck Dodge (1805-1895); Henry's sisters Maria and Martha were, respectively, the first and second wife of W. R. Remsen of Great Neck. Henry's other sister, Sarah, married Joel Davis.

The Dutch were still around in 1906, as the Beers and Comstock atlas shows. Mrs. E. E. Van Nostrand owned property on Sands Point Road near the Tibbits House. Miss Van Wyck owned property in Flower Hill that went down to Hempstead Harbor. The Monforts still held onto their property. Tunis B. Davis, son of Joel Davis, owned a big parcel that later became the Davis and Richard Roads area of Port Washington. Henry Remsen Tibbits owned the old Benjamin Sands House, now a Sands Point Village Landmark. However, a land-holding Dutch family disappeared from Cow Neck when Peter Luyster Bogart sold 276 acres bordering Hempstead Harbor in 1873 for the burgeoning sand mining operations.

THEN THE DUTCH LOSE OUT

While the Dutch had a head start in establishing themselves along the Hudson and on Long Island, they didn't hold their lead. They had money and talent and enthusiasm, but most Dutch citizens were happy at home in Europe and had little incentive to abandon their good life for one on a rough frontier (some, such as Peter Stuyvesant, remained in New York after the British conquest, probably because they had acquired large New World land holdings).

The Dutch Governors, from Peter Minuit to Peter Stuyvesant, who lost New Amsterdam in 1664, did not have the resources to manage properly the amount of territory they were expected to govern.

The governors in the New World also had to deal with the often uninformed decisions of the company directors back in old Amsterdam. And the directors were not always wise in their choice of New World governors.

While official Dutch eyes were focused on the Hudson Valley, English settlers began to infiltrate Long Island. When the Dutch finally began to pay attention to the island, the Algonquian tribes resorted to murder and arson in retaliation for previous Dutch attacks.

NO BRITISH NEED APPLY

Minuit, who became governor in 1626, was reasonably competent. Known for negotiating America's most famous bargain, the purchase of Manhattan Island, he also strengthened the fortifications of New Amsterdam. The next governor, Van Twiller (1633-1638), was a heavy drinker and a quarrelsome fellow who, nevertheless, helped settle Long Island by granting several land patents to both the Dutch and English. Appointed in 1638, William Kieft mismanaged tribal affairs to such an extent that the result was a four-year war with the Mohawks, primarily in Westchester and Connecticut. Concurrently, Kieft tried to stem the tide of English settlers coming to Long Island. In 1640, he ordered his troops to chase away Lieutenant Daniel Howe and a group of Englishmen from Lynn, Massachusetts, who had landed at the head of Schout's Bay (now Manhasset Bay). That group, which had not previously asked the Dutch for permission to settle, got back aboard its small boats and sailed along the north shore to settle in present-day Southampton.

The next Englishmen to come to Cow Neck were a bit smarter. When Robert Forman, John Carman, and their party arrived at Hempstead Harbor from Stamford, Connecticut, in 1643 and subsequently purchased the land that comprises the present Towns of Hempstead and North Hempstead from the natives, they secured a confirmation of purchase from Governor Kieft. Military hero Peter Stuyvesant replaced Kieft in 1647 and remained in office as governor for 17 years, despite constant complaints about his autocratic rule.

THE ENGLISH BECOME RESTLESS

Settlers on Long Island who desired the same civil and political rights as residents of New Amsterdam began to issue petitions and hold meetings. The still all-powerful Dutch West India Company sent orders to Stuyvesant to divide governance with the British and establish boundaries within Connecticut and Long Island. New Netherlands retained the territory on Long Island containing the five Dutch settlements west of a line drawn from Oyster Bay to the ocean. But

that didn't settle all the complaints. Traders wanted lower taxes. Long Island towns such as Hempstead, which had copied the New England system of autonomous church congregations and cooperative land holding, wanted more say in managing their affairs. In 1653, rebellious citizens of Flushing demanded union with England.

While Stuyvesant contended with the stubborn, hardworking, determined English settlers in the Dutch territories, the English King Charles II and his advisers turned their greedy eyes on New Amsterdam. In 1664, Charles awarded his brother, the Duke of York and Albany, "all the land from the West side of Connecticut River to the East Side of De la Ware Bay," and dispatched four warships to seize it. That action brought about Stuyvesant's reluctant capitulation. The terms of surrender granted full property and inheritance rights to the Dutch on Long Island and up the Hudson. (The English recognized productive citizens when they saw them.)

LEADERS IN A NEW LAND

As the population of Long Island grew, the Dutch strengthened the Dutch Reformed Church in Manhattan, Brooklyn and Flushing and founded new congregations in Manhasset and Brookville. Dutch settlers established some of the first schools in the new world. (The first school on Long Island was established in 1661 in Brooklyn.) They were landholders and merchants, community leaders and government officials. Dutch names are still visible in towns such as Remsenburg in Suffolk County. There's Onderdonck Avenue in Manhasset, Vandeventer and Bogart Avenues in Port Washington, Remsen Avenue in Roslyn and Schenck Avenue in Great Neck. The Van Wyck expressway is a major Long Island artery. In Sands Point, the only place names that acknowledge the Dutch are Half Moon Lane and Half Moon Bay, named either for their geographical shape or the famed ship of explorer Henry Hudson.

The c. 1695 barn on the grounds of the Cow Neck Historical Society's Sands-Willets House property, and the Thomas Dodge house, c. 1721, both in Port Washington, were built in the Dutch style. The barn started its life on land once owned by pioneer Samuel Sands and was donated to the Historical Society in 1982 by Dana Backus, son-in-law of James Laidlaw,

Dismantled and moved from Sands Point, this 17th century Dutch barn was reassembled on the grounds of the Cow Neck Historical Society at 336 Port Washington Boulevard in 1978. The Historical Society property was once the home of Revolutionary war hero Col. John Sands IV. (Courtesy, Cow Neck Historical Society)

the first mayor of Sands Point. It was taken apart, moved piece by piece, and reconstructed on the Society's grounds at 336 Port Washington Boulevard.

One reason that Dutch families have disappeared from Cow Neck appears to be that they "daughtered out" of the Dutch surname. For example, Supervisor Remsen and his businessman brother each had two daughters. Marie Dodge Ross, an Onderdonck descendant, died childless in 1998. Martha Knowles, who owns a local funeral home, is a Monfort. Local real estate broker Louise Hutchinson is a Hegeman.

AN INDIAN PRESENCE REMAINS

The fate of Native American families on Long Island was not as happy as that of the Dutch. A smallpox epidemic swept east from Montauk in 1658, afflicting the entire island. In the course of its two-year rampage, the disease killed nearly two-thirds of the native population despite stringent efforts to control the spread of the epidemic by limiting movement of the

Indians. By the end of the scourge, the native population had been reduced to around 1,000. Other diseases brought by the Europeans took their toll, and the introduction of alcohol didn't improve their health.

By 1700, there weren't many Indians left to visit Cow Neck. However, a small map of the Baxter property on the shores of Manhasset Bay, dated 1748 (which now hangs on a wall of the Cow Neck Peninsula Historical Society's Sands-Willets House), delineates the boundaries of the early Long Island farm in typical fashion with trees, brook, pond—and a small structure that looks like the horizontal half of a giant basketball. That building is a wigwam, the type of shelter made from tree branch and bark that was used by Indians throughout the northeast.

Intermarriage between blacks and Native Americans and the imposition of English as the language of trade and commerce led many Native Americans to abandon their language and dialects. However, contrary to beliefs of the press, which had been announcing the demise of "the last full-blooded Long Island Indian" since c. 1879, Native American culture on Long Island is still alive. The Shinnecocks sponsor an annual festival at their Southampton Reservation and are in the process of reconstructing their language. The Matinecocks and Montauketts have had a more difficult time maintaining old traditions, as they are scattered across the island. Nevertheless, groups such as the Matinecock Longhouse organizations in Nassau and western Suffolk perform many of the traditional ceremonies. Some of the groups have started a movement to reclaim their land. (Sands Pointers need not worry. The focus seems to be further east!)

While there is no visible evidence of the Native Americans who once were an important presence on Cow Neck, there are cultural reminders. Indian place names abound in neighboring communities. Our children play the Indian game of Lacrosse. The Town of North Hempstead's logo proudly displays the head of a long-vanished Chief. The Sachem Tackapusha is believed to have spent his last days in the Sands Point area. His remains may well lie not far from those of the white men who took it all away.

CHAPTER 2

1650-1750
THE FIRST FAMILIES OF SANDS POINT:
ENGLISH SETTLERS CLEAR THE LAND

One thing that must always be remembered about the history of Sands Point is that, in the colonial era and well beyond, the present-day villages of Sands Point, Port Washington, Flower Hill, Manhasset, Roslyn, and Plandome did not exist. It was all just Cow Neck, an inviting, wooded peninsula jutting out into Long Island Sound. Very few people lived there. In 1647, there were 62 freeholders in the Town of Hempstead. Assuming each represented a family of five, that meant a white population of around 300 plus a sprinkling of Indians. In 1710, when the Gate Rights map was drawn, there were probably no more than 600-700 men, women, children, servants and slaves in all of Cow Neck. In 1790, the earliest year for which we have figures, 2,696 people lived in all of North Hempstead.

As time went on and more people arrived, various places in Cow Neck took on names—often those of the first people to settle there, such as Motts Point, Sands Point and Barkers Point. Most of those early settlers were New Englanders who came to Long Island, with its religiously tolerant Dutch government, to escape restrictive New England Puritanism. The early Cow Neck property holders were strong-willed,

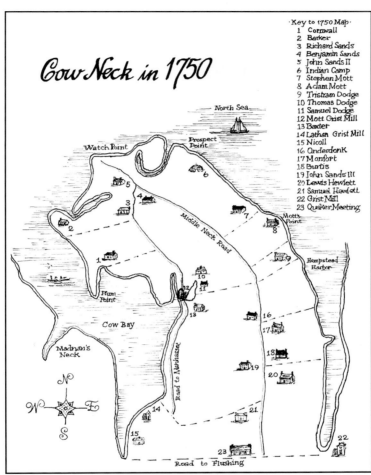

Cow Neck in 1750

Key to 1750 Map
1 Cornwall
2 Barker
3 Richard Sands
4 Benjamin Sands
5 John Sands II
6 Indian Camp
7 Stephen Mott
8 Adam Mott
9 Tristram Dodge
10 Thomas Dodge
11 Samuel Dodge
12 Mott Grist Mill
13 Baxter
14 Lathan Grist Mill
15 Nicoll
16 Onderdonk
17 Monfort
18 Burtis
19 John Sands III
20 Lewis Hewlett
21 Samuel Hewlett
22 Grist Mill
23 Quaker Meeting

industrious and independent-minded men and women. Most were farmers who raised cattle and planted orchards. Some, such as the Sands and Cornwalls, became rich shipbuilders and real estate investors. A few belonged to the Dutch Reformed Church, many to the Episcopal Church, and some descendants were soldiers in the War for Independence, the War of 1812, the Civil War. Some were men of peace who "fought" for abolition and helped slaves escape to freedom. The women worked hard in their roles as farmers' wives. Some ventured beyond their hearths and farmyards to take leadership roles in community activities and social movements.

COW COUNTRY

The Cornwalls were probably the first Europeans to actually build a house (c. 1676) on the peninsula, but not the first to live on the land. That distinction goes to the cattle pastured here in the second half of the 17th century. Town Records show the number of cows at 306 in June of 1657; the largest amount belonged to John Simons, who had 30. Cattle played a dominant role in the economy of the settlers, so keeping tabs on them was important. The first

The Cornwall House from the rear in 1999. The low section on the left was built around 1676 on land granted to John Cornwall by the British king. It was nearly destroyed by irate Hempstead townsmen who thought the family was trespassing on their communal pasture lands. (Photo by Will Wright)

recorded edict of the Town of Hempstead, dated "May ye 2d Anno 1654 stilo novo," directs that "all Ye Inhabitants that hath any rights to ye neck shall sufficiently make up Ether his or there proportion of fence at or before ye 16th day of May next Insuing ye date hereof, stilo novo. And every person or persons that is founde Negligent in soe doeing shall pay every rod defective twoe shillings and sixpence."

Pasturing cattle on Cow Neck began soon after Forman and Carman arrived at Hempstead Harbor in 1643 with their party of 30 men and women. The newcomers established farms on the flat and grassy Hempstead plains and pastured their cattle on the hilly, well-watered Cow Neck peninsula. As directed by the Town Board, each farmer built one "gate" per animal that he grazed on the public grounds. The result was a fence running from the tip of Manhasset Bay to the tip of Hempstead Harbor, roughly along the route of today's Northern Boulevard.

SETTLING IN

The Hempstead farmers regarded the Cow Neck pastures as their personal property. Unfortunately, the British governors thought it was theirs, and began awarding patents to friends, colleagues and other worthies. Tired of Indian attacks on white settlers in Rhode Island, John Cornwall I (which is also spelled Cornell and Cornwell) and his wife Mary moved down to Long Island in 1676 and settled on land on the northwest side of the peninsula between the area

now called Plum Point and the Soundview-Manhasset Isle areas of Port Washington fronting on Manhasset Bay, which was granted to him by Governor Andros. Their reception was not a welcome one. Cornwall, who had received his original patent of 116 acres from the crown in 1683, proceeded to build a frame house near the shore. Hempstead Town freeholders, who had cattle grazing rights to Cow Neck, were unhappy with the intrusion. Banding together, they voted to tear down the Cornwall house, a move duly noted in the Town Records: "At a Jenerall Meting Held in Hempstead by the maJer Part of those ho had Right on the Cow Neck the 14 day of October In the yeare 1676. It was fully agreed on and Concluded by them who had Right on the said Neck that they should all of them do down to the Cow Neck and Pull downe the billding that Cornwell had set up there. Nathaniell Pearell, Clarek." The righteous Hempstead men, disguised as Indians, tore down the house and set fire to the ruins (a recent discovery by the present owners revealed ancient charred beams under a plasterboard ceiling). The culprits were found guilty at a jury trial and fined for the damage they had done. After the judge in the Court of Assizes ruled that the Cornwalls had the right to settle in Cow Neck, they rebuilt their house on the same site.

The Town fathers were still having trouble over "squatters" in Cow Neck five years later. This time, they chose not to resort to force and turned to the courts instead. "At a Jenerll Town meeting Held in Hempstead the 28 day of November in the year 1681 it was Concluded by the MaJer Vote of the town that they would sue those Parsons at the Next Cort of seshons for trespasass that have settled them selfes on our land on the Cow Neck."

A MAP TO SOLVE DISPUTES

By 1695, the Town Board came to the conclusion that the grazing lands of Cow Neck could no longer be treated as common pasture; the time had come to parcel out the land. John Sands of Cow Neck and Jonathan Smith were authorized to tackle the task. The area contained 8,000 acres, some owned by British patentees. Each Gate entitled its builder to approximately 20 acres of land. The rest were apportioned amongst the fence builders.

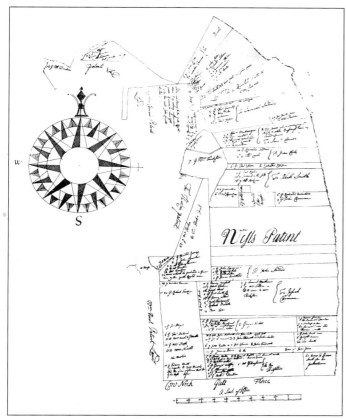

Copy of the original Gate Rights Map of 1709, drawn by Samuel Clowes, Surveyer. The Land on Cow Neck was divided among the men according to the number of "Gates," or lengths of fencing, which they had contributed when the peninsula was fenced in for three miles from Hempstead Harbor to Manhasset Bay, along what is now Route 25A. (Courtesy, Cow Neck Historical Society)

Most of the 61 Gate builders were assigned parcels of 120 to 200 acres, depending on the number of Gates they had built. The Gate owners were allotted long, narrow parcels running roughly from the present-day Middle Neck Road down to Hempstead Harbor. That way, each had access to Long Island Sound, which was so vital to transportation and communication. Most of the property acquired through royal patent, such as that of the Cornwalls and John, Benjamin and Samuel Sands, was located at the end of Sands Point and fronted on the Sound or Manhasset Bay. The map based on this apportionment was used by Town Clerk Thomas Dodge to settle disputes about property lines. It was stuffed into saddle bags, folded and unfolded many times as needs dictated to settle boundary disputes. By 1745, a copy was required, and the Town Board authorized Surveyor Samuel Willis to make one. This copy was used in 1910 to settle a dispute about the ownership of Bar Beach. The original is in the hands of the Cow Neck Historical Society. This map is important not simply because it is still in existence, but also because of the specific information it provides us about 17th and 18th century property owners and the role that the map played in preventing further acrimonious incidents.

THE CORNWALLS

The Cornwall family, which started the Town in the map-making business, grew and prospered. The original John (1647-1704) and Mary had six children. One of them, Mary, married neighbor James Sands; all four brothers, Caleb, Richard, Joshua and John I, owned shipyards. A fourth-generation Cornwall, another John, was also a successful shipbuilder; with his siblings, he supported the fight for independence. John's son, Hewlett Cornwall (1750-1828), served in the American Revolution in the regiment of Colonel John Sands, his cousin.

Some historians have claimed that the original Cornwall house is not the one at the end of Cornwall Lane, but a dwelling that once stood near the present intersection of Cow Neck Road and Sands Point Road. This conjecture makes sense in terms of the location of the family cemetery (now under the care of the Town of North Hempstead) on Cow Neck Road near Soundview Drive, and the location of the old Cornwall slave quarters on land bordering what is now Manorhaven Boulevard, not far from Sands Point

With the exception of the electric light fixture in the ceiling, this room in the oldest part of the Cornwall House looks much as it must have back when it was built c. 1696. The large fireplace was used both for cooking and heating purposes. (Photo by Will Wright)

Early Long Islanders lived hard lives and faced facts head-on. A skull and cross bones was a sometime gravestone adornment. The inscription on this monument at Sands Burying Ground reads, "Here lies buried the body of Mrs. Sybil Thorne, Wife of Mr. Stephen Thorne, Daughter of Mr. Edward and Mrs. Mary Sands. Died March 1759, aged 32 years." (Photo by Will Wright)

Road. However, the recent discovery by Ann and Vincent Mai of charred beams in the oldest section of their home at 48 Cornwall Lane, Sands Point, seems to substantiate the claim that their dwelling is the very first Cornwall house. The house in which the Mais live is a landmark to small-boat sailors and a splendid example of the commodious Long Island farmhouse once prevalent on the north shore. The major portion of the house was built in the mid-19th century. Kenneth Cornwall, a tenth-generation descendant writing in 1976, described the old section of the house: "The wing contains the kitchen, dining room, and three bedrooms, with a Dutch oven in the basement, and a great open fireplace on the main floor, still remains as originally built."

Later owners of the house, which the family called "Cornwallton," included Major Clarence Eagle, who commanded Port Washington's Home Guard during World War I; John Tibby of *Sports Illustrated* magazine; and Dr. and Mrs. Waldemar Herman. The house is a designated Village Landmark and listed on the National Register of Historic Places. John I and Mary Cornwall are said to be buried on the land that was theirs, but no record has been found as to where that is. Many of their descendants rest in the little cemetery by the side of Cow Neck Road: August Cornwall (1791-1840); Joshua Cornwall (1760-1822); Charles W. Cornwall (1802-1824); his mother, Elizabeth Willis Cornwall (1759-1844); Hewlett Cornwall; and several others, with the most recent known burial in 1868. Maintenance of the long-neglected Cornwall Cemetery was taken over by the Town of North Hempstead in the early 1960s. Unfortunately, an excess of housekeeping zeal led to the destruction or disappearance of several of these early gravestones.

WHY IT IS CALLED SANDS POINT

The large Sands Family Burying Ground, off Sands Point Road near the intersection with Middle Neck Road, also suffered the inroads of time. But thanks to the diligent research of the late Constance Bowen, a Sands family descendant, the names and antecedents of those interred from 1704 to 1867 (a total of 112) have been duly recorded and preserved for students and scholars as well today's Sands, none of whom live nearby.

The Sands who settled on Cow Neck trace their lineage back to Archbishop Edwin Sandys of England. They seem to have been an adventurous lot. The first one here, John Sands I (1649-1712), was a grandson of the Archbishop. John moved to Cow Neck from Block Island with his wife, Catherine Guthrie, in 1691. John was the son of James Sands (1622-1695) who came from Reading, Berkshire County, England, in 1642. James married Sarah Walker in Portsmouth, Rhode Island, in 1645. After what appears to have been 15 years of active participation in Portsmouth community life, James joined a group in purchasing Block Island from its Native American owners, obtaining a one-sixth share of the small island. He had seven children, five of whom settled on Long Island's north shore: John, Sarah, Samuel, James in Sands Point and Edward in Oyster Bay.

John I was a prosperous sea captain with a sheep farm back on Block Island when he first dropped anchor off Watch Hill, as the tip of Cow Neck was

This Sands House at 336 Port Washington Boulevard was built around 1735 by either John Sands II or John Sands III on property the family named Inland Farm, to distinguish it from their original Home Farm in Sands Point. The barn, which dates back to the early 1700s, was moved in 1978 from Sands Point to its present location. (Courtesy, Cow Neck Historical Society)

called then. Obviously, he had to build a house somewhere, but it is unlikely that the present Sands House, which sits serenely on the edge of the wetlands at 195 Sands Point Road, was his. The majority of local historians believe that house was probably built by John's grandson, Richard Sands (1729-1798), who acquired the land on which it sits on the death of his father in 1746. Richard, a prominent Quaker, probably built the house shortly thereafter. Early on, John Sands I owned 700 acres at Watch Hill. The house that was most likely John's is at 210 Sands Point Road, looking west over the wetlands. With its low ceilings and many fireplaces, the brown-shingled house exemplifies the New England influence on early Long Island houses. John is credited with introducing locust trees to Long Island from Virginia. The sturdy locust, which has tall straight trunks that were prized for making ships' masts, has flourished in Sands Point ever since.

Upon John's death in 1712, his Sands Point property, known as Home Farm, went to his son Nathaniel Sands (1686-1750). The Inland Farm property in the middle of Cow Neck went to his eldest son, John Sands II. Later, John II bought half of Nathaniel's property and acquired the old family home out on the point. He and his wife moved back to that

home and turned over the Inland Farm to his son John Sands III, whose greatest accomplishment was fathering seven sons who fought for independence. The Sands family held onto the Inland Farm until about 1840, when it was sold to Edmund Willets, a Quaker and leader in the abolition movement, who renamed it Homewood.

When John Sands II died in 1763, the Home Farm in Sands Point was given to his younger brother Benjamin, who had the misfortune to be a British prisoner of war during the Revolution. Benjamin sold it in 1800 to his son-in-law, Benjamin Hewlett (who, ironically, came from a family of devout Loyalists). The old house left Sands-Hewlett hands in 1852 when it was sold to Hall Jackson Tibbits (1797-1872), a clipper ship captain. The Tibbits family held onto it until 1959, when it was sold to Mr. and Mrs. Chandler L. Mackey. In the early 1990s, Jim and Sally Miller purchased the property and restored the old house and out-buildings to be as much like the originals as they could ascertain.

While John and Nathaniel Sands did well for themselves, Samuel Sands II (1690-1724), who inherited considerable land from his father, was not as fortunate. At one time, Samuel I owned a farm on Block Island in addition to the approximately 500 acres adjoining the Sands Point property of Captain John and another 200-acre property fronting on Middle Neck Road. The latter was sold to Richbell Mott of Madnan's Neck (Great Neck) in 1712.

NOTHING NEW ABOUT CATCH-22

There was a catch to Samuel II's inheritance: He had to provide for the other bequests in his father's will, such as dowries for his two unmarried sisters plus an annuity for his mother. Apparently, he ran up considerable debts in attempting to carry this out. One of his problems was being land rich—he owned a great many acres, but those he inherited from his father were entailed to go on his death to his eldest son and therefore could not be sold. In 1748, Samuel II petitioned the courts for permission to sell land in order to pay his debts, and was allowed to dispose of 200 acres. He was also allowed to transfer some land to two of his children. Ten years later, the hapless Samuel, with the agreement of his children, sold off the rest of his land to Stephen Thorn. The children arranged an annuity for their father; Thorn was to hold the purchase price, doling out the interest annually to Samuel. Upon his death, the capital was divided among the children.

Thomas Dodge house (c. 1721) interior shows original beams and fireplace with adjacent storage cupboards, which could also be used to warm food or outdoor clothing. (Photo by John Meehan, Town of North Hempsteaad)

WHY IT'S CALLED MOTTS POINT

The original portion of the much-altered Mott House at the end of Old House Lane was built around 1715 by Richbell's brother, Adam Mott II (1672-1739), on a 500-acre farm fronting on Hempstead Harbor. Their father had come from Essex, England, and settled in Hempstead Town in 1655. Adam I, a builder of the Gate Rights fence, is said to have been one of the irate Gate holders who tore down John Cornwall's house in 1676—which does not seem typical behavior for a member of the Society of Friends!

One of 13 children, Adam Mott II did not marry until he was almost 60 years old. His bride was 32-year-old Phebe Willets (1699-1782), member of another important Quaker family. Their wedding certificate survives; it states, in part, that Adam Mott "took Phebe Willets by the hand. Did in solemn Manner openly Declare that he took her to be his wife promising to be a faithful and loving husband...." The witnesses included William Mott (Cow Neck) and Joseph Latham (Plandome). After Adam's death, Phebe married Tristram Dodge from the farm next door. The productive Dodge farm was divided

between his sons, Stephen (1726-1813) and Adam Mott III. Stephen built his own house north of the old Mott homestead; his family and descendants lived there until 1895, when it was sold to Alfred Fraser.

The old Adam Mott II house remained in family hands until Martha Mott Fraser sold it in the 1950s. The somewhat ramshackle building probably started as a two-room affair with a central fireplace for cooking and heating. Other rooms were added during the years, with nothing demolished or altered until the late 1980s, when the home fell victim to renovation fever. Today, it barely resembles the old place described in 1890 by Mott descendant Thomas C. Cornell as an "ancient, low beamed two-storied shingled house." Peter Fraser, a present day Sands Point resident, remembers that "The metal numbers 1715 were affixed onto the arch of the porch roof over the smaller of the two doors on the front of the house."

The oldest part of the home built by Samuel Mott in the early 18th century, before extensive alterations, was at one time the residence of publisher Max Schuster. (Shown here in 1979.) (Photo, Conni Koldewy. Courtesy, Cow Neck Historical Society.)

The divided "Dutch door" at the Stephen Mott house is surrounded by small windows to let light into the hallway of the 18th century structure. (Courtesy, Cow Neck Historical Society.)

It was Adam Mott IV who built one of Port Washington's first grist mills (c. 1750) on the shore of Manhasset Bay, near what was soon to be, and still is referred to as, the Mill Pond. Mott's mill, long unused, was torn down at the turn of the century. (Another mill was built by around 1795, probably by Caleb Cornwall.)

THE DODGES DISCOVER HEMPSTEAD HARBOR

When Marie Dodge Ross died in the fall of 1998 at the age of 90, she was the last direct descendant of a family who arrived in Cow Neck in beginning of the 18th century. Her first Long Island ancestors were Thomas (1684-1755) and Tristram Dodge III (d. 1760), whose grandfather Tristram I had landed in Salem, Massachusetts Bay Colony, in 1660 with his four sons (Tristram II, William, John and Israel). Tristram I joined Roger Williams in moving from Massachusetts to Rhode Island, and later settled on Block Island. Thomas and Tristram III came to Cow Neck in 1718. Although they arrived some 27 years after John Sands I, it is not unreasonable to believe they may have learned about the attractions of Cow Neck from a Sands family member visiting old friends and relations on Block Island.

Tristram Dodge III, second husband of Phebe Mott, built his home in 1719 on 79 acres on Hempstead Harbor that were originally purchased by his brother Thomas from Samuel Clowes, the surveyor. The imposing shorefront house at the end of Harbor Road is considerably larger today than the original 18th century farmer's home must have been. Tristram served as father to Phebe's three sons as well as his own, and managed both his farm and the Mott properties. Certainly solid accomplishments, but the person who put this generation of Motts on the historical map was Phebe. The daughter of a large and distinguished Quaker family, she was an active elder of the Society of Friends, traveled widely and spoke throughout England on behalf of the Quakers. She was one of the first in the area to free her slaves.

Upon the death of Tristram III, the farm passed to his son Joseph (d. 1809). Members of the Dodge family lived and worked on the land for more than 100 years, when it was sold to Richard Mott. Mott, in turn, sold it to Jesse Bunnell in 1880 for $17,000. (The piece of property was roughly the size of Harbor

The Tristram Dodge House, located on Hempstead Harbor near the present Harbor Acres Beach Pavilion, had a string of distinguished post-Dodge owners including Hedley Donovan, one-time editor in chief of Time. (Courtesy, Port Washington Public Library)

Acres.) The property took on new fame in 1887, when 300 acres were purchased by W. Bourke Cockran, a rich and famous Congressman and orator from New York's 12th District. He built his own mansion, mostly as a summer retreat, and used the Dodge House as a guest house.

DIVERSE OWNERS

The next owner, Vincent Astor, paid $1,500,000 in 1926 for the estate; he, too, used the old Dodge house for guests. Most of the land was sold off for development in the 1930s. The old house had the good fortune to become the home of Hedley Donovan, editor in chief of Time magazine, and his wife Dorothy, who lovingly restored its historic architectural details.

Tristram II's brother, Thomas Dodge, built his house in 1721 on a 200-acre farm that ran from Manhasset Bay back to the middle of the peninsula. The brown-shingled Dutch-style house remained in the Dodge family until 1995, when it, plus the remaining one acre of the original farm, were purchased by the Port Washington Water Pollution Control Board as a buffer zone. The appealing house and two-horse barn are now maintained as a community museum by the local historical society. The seven-foot ceilings remain, as do the hand-carved pegs holding the beams together. Prior to 1909, the only heat source in the house came from open hearth fireplaces in the two principal rooms. And this was the home of a prosperous farmer!

This 1994 photo of the upstairs hall of the Thomas Dodge House (c. 1721) shows the original construction with beams held together by wooden dowels. (Photo by John Meehan. Courtesy, Town of North Hempstead)

THE SANDS WHO WAS A SLAVE

Unlike the cemetery off Sands Point Road, which has been in the public eye one way or another since it was established, another small Sands plot exists that attracted little attention until publication of the Environmental Impact Statement, prepared in 1998 as part of the Master Plan for The Village Club of Sands Point. Tucked away in a remote part of The Village Club's 208 acres at the edge of a wooded terrace is a small cemetery, measuring approximately 25 square feet, containing three headstones and two footstones marking the graves of Elizabeth Griffen Sands, Margaret Sands and Cato Sands. (The Club property was owned in the 18th century by Samuel Sands.)

The grave of Cato Sands, who died in 1854, is located in a small cemetery in a remote part of The Village Club's 208 acres. He is believed to have been the son of a freed slave, also named Cato. (Photo by Katharine Ullman)

The exact identity of the Elizabeth and Margaret buried there is not clear; Cato, however, is most likely the son of an African slave, also named Cato, who was freed in the will of Simon Sands, a grandson of John Sands I, in 1782. After receiving his freedom, Cato lived for a time near Motts Point. Later family members lived in a little house, still standing, by the Mill Pond.

Slavery on Long Island, though present in the colonial era and early 19th century, never played a major role in the economy as it did in the South, where huge plantations required the labor of many people. Most farms here were small holdings tended by the family. However, large land owners such as the Cornwalls, Sands and Motts of Cow Neck might have owned up to 10 slaves at one time.

A GOOD PLACE TO LIVE

There was no air pollution, no water pollution, no red tide in the early years of European colonization. Wells were dug to a depth of just 20 feet, and fresh water streams and ponds were everywhere. A plentiful supply of fish and shellfish came from Long Island Sound. No one lived more than two miles from Manhasset Bay or Hempstead Harbor. If you had produce to sell, you sent it to the New York city markets by boat or wagon, or perhaps sailed across the Sound to Westchester or Connecticut. For the most part, early 18th century farmers (and that's what all Cow Neck settlers were, except for a few wealthy ship owners) were subsistence farmers, growing what they needed to survive and thrive in the potentially bountiful new world.

BOOKS AND BOOK LEARNING

Entertainment was entirely self-generated and education was sketchy. If your grandmother had some lessons in her youth and lived long enough to teach you the ABC's, you were lucky. Most adults in colonial Cow Neck were illiterate. While the Town of Huntington engaged its first schoolmaster in 1657 and the Southampton Town Meeting hired Jonas Holdsworth for 35 pounds a year in September 1663, Hempstead "was very backward in the matter," said Dorothy Freemont Grant, writing in the *Long Island Forum*. "Sons and grandsons of the original settlers could neither read nor write. By the time the third generation reached maturity, well over 70 percent of

Known today as the Sands-Hewlett-Tibbits House after the families who lived in it, the shingled farmhouse at 210 Sands Point Road is the one generally believed to have been the home of John Sands I, who acquired 500 acres in Sands Point in 1691. (Photo by Will Wright)

the population was illiterate." It was not until 1702 that the first school was established in this area. In 1704, Rev. John Thomas was sent to establish the Church of England in Hempstead. He, in turn, appointed Thomas Gildersleeve as schoolmaster, a position the teacher held for 26 years. Gildersleeve was paid 10 pounds a year by the Society for Propagating the Gospel in Foreign Parts and received five shillings per quarter per child from the parents of his students.

Few Cow Neck children attended his classes, for Hempstead was a good half-day ride away. Those who did probably boarded with friends or relatives in the village of Hempstead. With such sparse educational opportunities in 18th-century Long Island, it's easy to see why the Town of North Hempstead's Official Town Record uses "creative" spelling in its early pages!

DIFFICULTY ANSWERING THE CALL TO WORSHIP

Worshipping God was also a problem for early Cow Neck settlers, who had no access to religious institutions closer than New Amsterdam. After the close of the 17th century, members of the Church of England could take a horse and wagon on a long, bumpy, dusty or muddy trip of three or four hours to St. George's Episcopal Church in Hempstead. Methodists faced an equally bumpy trip to the Methodist Church in Searingtown. The Dutch, who wanted to worship in the language of their forebears, could make their way to Lake Success where the Dutch

Reformed Church had established a congregation in 1730. The Quakers had an easier time of it; the Friends Meeting House opened its doors in Manhasset in the early 18th century.

WHY WATERFRONT LOCATIONS WERE POPULAR

What kind of roads did our intrepid churchgoers and market-bound farmers put up with? The answers are: not very many and not very good. In a study of historical transportation, Sylvia Meyer painted a forbidding picture of the long and tangled routes used by late 17th- and early 18th-century Long Islanders to travel to market, church and government offices. The north shore route westward to the East River and the ferries to Manhattan ran around the wetlands and tidal creeks at Little Neck Bay, where they cut deeply into the land, forcing travelers to go south to Jamaica and then into Brooklyn. Going eastward, the road followed bays and skirted wetlands to Huntington and beyond. To take produce to New York, a farmer would ferry the goods on his own vessel or hire a neighbor to do so.

By 1704, the government realized something had to be done for the poor travel-weary Cow Neck landowners. It provided for each Long Island county—Kings, Queens and Suffolk—to have three commissioners whose assignment was to lay out a highway from the Brooklyn ferry to East Hampton.

This photo taken in 1959 of the basement area of the Sands-Hewlett-Tibbits House on Sands Point Road shows the hand-hewn beams and locust posts used in its construction during the early 1700s. (Courtesy, Port Washington Public Library)

The road to Hempstead Harbor from Sands Point looked like this, little changed from its 18th century beginnings, when it was photographed in 1907 by Port Washington's John Witmer. (Witmer Collection, Cow Neck Historical Society)

Meyer explains: "In Kings County the road laid out by the commissioners came down Fulton Street, crossed Bedford Avenue and extended out to New Lots. Along Atlantic Avenue it ran through Queens into Jamaica." Residents who wanted a new road had to apply to the highway commissioners. And they had to pay for it though assessments or labor. "Eventually a network of roads branched out of Jamaica connecting all sections of Brooklyn, Queens and Long Island. Many are major arteries to this day," Meyer adds.

Despite the poor roads and absence of churches, schools, newspapers and entertainment in the early years, Cow Neck had much to offer. The soil was rich, fresh water plentiful and the natives—what few there were—friendly. (One story claims that Indians helped John Sands II build his Inland Farm home.) The English had firm control of New Amsterdam; the Dutch were good neighbors. News and problems from abroad were three months away by ship. Cow Neck was a fine place to live, and descendants of early settlers can still be found in the area.

CHAPTER 3

1750-1800
SANDS POINT'S ROLE IN THE FIGHT FOR INDEPENDENCE

here were about 150 property owners in 1750, living in what became the Town of North Hempstead. The total population of families, servants and slaves amounted to approximately 1,200—and perhaps as many as 1,400. (Forty years later, the first year of recorded census data, 2,696 were listed as living in North Hempstead.) A very few of them, owners of large farms for the most part, lived in the northern end of Cow Neck. These included men such as John (1721-1797) and William (1721-1797) Cornwall, who owned 398 Sands Point acres between them, and John Sands II (1684-1763), who owned about 250 acres at

the time. John Sands' nephews, Henry, Edward and Richard, also owned Sands Point property. The stalwart Phebe Willets Mott Dodge lived with her second husband, Tristram Dodge III, on more than 500 acres bordering Hempstead Harbor. And Thomas Barker, as in Barker's Point, was another early landowner. They were a small group, but they made up for the lack of numbers with their energy, enthusiasm, ingenuity, resourcefulness and cooperation.

John Sands II also owned property to the south of Sands Point, as did the Hewletts and the Baxters. The largest holding in the area was over 600 acres owned by the Latham family in Plandome. (The main house

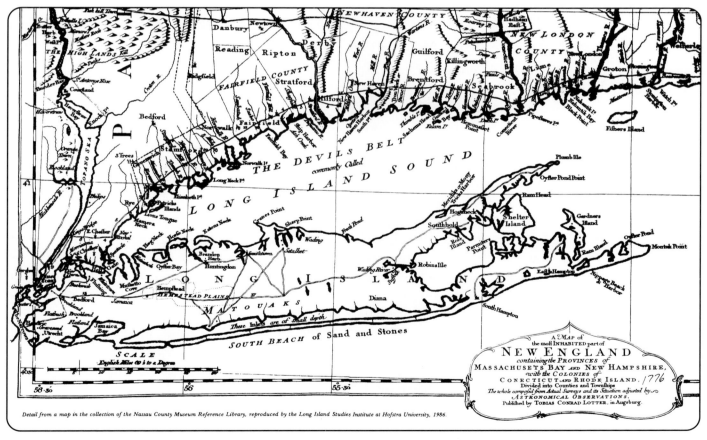

Detail from a map in the collection of the Nassau County Museum Reference Library, reproduced by the Long Island Studies Institute at Hofstra University, 1986.

Getting around during the Revolution wasn't easy due to a lack of roads (map presumably drawn c. 1776). The one road from New York ran from Brooklyn to Jamaica before dividing to go to Huntington and Hempstead. Apparently, Cow Neck did not amount to much in the eyes of the cartographer; there is no name on it. It's the peninsula above the "a" in Jamiaca. (Courtesy, Institute for Long Island Studies, Hofstra University)

The Sands family built houses all over Sands Point. This clapboard house is at 195 Sands Point. The oldest portion (left) is believed to have been erected by Richard Sands, grandson of John Sands I, around 1750. It was occupied by Hessian troops during the American Revolution. (Photo by Will Wright)

was called Plandome Manor by its builder, Matthias Nicoll, Mayor of New York City in 1674, who is credited with coining the name of "Plandome." The word came from the Latin *planus domus* meaning "plain" or "peaceful" home.)

When They Needed It, They Made It

Some of the Cornwalls were ship builders and some of the Sands were ship owners. All Cow Neck property holders farmed their land, sometimes with the aid of slaves. They grew corn, tobacco and flax, and maintained large orchards. They transported produce for sale in the New York City markets by sailing sloop and sometimes by wagon over roads that were little more than tracks. Life was fairly simple and, in some ways, truly primitive. Despite owning what would be seen today as a fortune in real estate, the early Sands Pointers lived in small houses with small rooms, low ceilings and few amenities. The houses were heated by wood fires, with wood cut from the owners' wood lots. Women spun flax and wool to make yarn that the neighborhood weaver made into cloth. The cloth, in turn, was sewn by women to make clothing—clothing that was worn until it was worn out. Food was whatever they could raise, shoot or catch. They put up vegetables for the winter, cooked for the men, tried to educate the children, and nursed the sick.

The Long Island colonial table featured shellfish, wild ducks, turkeys, geese and, occasionally, domestically raised beef, mutton and pork. Wild raspberries, strawberry, huckleberries and cranberries were plentiful in season. One popular dish was samp porridge, an Indian corn meal concoction adopted by the whites. In *Colonial Hempstead*, written in 1937, Bernice Schwartz gives elaborate directions for the labor-intensive preparation, which took all day. After the corn sat in wood ashes overnight, the husks were removed. The corn was then pounded in a hollowed-out tree stump with a 50-pound block of oak, rounded at one end, to make corn meal. The porridge was made by boiling the corn meal with water and salt pork or other meat in a large kettle. The resulting dish was said to improve on reheating.

Tea was gaining favor despite the cost, and the consumption of hard liquor, beer and wine continued to be nearly universal in the 1750s, for most people thought drinking water was unhealthy. (In many areas, it actually was safer to drink beer than water from streams and wells, which could so easily be contaminated by animal wastes.) Most people served spirits to visitors at all hours. Guests expected a "warm" welcome, even at 10 a.m. Men played whist, backgammon and dice in taverns and toasted their friends with grog or flip. Women and children entertained and drank at home.

Getting There Was <u>Not</u> Half the Fun

Despite the problems in traveling to church, services played an important role in the community and social life of Cow Neck settlers. In the early days, attending church meant a long trip to Hempstead or Flushing, where the nearest established congregations were located. After 1720, Quakers could go to the Meeting House in Manhasset. Because it took so long to get from place A to place B, roadside taverns were commonplace. There were three in Hempstead in the mid-18th century to serve the needs of those traveling to and from Flushing, and quite likely one in the Manhasset Valley.

Horse racing got men moving, too, both as spectators and participants. Men, women and children alike crowded into wagons and carriages for a day at the races, often held miles from home. This popular pastime owed its existence in this area to an expanse of flat land called Hempstead Plains. The first race course in the United States was established there in 1688 by

Governor Nicolson. By 1750, "a race engaged so much attention that over seventy chairs were brought across by ferry the day before and more were than a thousand horses were said to be on the grounds," Schwartz relates in her book. The exact location of that course has not been determined, but it's thought to have been somewhere in the area that now comprises Garden City and New Hyde Park. Other races were held in Jamaica, Newtown and Rockaway. Later, there was a race course in Cow Neck.

COMMUNICATION DIFFICULTIES

Because roads were hardly more than paths, travel by boat was preferable. A ferry north to Westchester is said to have been in operation prior to 1685. From their property on Hempstead Harbor, Tristram Dodge and his wife Phebe often sailed east to the opposite shore to make their way to the Matinecock Meeting house near Mosquito Cove (Glen Cove).

The population of Cow Neck, as in most of Hempstead, was close to illiterate for a long time. Teachers were scarce or non-existent. If you wanted your children to learn anything, you taught them yourself or sent them off to attend school and board in Hempstead or Flushing or Manhattan. The education light bulb went on for Cow Neck in 1748, when the first teacher was hired in response to this advertisement, which ran in the New York Mercury: "Thomas Dodge and Petrus Onderdonk want a man well qualified to teach school; on Cow Neck. He may be settled with reasonable support." Educational opportunities opened up for Cow Neck youngsters in 1757 when a school house opened in Flower Hill.

Tavern gossip was a welcome source of news about the outside world. Gossip, hearsay and an occasional letter from a friend in Boston or Philadelphia were the only ways people "heard" the news. No newspapers were

published in North Hempstead until 1846, when William H. Onderdonk of Manhasset founded the *North Hempstead Gazette.* The first New York City paper was established in 1725.

FRENCH AND INDIAN WAR

Though far from the battlefields, Cow Neck felt the effects of the sporadic French and Indian War (1756-1763). The conflict, a spillover of the Seven Years War in Europe, resulted from the perennial tug-of-war between England and France over who owned what lands and who could expand into which territories. Hostile Indians from northern tribes sided with the French and tried to recruit Long Island natives in rising up against white settlers.

One story relates that an Indian slave belonging to Samuel Sands was approached by a strange Indian who wanted to know how many white Englishmen were living on Cow Neck. The stranger, who claimed to be the son of the Sachem of Block Island, tried to recruit the local Indians for assistance. Nothing came of this plan, but after the loyal slave reported the incident to his master, you can be assured that muskets were stacked by doors and plenty of musket balls were cast. Another story tells of an English visitor from Rye who pulled his boat ashore and spied six strange Indians with painted faces darting into the woods. And a terrified Indian girl told of a strange Indian carrying two knives and a hatchet, who wanted to know how many houses were in Cow Neck. The white farmers combed the woods looking for signs of invaders but found nothing. Still, they must have been relieved when the war was over. The English had defeated the French and hostile Indians had returned to the Northern forests. Not only was the threat of Indian war over, but so was the need to supply food for men in the British troops.

This print of George Washington sitting awkwardly astride his horse was a British effort to belittle the American Commander in Chief. (Photo by Will Wright)

This print, published around 1870, shows George Washington directing his officers to "put none but Americans on guard tonight." Note the cannon and pile of cannon balls in the right-hand corner. (Courtesy, Janet and Harman Hawkins)

THE SEEDS OF REVOLUTION

It was during the French and Indian War that George Washington, serving as an aide to General Edward Braddock, began to develop strong anti-British sentiments. The arrogance of the British officers irked the young man from Virginia (he was 20 at the time he joined the militia). Washington opposed the Stamp Act of 1765 and became increasingly active in the Patriot cause. He was a delegate to the first Continental Congress in 1774 and became commander in Chief of the Continental Army, taking over on July 3, 1775, in Cambridge, Massachusetts. His appointment to this position was likely due to a combination of seven years' experience in the militia, success as a planter, and his commanding presence (Washington was over six feet tall at a time when most people were as much as 12 inches shorter). Washington is not known to have visited Sands Point, but many of its residents managed to meet him, spy for him, raise money for his military campaigns and serve in his army. The most famous were the seven Sands brothers, grandsons of early settler John Sands; all served in some capacity during the Revolution.

CAUSES FOR COMPLAINTS

The War for Independence didn't happen just because a group of men in Boston didn't want to pay new taxes on tea. It grew from many provocations. Over the protests of the colonists, the British government imposed one ill-advised new law after another to regulate trade and increase taxation. Particularly unpopular were the Writs of Assistance (1761), Sugar Act (1764), Currency Act (1764), Stamp Act (1765), Quartering Act (1765) and Duty Act (1767). Most annoying of all was the ban against settling beyond the Appalachian divide, which was imposed on the colonists as a money-saving measure. (The British were spending vast sums on wars with other European nations and could not afford to protect and govern more territory in the New World.) This did not sit well with the Americans, who coveted the forests and fertile plains on the other side of the mountains.

For years, the colonists had been treated with benign neglect, with the absentee government leaving them alone to run their own affairs. Now, however, seemingly without reason, restrictive steps were being taken. Colonists from Long Island to the western frontier were incensed. They already had reason enough to resent the British, who had billeted troops with area farmers for several winters. Though Cow Neck was a backwater of small farms and small merchants, the people knew what was happening in New England and the other colonies. The men made regular visits to the town seat in Hempstead and the markets in Manhattan, where they picked up news. Rumblings of discontent were also heard from visitors and read about in pamphlets and newspapers from other colonies

A TOWN DIVIDED

Long Islanders debated their next steps. The Town of Hempstead was about one-third Tory (loyal to the crown), one-third Whig (favoring independence) and one-third neutral with no desire for a visible part in the debate. Tories held sway in the southern part and Whigs dominated the north. Often, the individual's opinion was based not on ideology but on holding Royal appointments and overseas trading connections.

Grievances mounted. Then, in 1770, the British added fuel to the fire when several New Yorkers belonging to the Sons of Liberty were shot by a company of Britain's 16th Regulars. Irate citizens demonstrated in protest. Four years later, the New York Sons staged their own tea party. National leaders from all 13 colonies viewed independence from Great Britain as the only solution to their collective woes. On July 4, 1776, the Declaration of Independence was issued by the Continental Congress in Philadelphia. Written in eloquent language by Thomas Jefferson of Virginia, John Adams of Massachusetts, Benjamin Franklin of Pennsylvania, Robert R. Livingstone of New York, and Roger Sherman of Connecticut, the Declaration announced America's separation from Great Britain and presented a list of their grievances. Among the 55 men from the 13 former colonies signing the document, two were from Long Island— William Floyd from Mastic, in Suffolk, and Francis Lewis from western Queens

In Manhattan, Patriots protested by toppling a statue of King George III.

THE WAR BEGINS

Neither the British nor the Americans expected a long war or one that would envelop all of the colonies. However, the war did prove to be lengthy, arduous and particularly trying to Long Islanders, who suffered under British occupation from 1776 to 1783. Committees of Safety were proposed by the delegates

to the First Continental Congress in 1774 to help protect the colonists' assets. The first Committee of Safety was formed in October, 1774, by the Massachusetts Legislature. The Committees functioned throughout the Revolution and served important networking functions. Elected by counties and towns, the Committees soon became ad hoc local governments. They established militias and courts and formed provincial congresses. They suppressed Loyalist sentiment and watched the activities of all citizens. The Committees ceased to exist when state constitutions were adopted. (Richardson Sands, born on Cow Neck, was an agent for the Connecticut Committee of Safety.)

THE TOWN'S OWN DECLARATION OF INDEPENDENCE

Because most of Hempstead supported the crown, the Town officially pledged its allegiance to King George III. But the people of Cow Neck did not agree and formed a committee, led by Adrian Onderdonk, Martin Schenck, John Sands IV and Daniel Whitehead Kissam, to support the directives of the Continental Congress. In January 1775, the committee published a resolution supporting the Continental and Provincial Congresses.

The movement to spin off a separate Town of North Hempstead grew right along with the movement to create a new nation. North Hempstead issued its own declaration of independence from Hempstead Town on September 23, 1775. (The proposed town became a reality in 1784 after approval by the New York State Legislature.) The North Hempstead declaration said, in part:

"Resolved — That during the present controversy or so long as their general conduct is inimical to freedom, we will be no further considered as part of the township....in all matters relative to the Congressional Plan, we shall consider ourselves as an entire and separate and independent beat or district."

The declaration was sent to the Provincial Congress, whose members wrote the Cow Neck Committee that they "highly approve of their conduct therein." The Congress ordered the Declaration to be recorded on its books. One of history's minor mysteries is whether the original document still exists. It's not in the Town of North Hempstead archives (there was no Town of

North Hempstead then), which isn't surprising as it was directed to the state authorities. There must have been plenty of copies as it is reprinted in many early local historical works.

The document also listed those named to "be a committee for this beat or district"; almost all were Cow Neck residents (Daniel Kissam, Henry Stocker, William Thorne, Benjamin Sands, William Cornwall, John Cornwall, John Mitchell, Sen. John Burtess, Samuel Sands, Martin Schenck, Daniel Whitehead Kissam, Peter Onderdonk, Adrian Onderdonk and Thomas Dodge). Benjamin Sands was chosen chairman of the meeting and John Farmer, clerk. (The spelling of the names above and elsewhere in this book are as they appear in the document quoted. There were often several variations of one family name, i.e., Cornwall, Cornwell, Cornell; Burtess, Burtis; Hewlet, Hewlett, etc. Creative spelling prevailed in this era of limited schooling.)

COW NECK VOLUNTEERS

It was hard to entice men to enlist and hard to keep them once they did. Wartime discipline was difficult for men who were accustomed to working for and by themselves. Deserters, especially those with Loyalist sympathies, hid in swamps and woods and were hunted down by the militia. Fines were levied against militia men who failed to appear for monthly musters. When Thomas Wooley, a felt maker of Cow Neck, missed the monthly muster day, Captain John Sands seized a hat from Wooley's stock to pay the fine. Wooley turned up for the next meeting right on time but got into further trouble when he challenged Sands to a fight. He was arrested and hauled off to jail, and then released after a petition was presented saying that his offenses were more "from inadvertency than any design to offend."

BATTLE OF LONG ISLAND

War came home to Long Islanders when the British pulled out of Boston to concentrate their forces on strategically valuable New York. The Long Islanders' immediate concern was to keep their cattle (estimated at 100,000 head) and even more numerous sheep out of British hands. This led to a drive of livestock from Queens (including Cow Neck) to the eastern end of the island.

With the arrival of Lord Howe's fleet off the south shore of Brooklyn in 1776, the Loyalists of Hempstead Town actively began to provision them with fresh water, produce, meat and poultry. The Patriot forces retaliated by stepping up efforts to guard both the south and north shores. Colonel Sands, quartered in Westbury, ordered Lieutenant Jonathan Townsend to march with his troops to Matinecock Point (Oyster Bay Peninsula), set up camp and send an express rider to Westbury if the British were sighted. Sands directed his Uncle Simon to set a similar watch at Sands Point.

To rid Long Island of Tories, General Washington sent 1,000 troops to round up the leaders. Well-known Hempstead Town residents including Daniel Kissam, Samuel Clowes, Benjamin Lester, Dr. Samuel Martin, Charles Hicks, Benjamin and Stephen Hewlett, Isaac Smith, David Brooks, Joseph Gesewold, Dr. Adam Seabury, Samuel Lagdon, Whitehead Cornell and Richard Townsend were captured and exiled to Connecticut with their families.

Soon, more than 400 English ships carrying English guns and 31,000 well-trained British troops converged off Brooklyn, poised for attack on Manhattan. Washington had about 19,000 troops, mostly untrained and ill-equipped volunteers from the various colonies. Both sides sought control of Long Island and its plentiful supplies of timber, meat and produce. Both sides were determined to gain control of Manhattan and the Hudson River. The Americans fortified Manhattan and selected spots along the Brooklyn shore and waited.

The outcome of the Battle of Long Island was obvious before it began. On the morning of August 22, 1776, an impressive 15,000 British troops landed at Gravesend Bay in Brooklyn. One by one, American units were surrounded and captured. Among the American troops at the Battle of Long Island were 450 men from several militia units raised in Kings, Queens (which then included present-day Nassau) and Suffolk counties. As far as can be ascertained, they were never brought together to fight as a cohesive unit. The officers and men in the district of "Cow Neck, Great Neck" included Captain John Sands, First Lieutenant Thomas Mitchell, Second Lt. Aspinwall Cornwell and Ensign Andrew Onderdonk. Listed as sergeants were Richard Manes, William Hutchings, Joseph Akerly and William Hicks. Other troop members included

Cow Neckers Joshua Willis, Jonathan Mott, Henry Craft, W. Valentine, Elbert Hegeman, Daniel Kissam, William Dodge, Israel Baxter, John Allen, George Hewlett and Peter Monfort. There were four Sands and seven Cornwalls on the roster of about 140.

With 1,097 men taken prisoner, defeat was sure to follow—and it did. However, General George Washington, who was in charge of the American forces, planted the seeds of a future victory. Washington deceived British General Howe into laying siege to fortified defenses at Gowanus Heights as a diversion while 10,000 Continental troops retreated across the river to Manhattan, ferried by boats from Long Island and New England. Had the British triumph at the Battle of Long Island included the capture of those 10,000 men, the American army might well have been dissolved and American morale shattered. Following the battle, the Kings, Queens and Suffolk county militias were disbanded. Many members joined Washington's army on the mainland while more than 1,000 patriots and sympathizers fled to Connecticut to escape reprisals. Some of them became involved in guerrilla warfare, crossing Long Island Sound to raid British strongholds.

Long Island became occupied territory after Washington's withdrawal to Manhattan and remained so from August 1776 until the coming of peace in 1783. Long Islanders were forced to swear loyalty to the King and the majority did, for the penalties were stringent and most people just wanted to be neutral and avoid trouble. On the north shore, however, strong though surreptitious activity on behalf of the patriot cause continued.

THE WHALEBOAT RAIDERS

Long Islanders worked doggedly for their independence. Some joined Washington's army while others joined in whaleboat raids from across the Sound. Large-scale operations (50 to 100 men or so) against the British, sanctioned by the Continental Naval Militia, were carried out successfully from Sag Harbor to Lloyd's Neck. Smaller raids by one or two boats were more common (though not always with such a high purpose). Whaleboats were ideally suited to a quick sortie. Developed for off-shore whaling, the sturdy crafts were launched directly from the beach

The whaleboats in this lithograph by Gordon Grant were used for their intended purpose—catching whales. Their sturdy hulls and efficient design also made them popular with cross-Sound raiders during the war for independence. (Courtesy, Joan G. Kent)

into oncoming surf. The double-prow design made possible a hasty retreat from a whale's tail—or from a hostile musket. The boats could also be fitted with a single sail. These whaleboats usually carried six to eight men and a small cannon, but could hold more when the need dictated.

In an attack on the British encamped at Sag Harbor, American Lt. Colonel Jonathan Miegs brought 170 men in 13 whaleboats on May 23, 1777. The raiders burned 12 British ships, killed six men, and then packed 90 captives into their boats for the return trip across the Sound. The whole foray took 25 hours. Another notable whaleboat raid was led by Major Benjamin Tallmadge, an aide to George Washington, who sailed an 80-man contingent from Fairfield, Connecticut, to a spot called Old Man's (now Mount Sinai) on the north shore, and then marched across the island to capture and destroy the recently built Fort St. George in Mastic.

PLAGUED BY LOOTING

Not everyone from Cow Neck was on the side of George Washington, Colonel Sands and the angels. Whaleboat raiders lost their patriotic intent and resorted to looting and robbery. Any conveniently located, well-maintained house, barn or store became a target for raids that were motivated by greed, not service to an ideal. There were black marketeers (though the term had yet to be invented) as well.

Seemingly respectable citizens who publicly supported the American cause, they stole agricultural products from north shore farms or captured cargo on the way to market, and sold their hauls to the British in New York. They also smuggled imported British luxuries across the Sound to exiled Loyalists.

Popular history says that Cow Neck citizens watched from the top of the peninsula's highest peak, Beacon Hill, for British and Loyalist raiders. In reality, it was the British who used Beacon Hill, Harbor Hill in Roslyn, and other high ground along the north shore as sites for coded signal fires to relay news of hostile whaleboats. The citizens' greater fear was of outright marauders who attacked isolated homesteads in search of gold and silver. With no banks, no safe public storage of any kind and no way to invest, many owners of specie hid it and other valuables on their premises—under floor boards, up in haylofts, out in the fields, behind woodpiles. To most of the raiders, it made no difference if the homes were Whig or Tory or politically neutral. The British and renegade whaleboat raiders plundered the property of the Whigs (Sands, Cornwalls, Thornes, Onderdonks), the Tories (Baxters and Mitchells), plus the property of Benjamin Sands, chairman of the Sons of Liberty in the area. After the war, it is said, he dug up £800 buried in his cellar!

Citizens organized patrols to guard against raiders. Obviously, the Cow Neck patrols missed a few, as Henry Onderdonk recorded in *Revolutionary Incidents in Queens County*, published in 1846.

> *August 4, 1777: "Taken out of the pasture of Timothy Smith, Hempstead Harbor, a bay mare."*
>
> *September 12, 1777: "Two armed whaleboats from Middletown took two sloops, one at anchor in Cow Bay...."*
>
> *Oct. 20, 1777: "A whaleboat with 10 men from Byram River took a wood boat from Hempstead Harbor and returned for two others... but a few militia getting together, obliged them to row off with speed."*
>
> *May 25, 1778: "...a boat from Connecticut, with a 4 pounder, came to Sands Point and stripped a boat that lay there of all her sails and rigging."*

> *August 25. 1779: "A party of rebels under A. Cornell plundered the houses of Co. and Judge Ludlow at Hempstead Plains. They landed, it is supposed upwards of 50 men from seven whaleboats at the west side of Cow Neck."*
>
> *July 4, 1781: "On Saturday night last 40 rebels landed at the bottom of Cow Neck, 10 of whom marched four miles to the house of Justice Kissam."* [Near the present location of the Port Washington Yacht Club.]

Some households, such as Judge Onderdonk's, which was at the head of Roslyn Harbor and conveniently located for raiders, were robbed many times. Occasionally, civilians were killed or wounded. The teenage son of John Mitchell, whose home was near the present location of the Town of North Hempstead Dock, was one of them. When young Benjamin Mitchell and his father ran to the home of Cow Neck neighbor Israel Baxter for help, a robber seized the boy, dragged him outside and "shot him through the body with two balls," killing him on the spot. (The Baxter House stands at the corner of Central Drive and Shore Road in Port Washington.) Adam Mott II, whose Cow Neck house was close to the edge of Hempstead Harbor, was robbed several times by whaleboat men and mercenaries, both American and British, including Hessian soldiers stationed in Sands Point.

Once in a while, the good guys caught a bad guy. One of the latter was Barent Masters, a whaleboat raider taken prisoner in 1782. He is quoted by historian Henry Onderdonk, Jr. as saying: "I left Beekman Precinct in July, 1780, went to Long Island, and worked the farmers there, left Long Island six weeks ago; landed in Stamford and remained there five weeks; joined a whale boat crew, under John Hacksom of Long Island, consisting of John Thompson of Long Island; Townsend Hutchings of Cow Neck; and a man from Stamford. I went one trip with John Devore and six men; landed at Matinecock at the house of Avery Lawis; he was home; we got liquor; there was not plundering." The Quaker Richard Sands, who did not play an active part in the independence movement because of his beliefs, was another victim. His house, which faced Long Island Sound and often had small boats beached nearby, was an attractive and accessible

The oldest portion (low section on left) of this imposing house, shown in this c. 1875 photo, was the home of Captain, later Colonel, John Sands IV, one of Cow Neck's leading Revolutionary soldiers. Arms and ammunition were hidden from the British on his property and later smuggled to Washington's army by the Colonel's wife. (Courtesy, Cow Neck Peninsula Historical Society)

target. The former Sands home at 185 Sands Point road has a "secret" closet where the young ladies of the household hid from whaleboat raiders and plundering soldiers.

PATRIOTS RESIST

Some Cow Neck property owners hid munitions on their property, smuggling it to the Continental Army when opportunity presented itself. Naturally, this tended to take place at waterfront properties that opened onto the beach, with the contraband hidden in old wells or tunnels that had been built years earlier to circumvent British customs collectors from the port of New York.

While husbands, brothers and fathers were fighting with the Continental Army or leading raiding parties from Connecticut, the wives and mothers left behind kept the family farms going, protected the children, managed the servants and slaves, and helped the cause as best they could, with survival their priority. Some became actively involved. One of them, Nancy Strong from Oyster Bay, hung garments on her washline in a prearranged code to send signals for George Washington's intelligence network; another was Mrs. John Sands IV, the Colonel's wife.

SPIES IN SANDS POINT?

There is little information about the complex and efficient intelligence operation on the north shore of Long Island. Spies keep few records. It wasn't until 1930 that the identities of two spy masters, known as Culper, Sr., and Culper, Jr., were revealed to be Abraham Woodhull of Setauket and Robert Townsend of Oyster Bay, members of large and prominent Long Island families. These men, with their cohorts, supplied George Washington with a vast amount of useful information. Enlisting the aid of prominent Long Islanders, mostly from western Suffolk, they built an intelligence-gathering network that sent vital news of British plans and activities across the Sound or into the city, and eventually to General George Washington himself.

The names of those from Sands Point who aided the spy network are lost in unwritten history. However, in Morton Pennypacker's book, *George Washington's Spies*, there is mention that a fast way for couriers to get to Manhattan was to cross Cow Neck land. To evade the ever-present whaleboats on the Sound and their often piratical occupants, the relatively short trip from Stamford, Connecticut, to Cow Neck was favored over trips to more easterly harbors. The book also describes an elaborate plot to fool a British spy, starting with a whaleboat journey from Cow Neck.

FILLING THE WAR CHEST

Financing a war in a new and loosely organized nation, at a time when communication was slow and unsure, was not an easy task. The Continental Congress' initial efforts were badly conceived and ineptly executed. Both Congress and the states issued their own currency, redeemable in gold, but when the time came, the gold did not materialize. By 1780, a Continental bill was worth only one-fortieth of its specie value. Conditions changed after 1781 with the appointment of Robert Morris, a wealthy Philadelphian, as Superintendent of Finance. He cleaned up most of the mess, but he couldn't increase revenues. After all, people were fighting to get rid of taxes, not to create new ones! The State Legislature continued to meet and soon adopted a new state constitution. Still, financing the state government was difficult; many of the most prosperous citizens lived in occupied areas.

Governor Clinton looked for ways to go around the enemy lines and raise money from Long Islanders. Fortified with an introductory letter from the governor, prominent Whigs approached property owners of means who thought the way they did. One group from Cow Neck came up with £1000, to be repaid at six percent per annum. They were Major R. Thorne, £200; John Thorne, £200; John Sands, £400; and Daniel Whitehead Kissam, £200.

Getting the funds back across the Sound into the hands of the Continental government wasn't always easy—there were no neat checks drawn on the neighborhood bank and no easy-to-hide bank notes. Rather, there were pounds of gold and silver coins to transport. Major Hendrick Wyckoff of New Lots (Brooklyn) was a regular commuter, crossing the Sound from Connecticut, hiding out during the day at the Cow Neck home of Peter Onderdonk, going out to exchange Clinton's promissory notes for specie at night, then going back across the Sound when his pockets got heavy. Benjamin Sands, who could step out of his Sands Point House and sail across the Sound, also carried money to Governor Clinton.

Cow Neck suffered devastating hardships. Livestock was requisitioned. Forests, woodlots, and even orchards and fences fell to British demands for fuel and construction material. Vast acreage was leveled in the course of the occupation and the wood shipped by coastal sloops to New York City and other ports in British hands. Long Island and Manhattan were the only sizable portions of the colonies held by the British for any time. The island was occupied by British troops from the Battle of Long Island in 1776 until the surrender of the British at Yorktown, Virginia, in 1781. There were 20,000 troops in and around Manhattan. Some British troops were not Englishmen, and some of the Englishmen were not gentlemen.

AN OCCUPIED ISLAND

The occupying forces consisted of three distinct groups: detachments of the British Regular Army, a provincial regiment of American Tories, and Hessian Mercenaries. The British regulars generally conducted themselves in a proper military manner, but their allies did not. The Tory regiments "contained a high proportion of criminals who had enlisted merely to obtain the cash bounty. They were so hard to replace that punishments for crimes against the civilian population were seldom severe," John O'Shea wrote in the *History of the Town of North Hempstead*, published in the early 1980s. Historian Henry Onderdonk wrote in 1846: "The Hessians were a kind, peaceable people, inveterately fond of smoking and pea-coffee; their offences were of the sly kind, such as stealing at night, while the British and 'New Raised Corps' were insolent, dominating, and inclined to violence, robbery and bloodshed."

These often badly-behaved troops were billeted all over Long Island, and Cow Neck had more than its fair share. The school house on Flower Hill was occupied one winter, as was Samuel Latham's grist mill in Plandome. Hessians were quartered at Judge Onderdonk's Roslyn home; Hessian Colonel Janecke held sway at Dr. Latham's house in Plandome, while troops set up camp in a nearby orchard; and 12 Hessian soldiers were quartered in the weaving room of the Thomas Dodge house one winter, in a space about 15 feet by 15 feet.

Peter Onderdonk, whose house stood where the Port Washington Post Office is located today, was constantly called upon by the British to furnish supplies. He was a Whig, sympathetic to the cause of freedom, and expressed his frustrations in some notes written in the back of an old journal: "April 12, 1779 Be it remember that eighteen Canadian Frenchmen were billeted on me in order to cut all the wood belonging to William Cornwell and Richard Sands. November 13, 1782. Captain Westerhagen came here with his company to quarters and with violence drove my sick daughter Elizabeth and Jannetie Rapalye out of their sick beds. Ingratitude! He quit his quarters here Jany. 7, 1783 – a German hireling!"

Ogden's drawing from Harper's Weekly, October 20, 1883, commemorated the disbanding of a major part of the Continental Army at New Windsor, New York, in early November, 1783.

The British troops took over the property of small farmers and merchants as well as the homes and barns of the wealthy, especially the Quakers and known Patriots. Church buildings, other than those of the Church of England, were desecrated. The Presbyterian Church in Hempstead was used as a barracks, then a prison, and finally, after the floor was ripped out, as a riding school for the cavalry. Hessian troops were quartered at the Manhasset Friends Meeting House. The Flushing Meeting House was used as a prison, a hospital and hay barn. One winter, Master Elbert Hegeman had to close his school in Flower Hill because it was occupied by British troops. Hegeman had been a member of the Cow Neck Militia, fighting in the Battle of Long Island. Perhaps the British knew about his patriotic service and thus singled out Hegeman's school for troop housing.

LAFAYETTE TO THE RESCUE

While Long Islanders were enduring both personal harassment and economic disruptions, the Continental forces continued to fight up and down the eastern seaboard. Washington triumphed at Trenton and Princeton in 1777. General Horatio Gates defeated the British at Saratoga in 1777. The British captured Savannah in 1778 and Charleston in 1780. Then, American George Rogers Clark took the battle to the west, defeating the British on the frontier.

By 1781, despite increasing victories, the lack of public support weighed heavily on Washington's army. Continental currency was almost worthless and state governments would not honor requisitions. Men who weren't getting paid went home in droves, and General Washington encountered a stalemate. Then the Marquis de Lafayette came to his rescue, persuading French King Louis XVI to aid the Americans by sending an expeditionary force of 6,000 men under General Rochambeau. The French soldiers were followed by a large naval fleet, and part of it was instrumental in the successful defeat of the British at Yorktown. Still embroiled in conflicts with European neighbors, the British began to look for peace after Lord Cornwallis surrendered on October 17 as bands played "The World Turned Upside Down." Britain recognized American independence with the Treaty of Paris in 1783.

THE PRISON SHIPS

The Americans had a victorious end to the most successful rebellion in recorded history. From it grew the showcase of democracy, the most powerful and prosperous country in the world today—and probably tomorrow. There was a price, of course: shattered lives and a shattered economy. Battle deaths numbered 4,044, according to one source, 4,435 according to another. An additional 6,188 received non-mortal wounds. No figures are available on the total number of men who served in the Continental forces. It was difficult to get men to enlist and difficult to keep them in service. Volunteers came and went as the needs of their families and farms dictated. Much of the population was apathetic towards the rebellion or thought the grievances with the British were too petty to fight about. Still, the fighting directly or indirectly affected a large percentage of the people.

Nor does anyone know how many prisoners of war died. One historian estimates 8,500, but it could easily have been twice that number on prison ships; at least 16 fetid hulks anchored in the East River. No tally was kept—bodies were simply dumped overboard, to be disposed of by the tides or buried in shallow graves on the river bank. According to Dr. Myron Luke, Professor Emeritus, C. W. Post, "It is possible that more died in New York prisons than on all the battlefields of the Revolution. Those fortunate enough to be released during the war or those who survived to be released after the peace often died later of tuberculosis or other diseases caught on the ships." The most notorious of the prison ships was the *Jersey*, a former gun ship in which 1,000 men at a time were incarcerated. According to one prisoner who survived, they died at the rate of eight men a day.

But yes, it was possible to get off the prison ships. Anyone who immediately joined the British forces could be released. How many did so is not known. Some men benefited from prisoner exchanges. Others—we assume the good swimmers—managed to escape. Most, however, either died or waited out the war. One victim from Cow Neck was Wilkie Dodge, the captain of Comfort Sands' privateer *Sally*, who died in prison in 1778.

THE LOYALIST FLIGHT

The Loyalists did not fare well in the aftermath of the war. Many had lived comfortably on Long Island during the hostilities but afterwards, their property was confiscated and some were fined and imprisoned. During the final stages of the war, and for several years afterwards, many Tory families migrated to Canada, the West Indies and Europe, abandoning homes and property and leaving Whig friends and relatives behind.

Somewhere between 60,000 and 100,000 Loyalists left the country; about 35,000 were from New York State, many from Long Island. Approximately 5,000 Tories, mostly from Long Island, settled at the mouth of the St. John River in New Brunswick, Canada, where they founded the city of St. John. Colonel Gabriel Ludlow of Hempstead was that

Many of the men from Cow Neck who fought in the American Revolution, including Col. John Sands IV and Noah Mason, builder of the Sands Point Light, are buried in the Sands Burying Ground, located near the junction of Sands Point Road and Middle Neck Road on property once owned by Richard Sands. (Photo by Will Wright. Courtesy, Cow Neck Historical Society)

city's first mayor (1783-1795). The refugees bore familiar Long Island names such as Seaman, Hicks, Denton, Hewlett, Carman, Tredwell and Platt. Colonel Richard Hewlett, who had commanded a battalion of Loyalist troops on Long Island, led a fleet of a dozen ships, carrying around 2,500 Americans, to sparsely settled Nova Scotia in the fall of 1783. There may have been a Loyalist family or two from Cow Neck that joined the exodus, but if so, there is no record available.

The effect of the Loyalist departure from the Town of Hempstead was seen in a changing of the guard in the running of town affairs and a growing sentiment for a separate northern town. Most of what was soon to become the Town of North Hempstead, especially Cow Neck, had strongly espoused the cause of liberty.

ORGANIZING A NATION

As hostilities wound down, citizen soldiers straggled home intent on rebuilding their farms and villages. Women who had been keeping their farms going despite the ravages of British occupation turned their attention to domestic matters and the education of the young. Whigs returned from exile in Connecticut with depleted funds. As they reclaimed land seized by the British, they sought to restore their fortunes and take back their place in the community.

A few large-scale farmers found that some of their

The homes of affluent Long Island families in the 18th and centuries featured as many fireplaces as it was practical to build and stoke. Stoves, as we know them, were uncommon and central heating unknown. This photo taken in 1992 at the Tristram Dodge house shows a fireplace in the living room with another one directly behind it in the hall. (Photo by Katharine Ullman)

property had, quite literally, run away. Confusion during the Revolution provided the opportunity for slaves and servants to escape from their masters. While the slaves on Long Island were, in general, well treated, freedom still beckoned, despite the fact that many of them had no way to earn a living unless their former masters agreed to pay them a salary, which few were willing to do. One report claims that there were 319 slaves in 1722 in the Town of Hempstead and 212 in 1775.

After the Revolution, men gathered to plan for the future and share their opinions on how to shape it. How could a loose confederation of states with many conflicting interests become a unit, capable of taking its place among the nations of the world? A national constitutional convention was organized and a group of remarkable men from 12 of the 13 former colonies drafted a remarkable document that took effect after it was ratified by nine states. The Constitution of the United States became the law of the land in 1787. By 1790, all 13 of the original states had ratified the Constitution. The business of building a new nation was well underway.

HEROES IN THE FIGHT FOR LIBERTY

There may be some who think the incorporated village of Sands Point should have been called Cornwallville or some other variation on the name of the first family to build its home far out on the Cow Neck Peninsula. But anyone who has looked at the Revolutionary War

record of the Sands family can well understand the naming honor. Three of the third generation of Sands were soldiers in the Revolution—George, Simon and Benjamin, sons of John Sands II. Of the fourth generation, seven sons of John Sands III, all born at Inland Farm, actively participated in the war for independence, as did many of their cousins. So did John IV's wife, Elizabeth.

THE UNCLES

The Sands uncles (two of them not much older than their nephews due to their membership in a family of 13 children) included:

George Sands (1717-1777), born on Block Island, grew up on Cow Neck. He evidently lived in Westchester as he was a member of the 4th regiment of the Duchess County Militia and signed the Revolutionary Pledge in Poughkeepsie.

Simon Sands (1727-1782) married first Catherine Tredwell (d. 1769), and then Sarah Sands, daughter of James and Rebecca Bailey Sands. He supported the Provincial Congress and in 1775 voted "yes" to send representatives from Queens County to the Provincial Congress. He was a Sons of Liberty committeeman and is buried in the Sands Burying Ground in Sands Point.

Benjamin Sands (1735-1824) married Mary Jackson, daughter of John and Keziah Mott Jackson. Benjamin was an enlisted man in the Duchess County Militia. His early prominence in Patriot affairs, including serving as a delegate to the fourth Provincial Congress, led to his imprisonment, court martial and banishment to Connecticut during the British occupation of Long Island. While he was gone, the British made free with his property and he lost considerable value in livestock and cash. Family lore has it that, on returning to Sands Point, he exacted his revenge by selling the produce of his farm to the British commissary for such a handsome profit that he accumulated a very tidy sum—which he then used to help finance Washington's campaigns. He is buried in the Sands Burying Ground in Sands Point.

THE NEXT GENERATION

If they'd gone in for popularity polls at the Cow Neck School in the 1750s, John Sands IV (1737-1811) would undoubtedly have been voted the "Sands Most

Left: Joshua Sands (1757-1835), a captain in Washington's army during the War for Independence, served in Congress in 1803-05 and again in 1825-27.

Right: Comfort Sands (1748-1834), who supported the Revolution by serving on various provisional bodies and using the merchant ships he owned to aid the cause, was a paymaster for the militia. He later had a distinguished career in public service and banking. (Portrait Collection, Sons of the Revolution, Fraunces Tavern. Courtesy, Cow Neck Historical Society)

Likely to Succeed." The oldest of the seven sons of John Sands III, John IV inherited Inland Farm, "on the Road from Sands Point to Roslyn," in 1760. He was a charismatic leader who inspired men to action in the cause of independence. In 1775, Captain (later Colonel) Sands organized and led the Great Neck-Cow Neck-Hempstead Harbor Militia Company, which fought at the Battle of Long Island. Colonel Sands was with the army, actively or secretly, during the entire war, except for a brief period of captivity after he was arrested at his home in Cow Neck on December 1, 1776. He was pardoned by the British General Howe and released on parole. Though the Sands family suffered privation at the hands of occupying troops, John IV was able to contribute funds to Washington's campaigns. After the war he held various Town government posts and was elected to the State Assembly in 1784 and 1795. He continued to live in Cow Neck and, according to the author of *Patriots of the North Shore*, appears in the First Census of the United States, taken in 1790, and listed as having a household of eight free whites and three slaves.

Cornell Sands (1739-1793 served in the Land Bounty Rights Regiment of the Orange County Militia. Apparently, he moved from Cow Neck at a fairly early age.

Robert Sands (1745-1825) was with the sixth regiment of the Duchess County Militia. He later built a home (c. 1780) up the Hudson in Rhinebeck, where his descendants still live.

Comfort Sands (1748-1843) lived far longer than most people of his time and had an illustrious career like his brother, the Colonel. He married Sarah Dodge, daughter of Wilkie Dodge, in 1769. Her brother, also named Wilkie, was the master of the sloop *Sally*, a privateer owned by Sands. Comfort's second wife was Cornelia Lott, whom he married in 1797. A substantial businessman, he was a founding Director of the Bank of New York in 1784. Comfort was 17 when he was part a group that burned 10 bales of papers brought over from London. Four years later, he joined an association that vowed not to import goods from Great Britain until the repeal of the Tea Act and the Act imposing duties on glass and paint. In 1774, he was appointed by Congress to be a member of the Committee of 60, to carry out the non-importation resolution. He was subsequently elected a member of the Provincial Congress and also served on the Committee of Safety. Although he stayed away from Long Island and New York to avoid capture during the war, he supported the Revolution by serving on various provisional bodies. He also aided the cause using merchant ships he owned, and lost one vessel to the British that had a cargo worth £10,000. He later accepted an appointment as auditor general of the State of New York, a position he held until his resignation in 1782.

Stephen Sands (1750-1787) is known to have belonged to The Second Regiment of the Westchester Militia.

Richardson Sands was born at Inland Farm in 1754. He married Lucretia Ledyard of Hartford, Connecticut, and died in Philadelphia in 1783. Richardson worked at the store of his brother, Comfort, until 1776, when he moved to Philadelphia, presumably for greater business opportunities. He was an agent for the Hartford Committee of Safety throughout the war. The Sands brothers furnished supplies to Washington in 1782, nearly exhausting their funds. Not surprisingly, the British offered a reward for the capture of Richardson Sands.

Joshua Sands (1757-1835) followed in his older brother's mercantile footsteps by going to work at the age of 13 as a clerk in a rural store. Colonel Trumbull of Connecticut asked the young man to join the Commissariat Department of the American Army with the rank of Captain. After the army's defeat at the Battle of Long Island in 1776, Joshua joined his brothers helping to supply the Continental Army. At the close of the war he entered what was to prove a highly profitable partnership with his brother, Comfort. He served in Congress in 1803-05 and again in 1825-27.

Elizabeth Jackson Sands (1735-1796), wife of Colonel John, was a hero in the Revolutionary War in her own right. Colonel Sands, away serving with Washington, sent a messenger to his wife asking her to retrieve a cache of gun powder, which was hidden on their farm, and deliver it to a party of Continental Militia at the tip of Sands Point, some three miles distant. To get there from her home, Elizabeth had to pass a company of Hessian soldiers stationed on the Onderdonk property. Posing as a very old woman and accompanied by a trusted slave, Mrs. Sands slipped by the troops with the gun powder hidden in the springs of her carriage. Realizing they had been duped, the occupying troops set off in hot pursuit, galloping into view as the supplies were being loaded onto the waiting boat. Mrs. Sands made a split-second decision to join her husband in exile across the Sound. John Sands' will, published after his death in 1811, gave "my black man Michel Borough his freedom with the use of the House Built for him." Could this have been a reward for a wartime service?

THE YOUNGEST HERO

Colonel Sands' oldest son Benjamin (b. 1758, d. 1843), who is not to be confused with his great-uncle Benjamin or his cousin Benjamin, was just 18 when the Declaration of Independence was written. The Training List of Officers and Men in the District of Cow Neck-Great Neck, unearthed by his distant relative Constance Bowen in 1976, lists this Benjamin. A printed Payroll of Officers, non-commissioned Officers and Privates raised in Queens County shows a Benjamin Sands entering the service on July 12,

1776. That company was stationed part time at Cow Neck and part time at the New York Ferry. We know that Benjamin is buried in the Sands Burying Ground.

YOU DIDN'T HAVE TO BE A SANDS

The energetic and prolific Sands family did not have a lock on the title of Soldier of the Revolution. Others who lived in Cow Neck also made substantial contributions to the effort.

Noah Mason (1755-1841), best known as the builder and keeper of the Sands Point Light, joined the Continental Army at the age of 19. His military career was active, according to 19th-century Long Island historian Benjamin Thompson. Mason, a Massachusetts native, participated in the Battle of Long Island and was wounded at the capture of British General Burgoyne. After the war, he sailed a merchant ship out of New London; in 1809, he was engaged to build the lighthouse and later to become its keeper. Mason and his wife, Lucretia, are buried in the Sands Burying Ground in Sands Point.

Thomas Thorne (1752-1787) was first married to Abigail Sands and later to Sarah Onderdonk. He is listed among those who voted to send deputies to the Provincial Congress in 1775 and appears to have served as a private in Samuel Drake's Third Regiment of the Westchester Militia. He is buried in the Sands Burying Ground in Sands Point.

William Sutton (1735-1780) married Mary Sands, widow of Gideon Sands and daughter of Edward and Mary Cornell Sands. (How the Sands did intermarry!) Sutton served as a private in Captain Abraham Westfall's Company of Colonel Albert Pawling's Regiment of Levies. He is buried in the Sands Burying Ground in Sands Point.

Hewlett Cornwall (1750-1828), who married Elizabeth Willis, served in Colonel Sands' regiment in 1776. He inherited the Cornwall homestead in 1790 and helped bring religious institutions to Cow Neck by contributing money to build Christ Church (Episcopal) in Manhasset. Hewlett Cornwall and his wife are buried in the old Cornwall Cemetery in Port Washington.

Besides the people listed above, there were many others, with names like Dodge, Mott and Onderdonk, who served in various militias. Unfortunately, there has been little recorded about their contributions aside

Howard Pyle's drawing of the victorious Continental Army marching into New York at the close of the war.

When Hewlett Cornwall, who fought in the America Revolution under Col. John Sands, lived in the family homestead (shown here in a 1999 photo), it consisted of the low wing on the right. The center section was built around 1840. The wing on the left is c. 1900.
(Photo by Will Wright)

from an accounting of their names and units. Still others served throughout the long years of British occupation in non-combat capacities. One of them was Adam Mott IV, who was steadfast in his loyalty to the American cause. During this time, Hessian soldiers stationed in Cow Neck "lived off the land" (i.e., took food and fuel as they found it from the local farmers).

One of the troopers struck young Adam Mott with a sword when he refused to tell where his father had hidden the hay. Fortunately, the incident didn't seem to have had any permanent ill effect; Adam continued the successful farming tradition of the family and established a much-needed grist mill on Manhasset Bay, near the inlet that became the Mill Pond.

lighthouse was named an official landmark in 1992 by the Historic Landmarks Preservation Commission of the Incorporated Village of Sands Point. Though construction in the late 1990s of a massive new house near the site has made the lighthouse difficult to view from land, it remains visible to boats passing the tip of Sands Point.

Not far from Sands Point, Execution Rocks Lighthouse, shown in a 1960s photo, was built c. 1848 to warn mariners of the dangers for which it is named. (Courtesy, Port Washington Public Library.)

EXECUTION ROCKS

Some 40 years after the construction of the Sands Point Light, another aid to Long Island Sound navigation went into operation—Execution Rocks Light, located slightly less than a mile to the northwest. Congress authorized $25,000 for its construction in 1847. Its beam of light (which was red, to differentiate it from the white of Sands Point Light) was turned on in 1850. Just how Execution Rocks got its name has long been a source of conjecture. Many historians believe it was named for the number of ships wrecked on the treacherous rocks and the shoals around them. Others prefer the never-proven story that the British used the site for the execution of American prisoners during the Revolutionary War. That theory says that prisoners were chained to iron rings embedded in the rocks and left to die in the rising tide. However, those who are practical-minded point out that the rings were probably used to tie up small boats. At first, Execution Light was maintained by the keeper of the Sands Point Light. Separate living quarters on Execution Rocks, a lonely location indeed, weren't erected until 1867. The light was automated in 1979.

"IT AIN'T OVER 'TIL IT'S OVER"

Yogi Berra was referring to baseball in the 20th century with that statement, but a similar remark could easily have been made about the American Revolution by President James Madison in the first decade of the 19th century. Along the eastern seaboard and the western frontier, old animosities toward the British were flaring again. Bogged down by war with France and in desperate need of money and men, the British had begun to impress (a polite word for "kidnap") American seamen into service, often boarding American ships under the pretext of looking for British deserters. By 1807, the British had impressed close to 6,000 Americans. They then tried the patience of Americans even further by attempting to curtail trade with France through embargoes, and then blockades. American merchants and shippers suffered and seethed. Frontiersmen wanted access to Indian lands and British territories and pioneers took an aggressive stance against Britain. Careless farming methods by the American settlers were quickly exhausting the resources of the land, and they could prosper only if they moved on periodically to new lands.

Though President Madison was initially hesitant about involving the United States, with its limited resources, in armed conflict, Congress declared war in July, 1812. In what might be termed the second chapter of the War for Independence, Long Island once again became a key area of British operations. For many months, the British fleet was stationed in the eastern Sound, mostly off Montauk, blockading ports and harassing commercial and military shipping. Both the thriving whaling industry (operating mostly out of Sag Harbor), and the equally busy coastal shipping trade (engaged in by such Sands Point families as the Cornwalls and Sands) were severely hampered.

With little in the way of a navy, the federal government commissioned Long Island ships as privateers. Though regarded by some as little more than "licensed pirates," the privateers aided the American cause by capturing British vessels in Long Island Sound, along the coast and in the Caribbean. As in the Revolution, whaleboats were given naval duty, attacking British vessels anchored in East End harbors and at Huntington Bay. John Tredwell of Cow Neck was among those who manned the whaleboats for the "freedom of the seas."

During the clipper ship era, roughly 1830-1870, ships like this one were sometimes sighted off Sands Point on the last leg of a swift voyage to New York. Sands Point's Captain Hall Jackson Tibbits commanded one of the clippers in the China trade for thirty years. (Courtesy, Manhasset Bay Yacht Club.)

HERO OF 1812

Village tailor James Smith of Roslyn was the commanding officer of the Flower Hill Militia and Abraham Lyson Sands (1783-1840) served in his company. Captain Sands was the first man from Sands Point to attend the United State Military Academy, and he is buried amid the soldiers of the American Revolution in the Sands Burying Ground. A linear descendant of John Sands I, Abraham was a cadet at the academy from June 14, 1808 to February 18, 1809, when he graduated (apparently a four-year program had yet to be inaugurated) and entered the army as a Second Lieutenant in an artillery regiment. His 14-year career as a professional soldier was active. After serving at various posts along the Atlantic coast, he was assigned to recruitment duty from 1812-1813. He then went into action at Fort Charlotte, Mobile Harbor, Alabama, in defense of Fort Bowyer. In 1814, Sands became aide-de-camp to commanding officer Major General Andrew Jackson in the capture of Pensacola and the recapture of Fort Bowyer. Sands continued to be active on the Florida frontier (yes, there was one) from 1815 to 1819. By 1819, he was an acting Captain of the 4th Artillery and later adjutant-general of the 8th Military Department in Louisiana and Florida. He resigned his commission on November 1, 1823.

Sands' detailed resume appears in "Heitmans Register of Officers of the Continental Army." Unfortunately, the document doesn't tells us why he resigned. Could he have contracted malaria, then all-too-prevalent in the subtropics of the Gulf Coast?

Could he simply have been tired of soldiering? Or did he want to return home to go into business with one of his many Sands cousins? There is no clue. Abraham Sands died in New York on Christmas Day in 1840 and was honored for his service in the Bicentennial Year 1976 by the Veteran Corps of Artillery, Constituting the Military Society of the War of 1812. A marker was placed on his grave in the Sands Burying Ground at a ceremony attended by members of the Cow Neck Historical Society Board and Sand Point's Mayor Roy Olson.

WAR ON LONG ISLAND SOUND

With a powerful telescope and large rocks to jump behind should a cannonball go astray, it would have been quite possible to catch a glimpse of more than one naval operation from a Sands Point beach during the second war with Britain. In September, 1813, a flotilla of 30 gunboats passed from the East River through Hellgate, heading towards Sands Point in quest of British vessels that had been threatening American commerce. After maneuvering against a strong tide, the US gunboats spotted their quarry at two-and-a-half miles distance and began to fire. A British frigate managed to draw the Americans into a chase, allowing the other British vessels to return to their base to the east.

One boat that the British did capture, on May 14, 1814, was Aspinwall Cornell's sloop *Amelia*. Headed for Rhode Island with 600 to 700 bushels of rye and 10 barrels of flour hidden under the rye, the boat was carried by the ebbing tide toward Block Island, where it was boarded by men from a British war ship. Aspinwall, John Hegeman and Mark Lynch were passengers; Robert G. Cornell and two hired hands were the crew. The passengers were put ashore and the vessel and crew were sent to Halifax, Nova Scotia. All three passengers were arrested for treason and tried nearly a year later. They were acquitted by the jury for lack of proof.

Towards the end of the war, following the British sacking of Washington, it looked as though the enemy would again try to attack New York through Long Island. Frantic haste was made to set up defenses. Henry Onderdonk reports that, at one point in 1814, "There are one thousand two hundred of General Johnson's brigade of infantry from Kings and Queens counties now encamped on Fort Green, Brooklyn."

The tides of victory rolled in and out. American attacks on Canada were repulsed in 1813 and that same year, U. S. Commodore Perry won the battle of Lake Erie. The British captured and burned Washington in 1814 but failed to take Fort McHenry, birthplace of the "Star Spangled Banner." Both nations eventually grew tired of the expensive and exhausting war and reached a peaceful accord (Treaty of Ghent, December 23, 1814). There are some who would say that Andrew Jackson's post-treaty defeat of the British at New Orleans was the real end of the war, regardless of which event officially brought peace.

This bulletin appeared in the February 13, 1815 Boston Evening Gazette.

The people of Cow Neck were glad to see the end of the war. A contemporary account relates: "The news of peace was celebrated at Hempstead Harbor by firing volleys of musketry at seven A. M. The flags waved all day from the paper mill, factory and shoe-repair shop of Mr. Daniel Bogart. At noon and evening, salutes were fired by pistols. In the evening the houses were illuminated and appropriate toasts drank at the house of the Rev. David S. Bogart. Jamaica, Flushing and other principal villages on Long Island were also illuminated."

During the early part of the 19th century, Cow Neck homes were illuminated by whale oil lamps like the one photographed here. The large circular "tank" held the oil, which was fed to a flame in the center. The outer rim of the "tank" is ridged as a base for the globe. (Courtesy, Port Washington Public Library)

CULTURE AND EDUCATION

With the war over, Cow Neck residents had time for peaceful pursuits. Educating the children was one priority. The population of upper Cow Neck was still much too sparse to support a school, but children (mostly boys) could be sent to board in Hempstead, Flushing or Jamaica and attend classes in various academies. The Nassau Academy located in Hempstead announced the opening of its summer term on May 25, 1819, "under care of Rev. Timothy Clowes, A. M. Board and tuition $83 for the twenty-three weeks. French, Washing and bedding a separate charge." The Female Academy of Mrs. C. A. Taylor was scheduled to open the same day. (It is curious to see a school offering summer terms in an era when children were expected to help with farm chores, especially during the busy summer months. Perhaps, the expected students came only from wealthy families who hired extra hands or maintained slaves.) Closer to home, Christ Church Academy opened in Manhasset in October 1818. Meanwhile, in 1816, the Town of North Hempstead, somewhat wishfully, laid out nine school districts within its jurisdiction. Sands Point was included in district 5. The first school house in the district opened near the Mill Pond in 1825.

The men of Cow Neck were an intellectually curious group. Nineteenth-century historian Henry Onderdonk, Jr., records that, starting in 1800, The

Auroran Association of North Hempstead met Saturday evenings in the schoolhouse at Flower Hill, "for mutual improvement by reading and debating." The president was John Kissam and the secretary was Singleton Mitchell. Other members were "Geo. Baker, Isaac Bogart, John Burtis, Abm. Brinkerhoff, Richardson Cornell, Isaac Dodge, Wm. Dodge, Obadiah Demilt, Harry Demilt, Peter Demilt, Lewis S. Hewlett, Daniel Hoagland, Andries Hegeman, Jr., Peter Hegeman, Elbert Hegeman, James Mitchell, Peter Onderdonk, Minne Onderdonk, Lott Onderdonk, Joseph Onderdonk, Daniel Rapelye, Benj. Sands, Wm. Sands, Geo. G. Sands, Ray Sands, Obediah Sands, Geo. Seaman, John W. Seaman, Minne Schenck, Morris Salat, John M. Smith, John B. Thorp." All of these men came from Cow Neck, with nearly half from Sands Point. Ladies were not invited.

GETTING THERE WAS STILL MORE THAN HALF THE BATTLE

The biggest responsibilities of the Town during the first half of the 19th century were to determine routes and to construct and maintain roads, as well as allocate the use of common pastures. There were no utilities to contend with; water came from individual wells, waste was handled by cesspools and privies, and there were trash pits. Street lighting on rural roads, such as those in Sands Point, was unheard of. Each property owner was expected to provide labor or funds for the building of roads according to the amount of property held. Every section of the Town had its Overseer of Highways. In 1809, these included William Sands (bottom Cow Neck) and Lewis Hewlett (Middle Neck). Walter Cornwall and John Burtis, respectively, watched over the roads to Sands Point in 1818.

Despite the apparent attention spent to building and maintaining roads, travelling was a problem in the early part of the century. The roads, which were built by hand and pick ax, plus real horse power, were narrow and rutted, and they often washed out in heavy rains. Still, the rural infrastructure was not nearly as limited as it was prior to the Revolution. William Sands could ride his horse straight down rutted Middle Neck Road to meet his friends in Flower Hill and Singleton Mitchell from Plandome could go east on the road we now call Stonytown. This road was laid out sometime around 1770, after the Town Board

The Duryea House at 51 Cow Neck Road was probably built around 1845. It is one of the few surviving examples of the board and batten cottage-style home no doubt common to Sands Point before it was transformed into an estate area. (Photo by Will Wright)

passed a resolution that called for laying out a road "from the road Leading through the middle of Cowneck to the road Leading to Singleton Mitchell's Grist mill, three rods wide, Beginning near Daniel Ireland's Tavern." (Ireland's Tavern was apparently on the edge of the Burtis Farm.)

The Jericho Turnpike, an erstwhile Indian trail, continued to be the principal route for farmers to bring produce to market. It was a toll road for a good part of the 19th century—which did not stop the farmers from using it, as it was well maintained, saved time and reduced damage to their conveyances. The alternate route, while closer to home, required a long trip down Northern Turnpike, skirting the wetlands and ponds at the head of Little Neck Bay, and then travelling on to Jamaica or the East River to board a ferry. In 1823, a group of prosperous citizens decided to do something about this tedious trip and build a bridge over the watery obstructions. The *Long Island Farmer* reported on November 26 that Singleton Mitchell, Lewis S. Hewlett, Ben Haviland, Robert H. Van Zandt and Joseph Bloodgood planned to apply to the Legislature for "an act to incorporate the Little Neck Road and Bridge Company, with a capital of $10,000 to make a road from near the house of Henry Lawrence across the creek and meadows (by a draw-bridge) easterly till it reaches Elizabeth Mitchell's mill dam, Manhasset Valley...."

If you didn't have transportation of your own, you could take public conveyance. In the 1830s, Schenck's stage ran from the head of Hempstead Harbor to Cow Neck and on to Success and Jamaica. An important improvement took place in Cow Neck in 1833 with the construction of Flower Hill Road (called Main Street after 1912), a road "three rods in width" (a rod equals 16-1/2 feet) running straight from what is now the Port Washington Post Office to the steamboat landing, to the south of the present town dock. Property owners were compensated with sums fixed by a group of non-resident jurors. The Onderdonks, who owned the Post Office site, received $265; William Baxter received $220; Peter Cashow, whose property included the present site of the Main Street School, got $216.

LONG ISLAND SOUND AS HIGHWAY

For many, the sea was the preferred "highway." Homes built close to the shore, such as the Cornwall place on Manhasset Bay and the Mott and Dodge homesteads on Hempstead Harbor, had their own boats and anchorages (but probably no docks). Cargoes were loaded and off-loaded from sloops and schooners beached at the waterline. "The boats would sail in on high tide until they touched the bottom; when the tide went out, wagons could be driven down onto the sand until they came alongside the vessel for transfer of cargo," wrote historian Roy W. Moger. As the demand for both cargo and passenger facilities increased, piers and docks were built at such natural landing places as Roslyn's Steamboat Landing (under the present viaduct) and near Sands Point Light. This meant that loading schedules and sailings were no longer at the mercy of the tides.

Shipbuilding became a leading industry on Long Island in the 19th century. Some of the Cornwalls were shipbuilders, and the Dodge family had a shipyard on Dodge Island (Manhasset Isle). These craft were built for commerce and whaling, and later on for sport. Towards the end of the century, Roslyn became noted for the production of a racing boat called the *Roslyn Yawl*. Racing yachts for the New York Yacht Club were built at the Port Jefferson yard of W. J. Rowland, established in 1837. The nearby sail loft of R. H. Wilson became famous for supplying sails for America's Cup defenders.

PERILS OF THE SEA

The importance of the Sound as a major sea lane and the perils of 19th century sea travel were described in a fictionalized account published in the *Long Island Forum* in 1941. According to a Cow Neck housewife in the story, a blizzard of devastating ferocity started on December 23, 1811, with a sudden drop in temperature and winds that blew with "howling fury" for more than 24 hours. When the wind and snow stopped, leaving 10-foot drifts in their wake, those on shore learned that along the Long Island coast at least 50 ships had been blown ashore "smashed and battered and caked with ice." Many had died and the survivors were "miserably frozen." The Cow Neck farmers cared for the wounded and buried ten of the dead who had washed ashore. The "Light at Sands Point was burning brightly as usual during the storm, but who could see it? And no lighthouse can keep a ship off the rocks when the wind takes a turn at the tiller," said the narrator. The *Black Rock*, with Captain Gray at the helm, was one of 42 vessels that dashed ashore on Cow Neck. At Flushing, casualties "were very nearly as bad as here." At Whitestone, a new brig and six sloops were washed up, "all hopelessly damaged as much from ice as from rocks and wind." Cited among the wrecks were the *Traveller* under Captain Conkling of East Hampton, which went ashore at Eaton's Neck.

It is possible to get in plenty of trouble without help from a storm. Typical incidents were related by historian Onderdonk. Captain Abraham Brinkerhoff, sailing the market boat *Little Trimmer* in 1814 from New York to Cow Bay carrying a heavy load of bricks, took on water and sank off Plum Beach. The passengers and crew escaped in the long boat to Great Neck, except one who swam ashore in Cow Neck. In another episode, drunken boaters, returning from an expedition on the Sound, nearly drowned when they overloaded the small boat that was to land the passengers. The boat upset off the fishing rock, near Charles H. Willet's place on the west side of Manhasset Bay.

THE WHALING ERA

Though the ocean could be a cruel taskmaster, it also provided a great bounty to those who braved its perils. Whale oil for the lamps of America was greatly prized for most of the 19th century. Although the colonists had learned from the Indians how to hunt whales from the beaches, it wasn't until the introduction of off-shore whaling voyages in ocean-going brigs and clippers that whale hunting became highly profitable. Ships from Sag Harbor, Greenport, Cold Spring

Harbor and New Suffolk sailed the world, bringing back valuable cargo and tales of adventure. While there is no record of whaling ships sailing out of Hempstead Harbor, as several old-timers claim, some Cow Neck citizens no doubt invested in ships that sailed from other Long Island ports.

Built around the same time as the old Free Church, this simple one-room school at the head of the Mill Pond was attended by Sands Point children in the middle of the 19th century. (Courtesy, Institute for Long Island Studies)

SCHOOL DISTRICTS DEFINE COMMUNITIES

The emergence of individual communities on Cow Neck officially began when the area was divided into school districts, first in 1816 and then in 1832. The districts that covered Cow Neck were No. 4 Flower Hill, which included most of the property running along the western side of the Peninsula as far north as Tristram Dodge's house; No. 5 Bottom Cow Neck, which included most what is now Sands Point; and No. 6 Head of Cow Neck, which took in most of what is Plandome and Manhasset today and went as far south as the line of the old cattle fence.

In each location, distinct communities were forming, with clusters of houses at strategic locations marking the site of an emerging town center. The major concentration of people in the Bottom Cow Neck school district was around the Mill Pond in Port Washington, where two grist mills, a cluster of small houses and a tiny store or two were located. The growth of the little community, which served as a center for the Sands Point landowners, is succinctly described in a plaque erected by the Incorporated Village of Port Washington North on the 50th anniversary of its incorporation in 1982. It reads:

The Mill Pond Historic District Site of Cow Neck Village, first settlement in the area, dating to 1720. Originally Dodge's Inlet, it was enclosed by a dam forming Shore Road in 1795. Site of Port Washington's first school c. 1825, first Church for Cow Bay, 1857, and first Post Office, located in McKee's General Store, 1858. The Mill Pond derives its name from Cock's Mill c. 1750 and Cornwall's Mill 1795. Many homes in the area date from 1720 to 1860.

The growth of Cow Neck received a nudge upward in 1832 when Henry Cocks, who owned the Red Mill, planted oysters in a small pond near Manhasset Bay, where they flourished. After this initial success, Cocks and John Mackey planted oysters in the Bay itself, leading in later years to the development of commercial oyster farming. The oyster farmers, not surprisingly, chose to live near their work. More houses went up around the Mill Pond.

Slowly, North Hempstead's population grew, rising from 2,170 residents in 1810 to 5,419 in 1850. Only 200 people lived on Cow Neck as late as 1840; probably no more than 50 people of all ages lived in Sands Point. In a remarkable interview for the *Port Washington News*, published in 1908, Cornwall Willis provided the names of the Sands Point and Cow Neck farmers of 1848. Eighty-three years old at the time of the interview, a one-time "forty-niner" and a descendant of the Cornwall, Willis and Mott families, Willis related:

Beginning in Sands Point, the owners and tenants of the houses were as follows: Noah Mason who built the Sands Point Lighthouse, William Herold, Benjamin Hewlett, Abraham Sands, John Cornwall, Walter Cornwall, John Treadwell, Henry Treadwell, Peter Onderdonk, Leonard Mott, Samuel Mott, Henry Eato, Isaac Dodge, Henry Dodge, John Burtis, Jeremiah Remsen, Andrew Hegeman, Phebe Burtis, Israel Baxter, William Baxter, Jacob Covert, Whitehead Mitchell and Joel Davis.

(The Davis house is on Yacht Club Drive, the entrance to the present day Port Washington Yacht Club.)

This amounts to approximately 22 homesteads along a two-plus mile stretch of road. Some of the old farms changed hands; in 1852, George Guthrie

Hewlett and his sister Germina Hewlett Hicks, who inherited the property from their father, Benjamin Hewlett, Jr., sold the old Sands home to Captain Hall Jackson Tibbits, a sea captain who sailed his clipper ship to Alaska, China and other far parts of the world. His son married Sarah Remsen of Great Neck, daughter of Henry D. Remsen, Town Supervisor in 1870-72 and 1874-75. Their son Henry Remsen Tibbits (b. 1873) continued to live in the old house and became a prominent local banker and real estate man. John Sands V sold Inland Farm, home of all those Revolutionary war heroes, in 1841 to Edmund Willets, a New York merchant and a prominent Quaker. Abraham Sands, veteran of the war of 1812, still lived in the house at 185 Sands Point Road that he inherited in 1840.

FINALLY, CHURCHES NEAR HOME

At the beginning of the 21st century, when lapsed Catholics, non-practicing Protestants and non-religious Jews are almost as large a segment of the American citizenry as the devout, it may be difficult to realize the important role of religion in the life of 19th century Long Islanders. Houses of worship were not solely for worship; they also acted as community centers, sponsoring social activities, helping the poor and the sick, taking on active political roles, and providing both religious and secular education for the local children.

The folks who lived in Cow Neck in the 17th and 18th centuries made tedious trips of three and four hours each way to attend church in Hempstead or Flushing. That changed in the first quarter of the 19th century when a stretch along North Hempstead Turnpike in Manhasset, between the "Road to Hempstead" (Shelter Rock Road) and the "Road to Sands Point" (Plandome Road), became the religious row. First to build were the Quakers, in 1720, followed nearly a century later by the Episcopal and Dutch Reformed Churches. The very first church building constructed in Port Washington—the Free Church—went up at the head of the Mill Pond in 1858. It was built to house religious services of various Protestant denominations and its construction was financed by contributions that were solicited from all those of "the Protestant Christian faith." The boxy, shingled building with its square steeple, which stood on the

The first Church building to go up in Port Washington was the Free Church at the head of the Mill Pond in 1858, built to house religious services of various Protestant denominations. Church goers came from Sands Point, Port Washington and Flower Hill. Before then, they had to travel to Manhasset or Roslyn. (Courtesy, Port Washington Public Library.)

corner of Pleasant Avenue and Harbor Road on land donated by Jacob Cocks, cost $2,000 to construct. Methodists, Quakers and Baptists met there until the separate congregations established permanent homes of their own. The old Free Church continued to be used for recreational and civic purposes until it was demolished in the 1920s.

Sands Point didn't have a house of worship within its borders until 1953, when the Community Synagogue on Middle Neck Road opened. However, Sands Point had its share of religious leaders. David Sands, born on Cow Neck in 1745 to Nathaniel and Mercy Sands, both Presbyterians, grew up in Cornwall, N.Y., and joined the Quaker Society there at the age of 25. He rose from modest beginnings as an occasional speaker at Meetings, to a man who preached widely in New England, Great Britain and Europe. Cow Neck's Phebe Mott toured England as a Quaker preacher in the 18th century. Lucretia Mott, her distant in-law, was a preacher, along with many other accomplishments.

SANDS POINT FAVORS ABOLITION

As the century progressed, three great movements emerged that changed the social structure of America. These were the abolition of slavery, the right of women to vote and the prohibition of the sale and consumption of alcoholic beverages.

Anne and Adam Mott (c. 1848). The Mott family were supporters of the abolition movement and purportedly involved in the Underground Railroad. (Courtesy, Cow Neck Historical Society)

The strongest support for nationwide abolition of slavery was in the North, where the institution of slavery had the least effect on the economy. Unlike the labor-intensive Southern plantations, the relatively small Long Island farms had no need for slave labor. Even so, during the colonial era, affluent farmers in North Hempstead owned one or two household slaves; any more than that number was unusual but not uncommon. Old census records show Col. Sands with five slaves at Inland Farm. In his will, drawn up on January 4, 1746, Caleb Cornell of Sands Point bequeaths "unto my well beloved wife Phebe Cornell for and in the Consideration of her Right of Dowry one Negro woman Named Hannah and one Negro girl named Nell." Simon Sands owned at least five slaves. At Plandome Manor, there were as many as ten. The Cornwall's slave house stood on what is now Manorhaven Boulevard (it was demolished in the 1960s).

The Quakers objected to slavery on the grounds that God is in each of us and therefore no one person of God could own another. In 1776, the members of the Westbury Meeting freed 154 of their own slaves. Cow Neck's Phebe Mott Dodge was among the manumitting Quakers. The document she signed, witnessed by her two sons, reads: "Cow Neck, 3rd m. 1776. I, Phebe Dodge of Cow Neck, having for some years been under a concern of mind on account of holding negroes as slaves and being possessed of a negro woman named Rachel I am full satisfied it is my duty, as well as a Christian act, to set her at liberty, and I do hereby set her free from bondage."

BOWING TO PRESSURE

Bowing to growing citizen pressure, the state of New York enacted a gradual emancipation law in 1799. However, preaching by black abolitionists such as Sojourner Truth revealed that such laws had little effect. Eventually, public support forced New York to pass a law in 1817, which emancipated all slaves over age forty and younger slaves within the next ten years. By the 1830s slavery had ceased to exist in the Northeast but lingered on in other parts of the nation. The issue of slavery continued to fester as new territories opened up and the "slave vs free" debate was carried west. Many people in the northern states became fervent abolitionists and were no longer regarded as crack-pots and zealots, but as part of a powerful political force. Most Southerners defended the institution they considered the bedrock of their economy.

Among the developments that affected the Long Islanders' thinking was the 1820 Missouri Compromise, which provided for the admission of that state to the Union as a slave state, but forbade slavery in the northern part of the Louisiana Purchase. In 1833, slavery was abolished in the British Empire. That same year, an anti-slavery journal appeared in New York City, and the New York State Anti Slavery Society was established shortly thereafter. Diverse opinions split political parties, leading to the eventual formation of the Republican Party of Abe Lincoln. Poet and editor William Cullen Bryant, a favorite citizen of Roslyn, was among the supporters of the antislave segment of the Democratic Party.

EMANCIPATION MOVEMENT GAINS MOMENTUM

The Jericho and Westbury Society of Friends fostered the work of the Charity Society, founded in 1794, for

Edmund Willets (left), a prominent Quaker, and his wife Martha Whitson Willets bought Inland Farm, the Sands property on Port Washington Blvd., in the 1840s. These studio portraits feature a renaissance revival chair, an example of a furniture style popular at the time. (Courtesy, Port Washington Public Library)

LUCRETIA MOTT, A FIGHTING QUAKER

Lucretia Coffin Mott (1793-1880), wife of James Mott of Sands Point, a leader in both the antislavery movement and the movement to obtain voting rights for women, was most likely involved in Underground activities as well.

Lucretia Coffin Mott (1793-1880), a native of Nantucket, married James Mott of Sands Point and became famous as a Quaker preacher, abolitionist and women's rights advocate. (Courtesy, Cow Neck Historical Society)

"the relief of the Poor among the black people, more especially for the education of their children." Many Quakers from the north shore were drawn into the work of the increasingly busy Underground Railroad as more and more blacks sought the freedom of the northern states and Canada. Among the Cow Neck homes believed to have been stops on the way north were Plandome Manor, the Sands-Willets House on Port Washington Boulevard, and the Adam Mott House near the water in Sands Point.

Aiding the escape of slaves was dangerous and illegal in the South and risky and illegal in the North. Facilitated by both slave and free blacks as well as educated and sympathetic whites, the Underground Railroad's mission became more hazardous when the Fugitive Slave Act of 1850 was passed, which provided severe penalties for escaped slaves who were captured, as well as those who aided them. The operators of the Underground Railroad, of necessity, kept few written records. But folklore and post-Civil War memoirs contain many revealing anecdotes. One local story has it that a fugitive was smuggled into Glen Cove in a barrel and onto a boat crossing the Sound. Another tells that Robert Hicks disguised a slave in his wife's clothes and led her past her owner's house on the way to a sloop that was waiting at Samuel Motts' home on Hempstead Harbor.

Lucretia was an amazing woman for her time—or any time, for that matter. Born to a Nantucket Quaker family in 1793, she met Sarah Mott and her family, of Sands Point, when the young women were attending The Nine Partners Boarding School in Duchess County, N.Y., in 1809. Lucretia was impressed with the Mott family's antislavery stand. After two years of teaching, Lucretia married Sarah's brother James, the oldest son of Anne and Adam Mott IV. Seven years later, she began to preach.

As her commitment to abolition increased, she became more active in the movement. Lucretia was a founder of the Philadelphia Female Anti-Slavery Committee in 1839 and attended the world Anti-Slavery Convention in London in 1840. By 1848, she was planning the first women's rights convention with her friend, Elizabeth Caddy Stanton. She also found time to shock her more conservative mother-in-law by entertaining black friends in her home. Lucretia's husband, James, was a noted abolitionist as well, and founder of the Free Produce Movement, which boycotted the use of products—from foods to fabric—produced by slave labor.

RUM AND OTHER DEMONS

Heavy drinking was as prevalent in early 19th century society as in colonial days. The Puritans who arrived in the Massachusetts Bay Colony in 1630 brought 10,000 gallons of beer, 120 hogsheads of brewing malt and 12 gallons of distilled spirits. The colonists drank beer or hard cider at breakfast because they didn't trust the usually muddy and unpleasant-looking water, and they had no way to keep milk cold. Also, they believed hard liquor gave them extra strength for laborious tasks and kept them warm in winter. Workers in the field, sailors aboard ships and clerks in the counting house all received daily rations.

The tavern was not generally frequented by women, but that didn't keep women and children from drinking at home. Taverns provided space for community meetings. Revolution was fomented there. Politicians held court on tavern steps and bought drinks for potential voters in cozy tap rooms. Many believed that the fabric of society was held together by alcohol. Others saw alcohol as a negative force tearing at that society. By the 1780s, a temperance movement was emerging. The influential Dr. Benjamin Rush, a signer of the Declaration of Independence, published a tract with the descriptive title, "An Inquiry into the Effects of Spirituous Liquors upon the Human Body and Their Influence upon the Happiness of Society." The impact of this publication, coupled with stepped-up efforts by the Quakers and Methodists (traditional adherents of moderation), gave impetus to what was eventually to become the prohibition movement.

Due to religious belief or moral conviction, some felt obligated to rail against alcohol as a demon. Others could plainly see the damage that was inflicted upon the spouses and children of alcoholics (who were predominantly men in this era). Perhaps because of the heavy Quaker population, many men and women in Cow Neck were early supporters of the temperance movement. "A society to suppress vice and intemperance was organized at Oyster Bay, July 1st, 1815," reported a contemporary Long Island newspaper. The members met at the schoolhouse in Jericho, and a committee, formed to draft a constitution, included Elbert Hegeman, the Cow Neck school teacher. The Town appointed the 19th century version of the State Liquor Authority in 1818, "whose duty it shall be to prosecute all offenders against the people of this State committed within this Town or that shall come to their knowledge, In the unlawful Selling of Spirituous Liquors."

There was no division of opinion about the horrors of infectious disease. Unfortunately, not even the medical profession had much to offer in preventative measures other than advising people to stay away from the afflicted. The cholera epidemic of 1832 was met, for the most part, by sensible steps such as quarantines and restrictions on out-of-town visitors. The Board of Health of the Town of North Hempstead seemed to be ahead (or behind) the times in its belief in the power of mind over disease. "As the inhabitants are agriculturists on a large scale," the Board advised, they should tend "closely to their farming from early day till evening, that the energies of their minds may have full play and then the subject of cholera will not enter their thoughts."

GOING WEST...

Another important national movement was as old as the first settlements: continuing expansion of the population into western territories. No significant number of Long Islanders spent much time looking towards the west until the discovery of gold in California in 1848, the beginning of the gold rush. Long Island whaling ships were promptly refitted to transport prospectors around Cape Horn and north to California. Once in San Francisco, the charms of home were quickly forgotten as the crew joined passengers in the frantic search for precious gold. Ships were left to rot in San Francisco Bay, as there was no one to sail them back. How many Long Islanders went west is not known, but one estimate has as many as 600 going from Southampton Town alone, so 4,000 from Suffolk and western Queens might be a reasonable guess.

Some prospectors remained in the west and settled there. Old Long Island family names can be found in today's west coast telephone directories. One Sands descendant lives in Orland, California. Some people made their fortunes and returned East to enjoy them; many more returned penniless. Interviewed in 1908, Samuel Cornwall Willis said, "In 1848 some of the people got the gold fever. I was one to go, leaving for California on Dec. 22 of that year; I went on a vessel around Cape Horn. On Dec. 22, 1850, I landed in New York, coming back by way of the Isthmus."

Not every migrant went westward. Many New Englanders went south, settling in New York City and Long Island. Connecticut men and women had been crossing the Sound to settle on Long Island since 1640, and they kept coming. Sixty-five percent of the people in New York in 1820 could claim New England origins. Well into the 19th century, the population of Long Island was almost completely New England stock, except for a few Dutch enclaves.

STAYING IN COW NECK

Samuel Willis lovingly described what New Englanders found on Cow Neck, including Sands Point. The principal business was farming, and in addition to growing hay and grain, Willis reported that "a good many sheep were also raised." Market produce for sale was shipped by packet boat to the city. Horse manure from the city came back to fertilize the Cow Neck fields—an efficient bit of recycling. "Grain was brought there from miles around" to the grist mill owned by Henry Cock, who employed his brother Solomon as the miller.

Edmund S. Hyde operated a shipyard on Dodges Island. The occasional passenger could get to Manhattan on a packet boat, even though it was a tad smelly, or ride over to Manhasset to board the mail stage that made one round trip a day between Roslyn and Flushing, or get off at Great Neck and continue to the city by steamer. (The first commercially successful steamships in the U. S. was launched by Robert Fulton in 1807.) Rail travel was on its way; a line from

The imposing wing, shown in this 1890 photo, was added to the settlement-era Cornwall house in the mid 1840s. An additional wing was added on the left sometime after this photo was taken. (Courtesy, Susan Coleary.)

Brooklyn to Greenport was established in 1844. Ten years later, another line opened, running from Hunters Point to Flushing.

On the surface, the hamlets of Cow Neck didn't seen very different in 1848 than in 1784, when the Town of North Hempstead was established. The population of the Town had grown from 2,423 in 1800 to 4,291 in 1840—hardly overcrowding in an area of 33,770 acres! At mid-19th century it was little less isolated, perhaps, than before, but the people living in this bountiful rural area were still mostly white, mostly Protestant and mostly farmers. However, the forces of national and world social trends and political events, together with a local transportation revolution, soon brought momentous changes in the second half of the 19th century.

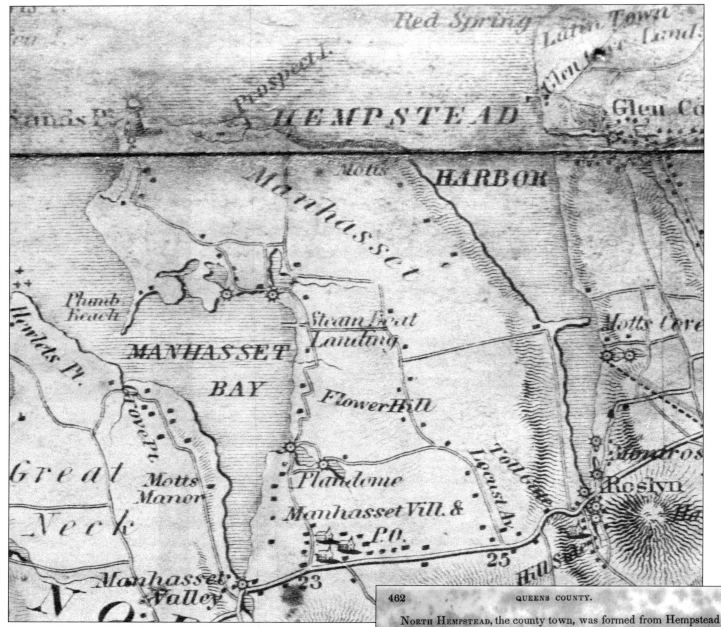

Segment of map of New York City area drawn in 1844.
Note churches in Manhasset. (Photo by John Schaub,
Courtesy Stephen and Natalie Lapham)

The Town of North Hempstead as
described in Historical Collections of the
State of New York by John W. Barber
and Henry Howe, published in 1842.

462   QUEENS COUNTY.

NORTH HEMPSTEAD, the county town, was formed from Hempstead
in 1784. This town has produced several eminent men, among
whom was the late Samuel L. Mitchell, Professor of Natural History,
&c., in Columbia college. He was born August 20, 1764, and died September 7, 1831. Manhasset is the name lately substituted for Cow
Neck, and designates a rich and fertile tract in this town. Situated on this tract, on the North Hempstead turnpike, is a small cluster
of buildings, consisting of three houses of public worship, a tavern,
academy, and a few private dwellings. At the most northerly part
of Manhasset is the Sands' point lighthouse, in the vicinity of which
formerly was the celebrated *Kidd's Rock*, near which it is generally
believed that notorious freebooter made valuable deposits. During
the revolution bands of marauders were accustomed to land upon
these shores in the night, and rob and cruelly treat the inhabitants.
In one instance a Mr. Jarvis, aided by an old lady living in the same
house, succeeded in beating off one of these gangs, killing and wound-
ing several of the assailants. Three miles easterly of the Manhasset
churches, beautifully located at the head of the bay, is the village of
Hempstead Harbor, containing about 40 dwellings. North Hempstead and Lakeville are small settlements; at the former are the
county buildings. The first paper-mill erected in the state was established here about a century since by Andrew Onderdonk, ances-
tor of Bishop Onderdonk of the Episcopal church. Pop. 3,891.
  OYSTER BAY embraces a larger extent of territory than any other

stage proprietor, gardener, tavern keeper, mason, wheelwright, attorney, lighthouse keeper. There was also a 20 year-old listed as "none." Many of the laborers were described as "alien." Names such as Richard Calahan, William Carney and Thomas O'Bryne reflect the influx of Irish immigrants at the time.

To complicate the matter, the draft act provided that any draftee could be exempt from military service if he furnished a substitute or paid $300 for one. This provision, which enabled the rich to avoid military service, was bitterly resented by those who could not buy their way out of the draft and led to the notorious New York City Draft Riots. In the north, many a prominent person and/or wealthy man such as J. P. Morgan and future president Grover Cleveland sat out the war by paying a substitute to go in his stead.

THOSE WHO FOUGHT

Though there is no record of violence on Long Island other than a disturbance in Jamaica, one can be sure that the working men of North Hempstead were not happy that their names were on the enrollment list. The names of the men who actually went off to war from North Hempstead, either as proud volunteers or reluctant draftees, were contained in lists that each Town drew up at the close of the war, which was required by the state. Unfortunately, North Hempstead's copy of the official list seems to have disappeared. There is, however, a useful compilation in the Bryant Library headed "List of Volunteers from the Town of North Hempstead." No date is shown, but it must have been done after the end of the war as it indicates that the redoubtable Benjamin Willis, finally a Colonel, was "home." (The Willis' Company was not mustered out until June 21, 1865.)

Ninety-four names, with military status, are shown. The list has nine men dead, three deserters,

This illustration from D. T. Valentine's Manual, 1862, shows the interior of the state arsenal, 57th St., occupied by the 7th N.Y.V. Steuben Regiment), 1861. Note the rifles on the right, which were taller than some of the men who were assigned to carry them. (Courtesy, Cow Neck Historical Society)

three discharged or "home," one in the hospital, one imprisoned, one since drafted and one missing.

NOT MANY PEOPLE IN SANDS POINT

Shipbuilder John Hewlett Cornwall (1816-1887) of Sands Point served as a captain and paymaster in the 2nd Regiment lst Div., NY Volunteers. (This writer has been unable to identify any other Sands Point resident in Union service. Lists of volunteers and draftees often show only names and town or county.)

It should be pointed out that there just weren't very many people in Sands Point in the 1860s. The H. J. Walling map of the New York metropolitan area published in 1863 shows 29 little black squares indicating buildings with owners' names printed nearby. Names on the west side of Middle Neck Road from the Sands Point Light south include Sands Point House (a hotel), B. B. Nostrand, Prop.; E. Nostrand; Mary J. Sands; and W. J. Cornwall. On the east side of Middle Neck Road, starting at Prospect Point, the names are E. E. Nostrand; E. F. Sloane (Sloanes Beach Road is indicated by a dotted line); I. Mott; Burdett; E. W. Mott; D. Cornwell; L. J. M. Hicks; A. Mott; W. Mott; S. Mott; E. H. Denton; and J. H. Onderdonk. Almost all of the houses are along one shoreline or another. (A copy of the 6-foot by 6-foot map hangs on the wall at the Sands-Willets House.)

Typical of the smaller homes built by local farmers and merchants in the Sands Point area around the time of the Civil War, this Gothic Revival gatehouse is at 220 Middle Neck Road. (Photo by Will Wright)

WAR AT SEA

Action at sea played an important role in the war, and Long Island played a part in the action. The North's blockade of southern ports is credited with destroying the economy of the Confederacy and ultimately bringing about its defeat. When the continued destruction of Yankee shipping led to plans to blockade Charleston Harbor, Union forces called for dynamiting and sinking ships at the entrance to this major southern port. Among those sailing in the "Stone Fleet" were the *Timor* and *Emerald* from Sag Harbor. That village's newspaper lauded the armada of ships sailing south by proclaiming, "With this formidable fleet, the loyal blubber hunters of the North, to the hotbed of Seceshia, send greetings!" While the sacrifice of those ships may have caused financial hardship for their owners, it should be noted that the whaling industry on Long Island was already in decline. The last whaling ship to sail out of Sag Harbor was the *Myra* in 1871.

Sands Point shipbuilders were surely interested in the most famous vessel ever built at a Long Island shipyard, the steel-plated *Monitor*. Built during the Civil War at a Brooklyn shipyard for $275,000, it was produced in response to the rumor that the South planned to cover a wooden fighting ship with steel plates. The *Monitor* is credited with changing naval warfare forever. The *Monitor* was not a refitted wooden ship; it was designed specifically as an "iron clad" and featured a revolving turret with two 11-inch guns. The

ironclads instantly made wooden warships obsolete. (In post-Civil War days, many old wooden fighting ships ended up in the salvage yards in Port Washington and off Plum Point.)

ESCAPE FROM PRISON CAMP

Some Cow Neck men had the misfortune to become prisoners of war. William Post of Port Washington was held at the notorious Andersonville prison and lived to return to Cow Neck. His hometown neighbors, Alonzo Childs and George Lewis, died at Libby Prison. Roslyn's Sgt. William H. Wood, Second New York Cavalry, made a "grand tour" of the Southern prison camps. Captured at Liberty Mills in Louisiana, he was sent first to Libby Prison outside of Richmond, next to nearby Bell Island, later to Andersonville in Georgia and then, as Sherman's army approached, to Charleston, South Carolina. Here, Wood and 11 other prisoners managed to escape by mixing with a crowd of sick and wounded Union prisoners who were to be exchanged for Confederate prisoners.

Confederate prisoners of war wanted to get home, too. David's Island, across from Sands Point near the Westchester shore, was the site of a military hospital that treated both Rebel prisoners and Union soldiers. Cornwall family history tells that an escaped Confederate prisoner was discovered hiding in the cellar stairs at the Cornwall House on Manhasset Bay by one of the women of the household. She told no one until the next morning, when the Rebel was nowhere to be found. Did he make it home by a reverse Underground Railroad? Who knows. But it certainly was easier to travel through enemy territory when you knew the language of the natives.

THE PRICE OF WAR

Early volunteers left for war in a burst of patriotic pride and little knowledge of what to expect. They soon found reality. Captain Willis wrote in a letter, published in the *Hempstead Inquirer* on February 14, 1863:

> *…I have lost by death three members of my Company Sergeant Charles A. Marshall, Private James Demott and Sergeant Michael Donnor, each of them was a true patriot and fearless soldier— Each of them won my love by their fidelity to duty and adherence to truth; each now sleeps in the cold*

This Civil War memorial in Roslyn Cemetery was photographed prior to the theft of the handsome bronze statue atop the granite pillar, still standing today, on which the names of members of the Elijah Ward Post #654 of the Grand Army of the Republic are inscribed. The Post drew members from all over North Hempstead. (Courtesy, Institute for Long Island Studies, Hofstra)

sod of Virginia never more to wake—each died a martyr to a holy cause—and each died a victim of cruel treason.

The Union forces numbered 2,213,363. Of these, nearly 30 percent (364,511) were killed, died of disease or wounds, or accident. (A monument to Long Islanders who fought at Gettysburg is located on Culp's Hill where they took part in the second day of the three-day battle of July 1, 2, and 3, 1863.) Confederate figures are incomplete, but at least 133,000 died on the field and another 30,000 or more died in Northern prison camps. The combatants used Springfield Rifles and Enfield Rifles and had cannons and mortars, horse-drawn artillery, guns on flatbed railroad cars and gun-mounted rotating turrets on steel-clad warships—but they didn't have antibiotics. Soap and water was the antiseptic, and it wasn't always used. Field hospitals were frequently overcrowded, understaffed and appallingly unsanitary. Anesthetics

North Hempstead veterans of the Civil War attended Memorial Day ceremonies in the Roslyn Cemetery at the turn of the century. The veterans organization of the Northern forces, the Grand Army of the Republic, was the most powerful political force in the nation for the quarter century after the end of hostilities. (Courtesy, Bryant Library)

were in short supply and whiskey was often the substitute for scarce chloroform and ether.

WAR BRINGS CHANGE

Besides exacting a terrible price in death and destruction and shattering the southern economic system, there was an another unhappy result of the Civil War, though it may not have been widely recognized at the time. The War brought new and more numerous taxes. The Internal Revenue Act, passed in 1862, provided for the country's first income tax. (The rate was 3%!) There were also taxes on tobacco, liquor, jewelry and inheritance. Though the tax burden was lifted after the end of the war, the concept of federal income tax did not go away. In 1913, income taxes once again became the law of the land when the 16th Amendment to the Constitution was ratified.

Slavery was now outlawed; the 14th Amendment to the Constitution, ratified in 1868, granted civil rights to all former slaves. However, the free black men and women did not automatically achieve equal treatment and acceptance, even by those who had fought for the abolition of slavery. (And despite legislation and good intentions, racial bias continues to be a disruptive force in American society nearly 132 years after the Civil War ended.)

The Civil War did not have a physical impact on Cow Neck, as the American Revolution did. No battles were fought on or off its shores. No troops occupied its countryside. Death was, however, a part of daily living as people scanned newspaper accounts of the war's progress and read the casualty lists.

While concerned about the welfare of the Union troops, especially those from their own communities, Long Islanders still managed to go about their business of farming, fishing and marketing with profitable aplomb during the hostilities. People quarreled about road construction and fence divisions. The Long Island Railroad reached Roslyn and Great Neck in 1866. And the steamboat landing at Sands Point was changing the character of the tiny rural community. Steamship passengers came and went every day. Day-trippers and boarders came to the Sands Point Hotel, which was not far from the remaining lands of the founding Motts, Cornwalls and Sands.

The Brooklyn ferry steams across New York Harbor c. 1860-1870 in this print published by G. K. Richardson. Note the team of horses and wagon loaded with what appears to be hay. (Courtesy, Joan G. Kent)

THE STEAMSHIP ERA

Steam competed with sail boats for Cow Neck customers as early as 1837, when a Captain Seaman scheduled a daily boat trip to the city from a spot near the present Town Dock. The idea didn't catch on then, but steamships soon became an entrenched part of the shipping mix. A lithograph of Hempstead Harbor c. 1840 shows three tall-masted schooners, two sloops, a ketch and two steam vessels, one headed straight towards Sands Point. It wasn't too long before every village along the North Shore from Glen Cove to Whitestone had its own steamboat landing. Sands Point had two: one on the Hempstead Harbor side, at the foot of today's Harbor Road in Harbor Acres, the other on the Sound near the Sands Point Light. Two

early steamers that offered service from Glen Cove to Manhattan, with stops along the way, were the *Glen Cove*, built for the short-lived Glen Cove Steamboat Company in 1853, and the *Long Island*, built in Brooklyn in 1859. The latter was bought by the government at the start of the Civil War.

Some of the independent lines were later taken over by the Montauk Steamboat Company, which was controlled by the Long Island Railroad. One of its better known vessels, according to Steamboat historian Fred Erving Dayton, was the *Shinnecock*, which ran from New York to Greenport. Built in 1898 at Wilmington, she was 220 feet long and still steaming in 1924 when she was assigned the Sag Harbor-New London run.

Most famous of the steamships on the Glen Cove-New York run was the *Seawanhaka*, built in 1866, for the Long Island North Shore Freight & Transportation Company. Engravings and post cards show an impressive double-decked, side-wheel, shallow draft white wooden boat. Originally 200 feet long, she was later lengthened to 230 feet. The *Seawanhaka* made daily trips between Roslyn and Peck Slip, stopping along the way at Glenwood Landing, Sea Cliff, Glen Cove, Sands Point, Great Neck and Whitestone. The *Seawanhaka* was considered a fast commuter boat, making the trip to New York City in about three hours, and she established a record for speed on the run between the East River and Execution Rocks. (The same trip in a fast sloop, when the wind is right, takes a day.)

THE SANDS POINT HOTEL

Steamboats hauled freight for Sands Point farmers and goods for Port Washington merchants. They brought city people to visit relatives in the country and allowed wealthy Sands Point landholders to keep tabs on their New York City enterprises with comparative ease. (After the Long Island Railroad reached Great Neck, the railroad itself ran a boat from Glen Cove to Great Neck, where commuters could take a stage from the boat to the Great Neck train station.) Steamships also brought New Yorkers to stay at the Sands Point Hotel and Seaman's Boarding House for the summer, and carried working-class day-trippers on excursions to the country.

The Sands Point Hotel, later called the Dunnsaugh & Doolittle Hotel (1873) and Peck's Hotel (1891), was built by B. B. Nostrand in 1850. Despite the name changes, patrons and local residents always referred to it as the Sands Point Hotel. It is described by Ernie Simon in a "Port Remembered" column as a "fashionable resort of the Victorian era." The hotel, which drawings indicate had 80 to 100 rooms, was located on the east side of the Sands Point Light. Contemporary illustrations show an impressive three-story white structure on the top of a hill with a pavilion and bathhouse on a lower terrace near the beach front. Activities included bathing and boating and dancing nightly on the lantern-lighted piazza. Besides attracting visitors who stayed for the entire summer, the grand hotel drew in local residents who came by stage from Port Washington to enjoy the hotel's amenities. But fire, which destroyed so many Sands Point buildings, leveled the hotel in fall of 1892 and it was never rebuilt. Perhaps by that time many of its regular clients had purchased their own Sands Point and Port Washington homes.

The Sands Point Hotel attracted vacationers from the city and day-trippers from Long Island for nearly half a century, until the wooden structure was destroyed by fire in 1892. It is believed that the building was erected around 1850. (Courtesy, Port Washington Public Library)

The former Seaman's Hotel on Lighthouse Road, now a private residence, is shown undergoing renovation in 1999. The Queen Anne-style structure was built around 1860 and served as a boarding house in the summer and a home to the Seaman family the rest of the year. (Photo by Will Wright)

On a more modest scale, W. E. Seaman built a white Queen Anne-style house down on the shore to the west of the lighthouse, which he called Seaman's

Hotel. It is still standing and is a private residence. Sands Point was not the only site of resort hotels on northern Cow Neck, though it was one of the first. The Central Hotel went up on the corner of Shore Road and Main Street in 1872 and the Port Washington Hotel was built across from the Town Dock that same year. Others followed after train service to Port Washington arrived in 1898.

DODGE'S DOCK AND OTHER THINGS NAUTICAL

Another early boost to transportation and commerce was Dodge's Dock. Though what we call Sands Point today was but a half-dozen big farms and one or two country houses on plots of several acres, like the rest of Cow Neck it was dependent on trade with Manhattan and New England. Its residents must have been delighted when William Dodge set to work on a large (for those days) commercial wharf adjoining Mill

Pond in Port Washington, near the grist mill. Dodge presented a petition to the Town on April 1, 1845, seeking permission to charge fees for use of the dock and its storehouse. The facility is described as, "one hundred and twenty six feet wide adjoining the dam, eighty four feet long on the south side; sixty eight feet long on the North side, and forty feet wide on the front adjoining the Bay." Dodge went on to request that, "for so useful an improvement, permission be granted to said petitioner to charge such reasonable wharfage to the Captains and Commanders of the Vessels as he the petitioner shell deem proper...." The petition was granted by the Town board which, for business and civic reasons, undoubtedly was pleased to have the dock available.

Jane Warner Tibbits, the Captain's wife (1802-1886). (Courtesy, Port Washington Public Library)

Captain Hall Jackson Tibbits (1797-1872) retired to Sands Point in 1852. Painting by Cole, when the Captain was 30. (Courtesy, Port Washington Public Library)

UNWANTED ROADS AND FENCE VIEWERS

The presence of commercial docks brought a demand for better and/or shorter roads to get to them. Like most new roads, the one proposed for Sands Point in 1858 would have benefited some property owners and caused a loss for others. The plan of the Town's road commissioners called for a new thoroughfare "running northerly through the lands of John Treadwell, Walter J. Cornell. Northerly and Westerly through lands of Leonard Mott, Hall J. Tibbits, Benjamin B. Nostrand, J. D. Beach, Benjamin B. Nostrand, Epentus Nostrand, O'Gorman and Dillion and Epemtaus and Benjamin B. Nostrand, to Sands Point Steamboat Landing." Translated into current terms, that means running roughly along the route of Cow Neck Road from Shore Road to Middle Neck Road, with a spur down to the steamboat dock near the lighthouse.

The road commissioners proposed that the affected property holders be paid compensation of $1.00 each. This was not very popular with the property owners, who came back with their own petition, addressed to the County Judge of Queens County. It pointed out that the steamboat landing was already served by a perfectly good road that was one-quarter mile shorter and could be improved at far less cost to taxpayers than building a brand new road. And they contended that the road would cut some properties into difficult-to-use wedge shapes, reducing their value. The petition was signed by Hall J. Tibbits, Walter J. Cornwell, John H. Treadwell, John H. Burtis and Benjamin Mott. A hearing was held at Nostrand's Hotel in Sands Point, and the jury awarded more realistic compensation: $72 to Treadwell, $10 to Walter Cornwell, $253 to Tibbits and $92.50 to James D. Beach. The proposed route would bisect Tibbits' land.

WHAT WAS A FENCE VIEWER TO DO?

The Gate Rights fence had crumbled under the onslaught of greater population density and the growth of village centers. There was no way the whole peninsula could remain a cow pasture any longer. But out towards the top of Cow Neck, and in Sands Point in particular, large holdings still flourished and fences remained important. The fences, usually simple split rail, marked boundary lines and prevented livestock from straying. The Town put the onus of fence maintenance on the property owners and sent officials out to settle disputes. Since colonial times, men appointed by the Town as Fence Viewers made sure that property holders kept their fences in good repair. In April of 1867, Daniel A. Cornwall and Edward W. Mott, who owned property on the west side of Sands Point, were asked to settle their fence maintenance differences. Silas W. Albertson and James D. Smith (not of Sands Point, the Town Record for 1867 clearly states) were selected as fence viewers to decide how to divide the line fence between the two properties commencing at "the new road running from Sands Point Steamboat Dock easterly in the direction of Hempstead Harbor." (No such road is shown in the 1873 atlas, so it is possible that the road was not put in as soon as anticipated.) Mott and Cornwell were each ordered to "make and keep in repair" half of the needed fencing.

SAND MINING AT SANDS POINT

From the 1870s to the 1940s, sand mining operations dominated the economy of Cow Neck, changed the landscape and brought in a new population mix. Today it is hard to visualize the mining operations, except when traveling across the roads around Hempstead Harbor. It is particularly difficult to believe that sand mining had any effect at all on Sands Point except to make a few lucky people who owned land on Hempstead Harbor a great deal richer. Yet, the very first official Town mining permit to be signed and entered in the Town Records is all about Sands Point and sand banks. On June 1, 1870, North Hempstead Highway Commissioners Smith, Valentine and Mott signed an agreement with John Gallagher and John Murray of "the City and County of New York" allowing them "to lease the privilege of digging and carrying away sand and gravel from the beach on the Shore of Long Island Sound and Sands Point... between the Mouth of West Creek and Sands Point Northwardly to a point 600 yards Southwardly from the Steam Boat Dock," for a period of five years. This was the area we now call Half Moon Beach. The leaseholders were not permitted to erect buildings, only to "dig and cart away sand." They had to pay for "such privilege, the yearly rent, a sum of One hundred dollars, payable in advance, on the first day of June in each year."

Sand mining was no easy job. The Port Washington Library's Oral Historian Elly Shodell described the process in *Particles of the Past:* "laborers dug the sand by hand and pushed wheel-barrow loads of sand up planks and aboard waiting schooners and scows for delivery into New York City." The scows carried about 500 tons each and were towed by small steam boats, forerunners of the sturdy tugs that still ply the Sound.

There doesn't seem to have been any more digging at Sands Point after 1875. Perhaps digging up the beach didn't prove profitable; that sand was less suitable for construction than the sand in the nearby bluffs. The sand in the hills was composed of glacial deposit left behind 20,000 years ago when the last ice age defrosted. Not as fine as the beach sand, the coarse mixture of grain sizes and shapes was considered ideal for mixing with cement and water to make a durable building concrete. Other sand mining operations near Sands Point dug out part of Baxter Estates and the old Cocks farm, flattened hilly Dodge Island (Manhasset Isle) and extended as far south as Plandome Heights. The largest mining area was along the west side of Hempstead Harbor, a stretch of steep cliffs running from the foot of Beacon Hill nearly to the edge of Roslyn Village. Land that had belonged to the Motts, Sands, Bogarts and Willets for generations was sold and names of sand mining operators such as D.B. King, Patrick Goodman, Metropolitan Sand and Gravel, John Gallagher, Cornelius Gallagher and Murray and Reed replaced them on the property deeds.

Hand shovels were soon exchanged for steam shovels and wheelbarrows for small railroad cars. Giant shovels filled with Cow Neck sand were ladled directly into small dump cars which followed narrow-gauge track to the docks, and the sand was then loaded directly onto barges for transport to metropolitan building sites. More people were needed to do the work than there were workers available in Cow Neck. Men came from Italy, Scotland, Poland and Nova Scotia to work in the sand banks. Many settled in Port Washington and Roslyn. Some of the mine operators, such as O'Gorman, became rich enough to live in Sands Point. And some of the immigrants later went to work on Sands Point estates.

SOCIETY CATCHES UP TO INDUSTRY

The world didn't have to wait for Thomas Edison to invent the incandescent electric light bulb (1867) to be on its way to a modern industrial society. News of the

This drawing, reflecting women's mission to bring comfort to serving soldiers, headed the chapter, "Women in the Civil War" in Women of the Century, published around 1900. (Courtesy, Cow Neck Historical Society)

Civil War had been flashed from the battlefields by telegraph. Steam engines pulled trains, propelled ships and ran mills. The sewing machine (1851) made mass production of clothing possible and New England mill owners richer. The golden spike was hammered into place on the transcontinental railroad in 1869, which brought young men west in the comparative comfort of the railroad car in just a few days, as compared to months-long trips around the Horn. Gail Borden gave housewives condensed milk in 1853. Gaslights improved street illumination in cities and villages. Typewriters began to appear in offices after 1867.

MOVING TO THE COUNTRY

Many of these modern developments made it easy to live and do business in North Hempstead. More people bought Sands Point farm land—but not necessarily with the intention of farming. Some were wealthy New York businessman who wanted country homes within a reasonable distance of Manhattan. The 1873 Map of Cow Neck shows 37 buildings (as opposed to 29 in 1863), several new unimproved roads (dotted line) from Middle Neck down to Hempstead Harbor, two steamship landings and the hotel, which was still at the same place near the light house. The new names included C. S. Sloane, D. H. Burdett, J. A. Parker, C. Dever, P. E. O'Brien, J. Deaver and L.H. Covert. One of the squares, near Plum Beach, is marked "club house." It is not shown on the 1906 map, though that map does indicate a Sands Point Golf Club at approximately the same location as the present club on Middle Neck Road.

Sand mine operator O'Gorman built a large gambrel-roofed colonial revival house at 240 Middle Neck Road. Its hilltop location had views of both Manhasset Bay and Hempstead Harbor. Mrs. Alvina Wiles, who owned the impressive home in the 1950s, fondly called it "Pheasant Hill" in honor of the large birds that strode majestically across its broad lawn. The house fell to the wrecker's ball in the 1990s. The appealing white 19th-century Duryea house (c.1860-70) can still be seen at 51 Cow Neck Road. The *Intensive Level Survey*, which was published in 1998 by the Sands Point village Historic Landmarks Preservation Commission, calls it "a rare example of the board and batten, vernacular cottage-style residence undoubtedly common to the area before the transformation of Sands Point with estate-era dwellings at the turn of the century."

James Mott, the abolitionist, and Silas Mott, the savings bank founder, played important roles in rural Sands Point as well as on the national stage during the Civil War era, but it was Thomas' daughters who saw Sands Point change from a rural enclave to a fashionable exurban community. Martha Mott was born in 1873, Caroline in 1875. They grew up to marry, respectively, Alfred Valentine Fraser and Francis Kendall Thayer, community-minded business leaders who built sprawling shingle-style family homes on Mott family land and became major shapers of turn-of-the century Sands Point. Sands Point had begun its evolution from farm country to country estates.

Detail of an illustration from Harper's Weekly shows the Sands Point steamboat landing. (Courtesy, Andrew Newman)

CHAPTER 6

1875-1900
SANDS POINT IS DISCOVERED: STEAMBOATS AND STEAM TRAINS CHANGE EVERYTHING

During the last quarter of the 19th century, Sands Point was transformed from a rural hamlet to a village that was considered a desirable place in which to live or maintain a country home by affluent businessmen and families. The local newspaper even began to call Sands Point "exclusive," perhaps because of the large size of the properties purchased by the new residents. That land became available when real estate prices rose due to the community's proximity to New York City and old families made more than they could operating farms by selling off parts of their holdings. Some oldtimers moved out altogether. Others remained to help build what would become an incorporated village in 1910.

The neighboring community of Port Washington, which Sands Point residents depended upon for services and servants, continued to prosper from shell fishing and sand mining. A number of old Sands Point families prospered with them, selling or leasing their land for mining. Because dangerous working conditions existed at the sand banks, some of the old Quaker families did not like to admit they had benefited financially from mining operations. According to her grandson, Richard Fraser, interviewed in 1999, Martha Mott Fraser never showed any concern about the horrific working conditions to which the

Harpers Weekly illustrated the charms of Sands Point (c. 1885) in this drawing. The Sands Point lighthouse is shown as is the old Mott Mill on Manhasset Bay. The beach on which the ladies and gentlemen stroll appears to be Sloane's Beach. (Courtesy, Andrew Newman)

miners were exposed—but she did worry out loud about the overworked cart horses used to pull wagonloads of sand.

Clam diggers and sand miners weren't the only ones who made a living from the sea. Shipbuilders and sailors, and canny proprietors of summer hotels and picnic grounds, all got their share. The sloops that transported the clams from Manhasset Bay were often built by local shipbuilders such as the Cornwalls of Sands Point, who had a shipyard on Dodge's Island (Manhasset Isle) before it was flattened by sand mining operations. Other schooners sailed from Roslyn, the head of Hempstead Harbor. (Some may have stopped to take on water, as they did in the colonial era, at a fresh water spring near the Tristam Dodge House on the west shore.)

Sailors expected to face risk and danger at sea, but sometimes there were dangers in port as well. Town officials were concerned about crime on both sea and shore. Town records show that on August 31, 1875, at a Town Meeting, the North Hempstead Board petitioned the Supervisors of the County of Queens to "offer a suitable reward of the apprehension and conviction of the murderers [of Mr. L. Lawrence, Captain of the schooner *John F. Pott*] who was murdered in the Harbor of Cow Bay." No other details are given, but judging by the wording chosen, it seems probable that the unfortunate seafarer was attacked aboard his ship while it lay at anchor.

FOUNDING A FREE LIBRARY

While Sands Point was developing a distinctive character of its own, its residents remained involved in the political and social happenings beyond Cow Neck Road. The activity with the longest-lasting benefit for the community was, perhaps, one that was started innocuously by Miss Caroline Hicks, who was staying at the Old House, and a group of women friends, many from Sands Point. Together, they decided to form a Port Washington woman's club under Hicks'

ENTERTAINMENT

GIVEN BY THE

Woman's Club of Port Washington

AT LIBERTY HALL,

Wednesday Evening, March 16, 1892

PROGRAMME.

PART FIRST.

Duett, Violin and Piano, Overture from Stradella . . . . Flotow
Miss Caroline Hicks and Mr. I. A. Willets.

Reading . . . . Selected
Mrs. Albert Messenger.

Soprano Solo, "Last Greeting" . . . . Levi
Mrs. Samuel C. Mott.

Duett, Piano, "La Malle des Gardes" . . . . George LaMootie
Mrs. C. A. Remsen and Mrs. D. Orr.

Recitation . . . . Selected
Mrs. Charles Sperry.

Soprano Solo, "Love's Sorrow" . . . . Shelly
Mrs. Anna L. Peck.

Duett, Violin and Piano, "La Ingenue" . . . . Arditti
Miss Caroline Hicks and Mr. I. A. Willets.

PART SECOND.
Social Tableaux From Life

And Popular Advertisements.

F. M. Eldredge, Steam Printer, 330 Grand Street, Brooklyn.

The Woman's Club of Port Washington, founded by Caroline Hicks of Sands Point, raised funds for good causes such as the Port Washington Library, which the club was instrumental in founding. (Courtesy, Port Washington Public Library)

leadership. What makes it worth writing about a century later is the basic reason the club was formed: to establish a circulating library. The charter members included Sands Point neighbors of Miss Hicks: Mrs. J. H. Tredwell, Mrs. Walter Cornwall, Miss Mattie Tredwell, Mrs. Annie Mott, Mrs. Messenger and Mrs. William Cornwall. The Port Washington Circulating Library opened in the Shore Road home of volunteer librarian Wilhelmina Mitchell on February 10, 1892 with books donated by club members from their personal libraries. Mrs. Benjamin Mott of Sands Point donated books dating back to 1777. The women's little 123-book lending library grew up to be the Port Washington Public Library, considered the best library of its size in the country today.

As the library evolved from a small circulating service into a free public library serving the entire school district, Sands Point residents continued to be important as volunteers. Library Board members from Sands Point have included Mrs. A. Valentine Fraser, 1903 and 1942; Hedley Donovan, 1960-1963; William I. Stoddard; 1971-1975; Henry A. Salomon, 1973-1984; Joan G. Kent, 1975-1995; and Daniel Kurshan, 1982-1998. Both Salomon and Kent served as Board Presidents.

INSTITUTING A "SAFE PLACE FOR SAVINGS"

Sands Pointers were also instrumental in establishing the Roslyn Savings Bank, the first financial institution of any kind to open in what is now Nassau County. It was founded with the high-minded purpose of providing a "safe place for savings...an institution to assist our people to build or purchase their homes."

A certificate of organization was issued by the Banking Department of the State of New York on December 17, 1875. The committee that organized the bank was a cross-section of the community leaders of the day. Members from Sands Point were Silas Mott, Daniel A. Cornwall, Thomas Mott and at least one Hicks. Former congressman Stephen Taber of Roslyn, a Quaker like the Motts, was named president. The fledgling bank opened for business on April 3, 1876, in a house owned by Henry W. Eastman, local attorney and the newly-elected bank treasurer. The bank took in $534.32 on its first day. The first bank in New York State was the Bank of New York, established by Alexander Hamilton and other federalists such as Comfort Sands (born in 1748 at Inland Farm on Cow Neck) as well as Tories.

BY IRON HORSE AND STEAMBOAT

The new bank, new library, new social and fraternal organizations, and easy access to shops and services all contributed to making life in Sands Point convenient and pleasurable. So did the charm of the verdant countryside, uncluttered beaches, and views of passing ships and distant shores. But what really turned Sands Point into the home of corporate executives, business leaders and just plain rich people was continuing improvements in transportation. In 1780, the trip to New York City for Benjamin Sands had taken a day; in 1875 the journey could be made in three hours by steamer; and in 1898, when the Long Island Railroad finally bridged Manhasset Bay, the time was down to just 45 minutes by train.

The steamboat Seawanhaka crossed the waters of Long Island Sound for many years, docking at Sands Point (see the lighthouse and hotel in the background) to take on passengers and produce. On July 28, 1880, the ship caught fire passing through the turbulent waters of Hellgate on the East River. Forty of the 300 passengers died in the blaze. (Courtesy, Society for the Preservation of Long Island Antiquities)

Steamboats had provided passenger and cargo service to ports on both sides of the Sound since the wooden 357-ton *Fulton* was launched in 1824. That first Long Island Sound steamboat ran from New York City to New Haven, New London, Newport and Providence. By the 1860s a number of ships were serving ports on both sides of the Sound and providing connections to the New Haven Railroad. Some were built here on Long Island. The wooden side-wheeler *C. H. Northan* was constructed in Greenport in 1872 for the New Haven Line and used on regular runs between New York and New Haven until 1898. The

Newport, which traveled the route between New York, Newport and Fall River from 1865 until it was ingloriously converted to a barge in 1890, was also produced in Greenport.

Towards the end of the century, picnickers at the Sands Point Light would have seen the 230-foot-long *Seawanhaka,* which carried as many as 300 passengers along the New York-Glen Cove route. Some of the passenger boats were operated by the Montauk Line, which was a subsidiary of the Long Island Railroad.

Commuting by steamship from Sands Point to New York City could be quite comfortable, with private staterooms available for those who could afford them. After the LIRR extended service out to Great Neck, the commute could be shortened by taking the boat to Kings Point, proceeding to the Great Neck station by carriage and then boarding the train. (The steamer docked on the west side of the Great Neck peninsula where the Merchant Marine Academy is located today.)

THE SEAWANHAKA BURNS

Like sail-powered vessels, the great steamboats were subject to the whims and rages of nature and the errors and negligence of human beings. Although collisions, wrecks, and sinkings took place closer to home, such as the 1859 sinking of the *Long Island* off Sands Point, no disaster made a greater impression on Cow Neck residents than the fire aboard the *Seawanhaka.*

The ill-fated Seawanhaka was replaced on the Sands Point run by the Idlewild, built in 1871. The vessel's timetable for June, 1885, shows that it carried horses and carriages. (Courtesy, Port Washington Public Library)

Six wooden warships, which Captain Elbert Stannard planned to dis-
mantle for salvage, and two coastal schooners anchored nearby burned
off Plum Point in 1889. The fire was so intense, the flames could be
seen from the south shore. (Illustration from Harpers Weekly. Courtesy
Ann and Vincent Mai)

Her captain was Charles P. Smith, a native of Merrick. On July 28, 1880, with a large number of women and children among those crowding the passenger area, the ship caught fire while passing through the turbulent waters of Hellgate on the East River. The quick-witted captain managed to maneuver the boat into shallow water, an act that probably helped reduce casualties. Still, the toll was fearsome— 40 of the 300 passengers, almost all from the Town of North Hempstead—are believed to have died in the blaze. One of the victims was two-year-old Minnie Beach, daughter of Judge Ross of Glen Cove. The survivors included shipping magnet W. R. Grace of Great Neck, author Charles A. Dana and book publisher John Harper.

The *Seawanhaka* was replaced on the Sands Point run by another steamer, the *Idlewild,* built in 1871. The June, 1885, timetable of the *Idlewild* showed that horses and carriages were carried on board. The timetable also listed departure information for a morning boat, *Accomack,* that left Peck Slip at 9:30 a.m. and made its way to Sands Point and Glen Cove. After the *Idlewild* burned at its winter quarters in Brooklyn in 1901, passenger service by boat from Sands Point to Manhattan was discontinued. That same year a heavy storm nearly destroyed the old Sands Point dock. However, neither fire nor Mother Nature killed steamboat commuting—that was done by the Long Island Railroad, providing faster, more efficient, more convenient service. Well into the present century, there have been sporadic efforts to revive regular boat runs on a smaller, speedier scale. But the faster, more economical service offered by the train has always defeated such ventures.

THE BIG WARSHIP FIRE

The advent of ships powered by steam engines, plus the introduction of iron-clad vessels, made much of the U.S. Navy's fleet obsolete. As a result, ship salvage became big business on Manhasset Bay. In 1887, Elbert Stannard, a retired clipper ship captain, acquired the old Mitchell Homestead (across the street from the present day Knickerbocker Yacht Club), where he ran a business of converting wooden warships into freight and passenger vessels, or breaking them up for parts.

Two years later, it was Stannard's ships that supplied the biggest illuminated display ever seen in Sands Point. Six wooden warships owned by Stannard and two coastal schooners anchored nearby went up in flames off Plum Point in 1889 . The fire, of unknown origin, started on the war ship *Colorado* and rapidly spread to the other vessels moored nearby. A contemporary newspaper account reported: "The bright light brought hundreds of villagers to the beach, who gazed in wonder at the fearfully beautiful sight. The heat was so intense that it was impossible to go near the burning ships, while the crackling of the flames sounded like the sharp crack of musketry." The fire could be seen from as far away as Rockaway, on the south shore of Long Island. The account also said that the "fire burned so fiercely that inside three hours nothing was left of the old defenders of America but a few charred planks and floating timbers." Captain Stannard estimated his loss at $100,000 and added: "Had the ships been serviceable, the loss would have been millions."

THE L.I.R.R. REACHES PORT WASHINGTON

In an unpublished manuscript, Peter Fraser, a present-day resident of Sands Point, describes the journey to Manhattan of his grandfather Alfred Fraser. The fur broker would "breakfast by a window overlooking Long Island Sound. When the city-bound steamer *Idlewild* passed the window, he would get into his carriage and the driver would take him to the dock at

Ashcombe, named after the family home back in England, was the country house built by fur broker Alfred Fraser c. 1892. The woman in the carriage with him is probably his wife Mary. (Photo from the collection of Peter Fraser)

the end of Sands Point. He would board the boat, and enter his private cabin (with a brass name plate on his door) and not speak to anyone until the steamer arrived at Kings Point." Fraser and his fellow commuters then clambered down the gangplank and boarded carriages that took them to the Great Neck railroad station. From there, they continued their journey by rail to Long Island City and then across the East River in ferries operated by the railroad.

Despite the luxury of his cabin quarters, it's no wonder that Alfred Fraser was one of the Cow Neck citizens who worked diligently to get the rail line extended past Great Neck to Port Washington. The first railroad on Long Island, running from South Ferry, Brooklyn, to Jamaica, Queens, went into operation in 1836 and was extended to Greenport by 1844. Ten years later, a line from Hunters Point to Flushing opened, and then came to Great Neck in 1866. At the same time, the Oyster Bay line reached Roslyn. Although talk about extending the tracks to Port Washington began almost as soon as the line reached Great Neck, railroad officials did not actively consider it until 1882 when Austin Corbin, president of the railroad, sent surveyors to map a route connecting Great Neck to the Oyster Bay branch station in Roslyn, and adding track from Locust Valley to Northport. The estimated cost of such an extension was $400,000, a high price tag for the times. The plan

was put aside, to be revived briefly in 1885 with no resulting action. However, the idea of the railroad extension was still alive in the minds of local farmers, businessmen and disgruntled Sands Point commuters. Finally, in 1895, a group of Cow Neck community leaders succeeded in getting the railroad to revive the extension project.

Surveys were completed and land acquisition started. Many property owners, eager to see the project go forward, donated rights of way; others, hoping for substantial profits, held out for high prices. A group of businessmen raised $8000 to buy up the holdouts. Fraser and his friend, Thomas Mott, were among those who subscribed, putting up $800 each. In 1897, the Kings Bridge Iron Co., a subsidiary of Carnegie Steel, took on the job of bridging Manhasset valley. The challenging job proved to be as difficult as anticipated due to areas of quicksand that swallowed up pilings. The trestle, 678 feet, eight inches long, and 181 feet high, was the longest and highest in the Long Island system. The excavation work was done by steam shovel and the debris was removed by donkeys and horses pulling heavily laden dump carts.

Thomas Mott (shown here) and Alfred Fraser were among those who contributed $800 apiece to pay for a survey of potential railway lines to Port Washington. They were tired of the complicated carriage, steamboat, train, and ferry trip to Manhattan. (Courtesy, Institute for Long Island Studies at Hofstra)

RAIL SERVICE AT LAST!

June 23, 1898, was the day a Long Island Rail Road locomotive first steamed into Port Washington for the first time and was met by nearly the entire population of the community and surrounding villages. A parade, refreshments and speech by

Sands Pointers donated funds and worked hard to help bring the Long Island Railroad to Port Washington, a feat accomplished in 1898. By 1904, the date of this photo, commuters enjoyed shelter at the station. (Photo from the Wittmer Collection, Cow Neck Historical Society)

Congressman/orator Bourke Cockran were the featured attractions. City dwellers who had come solely as summer visitors, and city dwellers who had considered Cow Neck much too far away for a viable commute, now looked differently at Port Washington and Sands Point. While no one wrote a song about it, the Port Washington station of the Long Island Railroad really was 45 minutes from Broadway.

Picking up people at the station seems to have been a good deal more colorful and exciting in the horse and buggy era than today, when second cars and parking meters predominate. It was even dangerous at times. *The Brooklyn Eagle* of January 23, 1898, printed a story about a runaway horse that caused pandemonium at the Port Washington station, injuring one, terrifying spectators and shocking returning commuters. A coachman came by horse and carriage to meet the 5 p.m. train, which was bringing Dr. D. W. Lambert out for a summer stay at the old Mott House. "As usual the station yard was crowded with conveyances of every description. Lined up alongside the platform were the wagons of S. Pell, Jeremiah Reid, A. Fraser, W. Bourke Cockran, John Murray and several other well-known residents," the newspaper relates. Something spooked the Lambert horse, and the driver was thrown from the carriage. The panicked horse crashed into Cockran's team, which broke loose and smashed into the wagon that Mrs. Reid occupied. When the train pulled in, Dr. Lambert went to work treating Mrs. Reid for damages caused by his own runaway horse.

THE NEW "FIRST FAMILIES"

Among the people met in style at the station were some of Sands Point's most prominent residents, including bank founder Tom Mott; Alfred Fraser, a new arrival at the time, whose descendants still live in Cow Neck; representatives of the publishing and academic worlds; and the still-forceful Cornwall family.

Alfred Fraser (1820-1915), who helped bring the trains to town, became acquainted with Sands Point in the 1880s when his family left its Brooklyn home to summer in Greenvale. Fraser was born in London and worked for C. M. Lampson, a fur brokerage firm with business partners in New York. He made several trips to this country before moving to the United States in 1876 with his growing family: wife Mary Crocker, the first six of their thirteen children, and two nursemaids. His office was at 50 Wall Street and his residence in Brooklyn Heights. In 1895, Fraser purchased 67 acres of land fronting Hempstead Harbor that had once belonged to Benjamin Sands. "It was an elongated pie-shaped parcel almost 8/10 of a mile from the waterfront up a hill to the Middle Neck Road." There he built a summer home, "a large brown shingled affair with enough rooms for all the family and their servants."

Alfred Fraser, 1820-1915, and his wife Mary Crocker Fraser. (Photos from collection of Peter Fraser)

Two of his sons, Alfred Valentine Fraser (1869-1931), the oldest, and Robert Fraser, Sr. (1882-1959), the next to last, married local women and settled in Cow Neck. For many years, Alfred Valentine and his wife Martha Willets Mott (the girl next door) lived in the Old House. He served as mayor of Sands Point from 1927-1930. Robert married Anie Franke of Beacon Hill. As a youngster, he attended Poly Prep in Brooklyn, where he established a high-jump record that lasted for 50 years. (Peter Fraser says his father was invited to try out for the Olympic Team c. 1904, but Alfred senior would not permit it because he didn't want his son associating with "all those foreigners.")

In the last quarter of the century and the beginning of the next, one Mott or the other, or a Fraser in-law, was active in the founding of Nassau County's first bank, or working to bring the Long Island Railroad to town, or taking part in the establishment of Village government. The women, not content with behind-the-scenes-roles, played important parts in the founding of the Port Washington Public Library and organizing charities.

Built around 1906, the Kendall Thayer house is shown here in 1915. The commodious clapboard house, still standing at the end of Forrest Drive, is typical of the country homes built on Long Island in the early part of the 20th century by well-to-do New Yorkers. (Photo from the collection of Peter Fraser)

Another newcomer was Kendall Thayer, who married Kanny, a sister of Martha Mott Fraser. (The big shingled house he built, overlooking Hempstead Harbor at the foot of Forrest Drive, is still standing.) According to the *Port News*, "Mr. Thayer was noted for his fine breed of horses and maintained a large stable near his mansion on Hempstead Harbor." An attorney who graduated from Columbia University Law School, he was among the founders of the Village of Sands Point.

Charles Alexander Nelson, chief reference librarian for Columbia University from 1893 to 1909, moved to Sands Point and lived in the Georgian style two-story house that still stands at 220 Middle Neck Road.

Drawing on the stories he heard from his parents and grandparents, Peter Fraser describes his family's Sands Point residence at the end of the 19th century as a self-sufficient enclave. There were four houses in the hands of "family": Ashcombe (the senior Frasers), the Old House (Martha Mott Fraser), the New House (Thomas Mott), and the Thayer House. All except the Old House were "large, brown, shingled turn-of-the-century country homes." All except the New House had central heating. "The owners," who were only there in the summer, Peter recounts, "more or less lived on the produce of the land, with additional supplementary needs furnished by McGee's grocery store." (Located in Port Washington.)

Captain John Hewlett Cornwall, March 30, 1816–December 17, 1887 and his wife Susan Reynolds Cornwall, May 18, 1828–April 1, 1892.

The Cornwalls, Sands Point's original family, were still a presence. John Hewlett Cornwall (1816-1887), a veteran of the Civil War, was a prosperous shipbuilder who lived in the old Cornwall home near

The stone arch built by Susan Cornwall is inscribed "Cornwallton, 1890." More than a century later it still welcomes people to the Cornwall homestead. (Photo from the collection of Susan Coleary)

View of the Cornwall farm in winter, 1890, from the Bay. The house (left) had five chimneys. The large barn in back was torn down in 1893; the smaller building burned in 1929. The granary burned in 1945 but was rebuilt by then-owner Herbert Pell. (Photo from the collection of Susan Coleary)

Rear of the Cornwall house facing up the hill, showing the oldest section of the house, the ell or kitchen, on the left. Miriam and John Cornwall built the Greek Revival house at right in 1840. The roads were of crushed oyster shells. The small brick smokehouse, behind the three women and child posing, is still standing. (Photo from the collection of Susan Coleary)

Plum Point. The house and numerous outbuildings, including a boat shed, made a striking picture of a prosperous Cow Neck farm. John's wife, Susan Reynolds Cornwall, was active in civic affairs and successfully operated the farm after his death. She was also the largest purchaser of bonds to finance a meeting hall for the Atlantic Hook and Ladder Company, which had been organized in 1887. Because of this, she was given honor of choosing the name, and she picked "Liberty Hall." The building on South Washington Street, Port Washington, was designed to house fire equipment on the first floor and meeting rooms on the second. It was dedicated in 1891 and is still in use today as a dance studio.

In an era when Sands Point houses were built almost entirely of wood, it is easy to understand the strong support of homeowners for the volunteer fire companies that were organized in Port Washington in the 1890s.

A LIVELY LIFESTYLE

Summer in Sands Point could be glorious, as the diary of an 1890's visitor tells us. The Frasers had kept in touch with their British relatives, and in 1894 and 1895 one of the cousins came to visit. The cousin kept a diary—and remarkably, a few pages have survived. They are in the possession of her distant relative, Peter Fraser. The pages do not mention the author's name but Peter believes it was Mildred Ella Fraser, a daughter of James Fraser, older brother of Alfred.

The diarist had a grand time during her visits, for life in Sands Point in those distant summers was filled with social activities, athletic outings, games and amusements, and domestic tasks. The writer described her journey across the ocean on the *Adelphia*: "Being over 500 saloon passengers there has to be a second edition of the meals. We belong to the first and whether you have finished or not you must go when the time comes for the second meal." Upon arriving in America, the British party went to the Fraser home in Brooklyn and departed the next day for Sands Point on "Railway cars all corridor cars then seats on each side...all same price (for long journey parlor cars). Guard takes all tickets during journey and calls out name of each station before arrival there. Arrive at Great Neck, found Val, Ethel and Robert (Fraser) there to greet us."

The English cousin had plenty to do in Sands Point. This is a typical diary entry: "Thursday: Helped straighten up the house. Carried borrowed lamps back to Mrs. Mott's Old Farm House, 200 years old, open fireplaces with dogs for logs. Went to meeting of the Thursday Afternoon Club. Mrs. Chapman and Mrs. Mott read papers." The group also took a breathtaking trip by parlor car to Niagara Falls in 1895. Ella reported in her diary, "There are no platforms at most of the stations; the spaces between the rails being boarded and a train passing through a station or street has the big bell on the engine ring continuously." They stayed at the Cataract House "from which we heard plainly the noise of the Falls." The cost of room and board was $4.50 per day.

GOLF AS A SOCIAL EVENT

Through the years, Sands Point has had several institutions of its very own. The Sands Point Golf Club, one of the best known, seems to have existed in several incarnations. The club was established sometime before 1899. *The Roslyn News* reported in the summer of that year: "The Sands Point Golf Club entertained their friends at luncheon and a tea on Tuesday at the links. The day was fine and the links presented a gay appearance with the scarlet coats dotted over them."

It seems that most of Sands Point attended the festivities, for the guest list included Mr. and Mrs. Alfred Fraser, the Misses Fraser, Martin Fraser, Mr. and Mrs. John Harper, Mr. H. R. Harper, Mrs. Gow, Mrs. Nostrand, Mrs Mott, the Misses Van Wart, the Messrs. Van Wart, Mr. and Mrs. Nelson, Mr. and Mrs. Slane, Mr. and Mrs. MacDonald, Mr. and Mrs. O'Conner, Mr. and Mrs. Newbold, Mr. Childs, Miss Childs, Mr. and Mrs. Faye, Mr. and Mrs Coffin, Mrs. Thomas Mott. The big mystery is the whereabouts of the actual course. However, the 1906 *Beers and Comstock Atlas of Long Island* does note the "Sands Point Golf Club" in an area to the north of the present club's site, near the corner where Cow Neck Road and Middle Neck Road meet.

GETTING THE WORD AROUND

Chances are that Mildred Fraser's visit was duly reported in the Port Washington Notes section of the *Roslyn News*, which covered town and county political news and devoted columns to Port Washington/Sands Point happenings prior to the debut of the *Port Washington News* in 1903. Because of its extensive coverage of Long Island, the daily *Brooklyn Eagle* was also widely read in the area. With the invention of the linotype typesetting machine in 1866, and the telephone in 1875, it became easier for editors to keep their readers abreast of national, international and local news.

While the Sands Point residents had to travel into town to get their mail, the fact that it was delivered to Port Washington every day was a vast improvement over earlier times, when mail was delivered to Great Neck or Roslyn and someone from Port Washington had to make a trip to collect it and bring it back. By 1882 there were seven post offices in the Town of North Hempstead: Old Westbury, Roslyn, Mineola, East Williston, Port Washington, Manhasset and Great Neck.

Telephone wires reached Port Washington in August of 1885 when the community's first telephone was installed at the A. C. Bayles drugstore, on the corner of Main Street and Shore Road. Telephone use did not spread like wildfire. When the *Port Washington News* was founded eight years later, it was assigned telephone number 35. However, the idea eventually caught on in Sands Point. Harvey Levine, who lived on Plum Beach Road as a teenager in the '40s, tells us that the telephone number assigned to the caretaker's cottage located on the Lehman estate was "3."

With the formation of local electric power companies, lights were turning on all over North Hempstead. Soon there was a power company in every village; later, they consolidated into the long-dominant Long Island Lighting Company (whose last president, William Catacosinos, was once a Sands Point resident).

LIFESTYLE CHANGES

As the economy grew in the 1890s, the ranks of successful businessmen and corporate managers grew too, and more of them found their way to Sands Point. It was easier to get there; the Brooklyn Bridge opened in 1884, ferries crossed the East River and there were direct rail connections.

Fraser family outing in Sands Point around 1884. The tall boy in back is A.V. Fraser, a future mayor of Sands Point. The small boy on the left is Robert Fraser, Sr. (Photo from the collection of Peter Fraser)

Life was improving at home, too. Most middle-class households had one or more servants—often a cook, a maid and a "hired man" who doubled as both gardener and coachman. Economic difficulties abroad prompted increased European immigration to this country, providing a ready supply of labor for the local sand mining and shellfish industries as well as a ready supply of household workers.

Lawn maintenance was simplified after the introduction of the rotary mower shortly after the Civil War. Indoor plumbing was common. Central heating replaced fireplaces and stoves. The insulated wooden icebox took over from the cold cellar and ice house. Welch's Grape Juice (1870) might be found inside. Markets on Main Street were happy to deliver produce and meat to Sands Point homeowners and summer visitors.

Because of vastly improved communications and transportation, Sands Point residents were well aware of what was going on elsewhere and could not avoid being affected by outside events and ideas. The nation's continuing love affair with westward expansion offered jobs and homesteading opportunities to young people, and money-making opportunities to financiers and entrepreneurs. The transcontinental railroad system opened the way for settlement; stimulated mining interests; kept the blast furnaces of Pittsburgh busy; brought food to distant markets including Long Island, and Long Island oysters out to Denver and other western cities; and, directly or indirectly, contributed to the founding of some of the great before-income-tax American family fortunes.

Some changes on the national level were not welcome. The country was horrified by the assassination of President Garfield in 1882, just as it had been horrified by the assassination of Lincoln 18 years before. The passage of the Sherman Anti-Trust act in 1890 signaled a new era of government regulation of business. Closer to home, the blizzard of March 1888, which has been talked about ever since, left Sands Point out of touch with the rest of the world—and it blanketed the Northeast, causing $25 million in damages and the loss of many lives.

YACHT CLUB IS WAR REFUGEE

Of the numerous international events of the time, including wars in China and revolts in the Sudan, the one that involved America most directly had a distinct local touch. Teddy Roosevelt of Oyster Bay and publisher W. R. Hearst, a future Sands Point resident, played catalytic roles in our country's war with Spain.

When war with Spain broke out in 1898, many people, military and civilian alike, feared that New York City would be attacked by the Spanish Navy, which was then on its way across the Atlantic. Two protectors of the Long Island Sound approach to the city (Fort Totten, in Bayside, and on the opposite

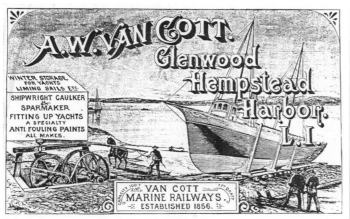

This advertising card was issued around 1900. (Courtesy, Port Washington Public Library)

shore, Fort Schuyler in the Bronx) were put on alert. As a defensive measure, Little Neck Bay was mined. This scuttled the Douglaston Yacht Club's 1898 racing season.

The club members looked longingly at the protected waters of Manhasset Bay. Luckily for them, property owned by the Murray and Reid sand mining interests, complete with a large residential structure and docks, was available on the east side of the bay. The club moved to Port Washington from Douglaston to escape danger from the conflict, and soon changed its name to the Manhasset Bay Yacht Club. It became Manhasset Bay's largest and most influential yacht club. (The establishment of yacht clubs on Manhasset Bay became one additional reason why Sands Point was such a desirable place to live.)

WAR WITH SPAIN

The Spanish-American War was, as wars go, comparatively popular as well as remarkably short. The United States was drawn into the Cuban rebellion against Spain mainly for economic reasons. A few feared that Cuba might become a black republic like Haiti, although it took a good deal of prodding on the part of a jingoist press, such as the *New York World* and the *New York Morning Journal*, owned by William Randolph Hearst. Businessmen felt that intervention would be in their best interest, because trade with Cuba had been $100 million in 1893. There were also heavy investments in Cuban sugar and mining industries.

The underwater explosion which destroyed the U.S. Battleship *Maine* in Havana harbor on February 15, 1898, killing 260 people, was ostensibly the reason

the United States took military action. Though responsibility for the explosion has never been established, as far as the popular press and the general population were concerned it was sabotage on the part of the treacherous Spanish government. "Remember the Maine" became a familiar rallying cry. Congress declared Cuba independent of Spain on April 19 and an understandably aggrieved Spain declared war on the United States on April 24. Despite a lot of flag-waving at the nation's Fourth of July celebrations, the war had little impact on the average citizen primarily because of its short duration. One local historian wrote, "The Spanish-American War was brief and, except for fighting in Cuba, was chiefly a naval affair."

Many of those who served in the all-volunteer Army trained at Camp Black on Hempstead Plains near Westbury. A few of the young men who went off to war were from North Hempstead. A *Roslyn News* article noted that Lt. Nostrand from Port Washington (perhaps a member of the Nostrand family of Sands Point) had been ordered to the *Buchanan* (berthed at Tampa), a vessel formerly owned by William. R. Hearst and purchased by the United States government for blockade duty.

ROUGH RIDING TO FAME AND GLORY

Teddy Roosevelt and the Rough Riders did not win the war by themselves. They had help from Commodore George Dewey, who defeated the Spanish at Manila Bay on May 1, and Admiral Sampson and Commodore Schley, who wiped out Spain's Atlantic fleet at Santiago, Cuba, in July.

The Rough Riders were not recruited from Roosevelt's Long Island neighbors; most were ranchers and cowboys from North Dakota and other western states, chosen for their riding skills, plus a few eastern seaboard gentlemen adventurers. The outfit's official name was the 1st Regiment of the U.S. Calvary Volunteers. It was organized by Roosevelt, who resigned his post as Assistant Secretary of the Navy to undertake the task, and General Leonard Wood. The Rough Riders saw action in and around the city of Santiago on foot, as they had been forced by lack of shipboard space to leave most of their mounts in Florida. Roosevelt, who managed to bring his horse along, led them to victory and himself to even greater fame when the regiment took part in the attack on San Juan Hill near the town of El Caney.

Theodore Roosevelt in his favorite role, "The Rough Rider."
(Courtesy, Institute for Long Island Studies at Hofstra)

Colonel Roosevelt brought his victorious but fever-ridden troops back to Montauk to recuperate. Some 25,000 Spanish-American War veterans arrived on the end of the Island to convalesce. Of the 5,462 American deaths occurring during the period of hostilities, only 379 were battle causalities. Yellow fever, malaria and other tropical diseases accounted for most of the rest.

The Rough Riders' exploits brought statewide and national fame and visibility to Teddy Roosevelt, who ran successfully that fall on the Republican ticket for governor of New York State. He never let any of his constituents forget his participation in the Spanish-American war — he had a bugler blow the "charge" before each of his campaign speeches.

NASSAU COUNTY IS ESTABLISHED

At the end of the millennium, the event with the greatest affect on the lives of Sands Point residents was the formation of Nassau County in 1899.

The first two organized efforts by the eastern Towns to separate from Queens—one in 1869 and one in 1875—failed to win legislative approval. Then, threat of annexation by New York City brought the idea back to life in 1898. New York City had already annexed all of Kings County and western Queens and now was turning its eyes to eastern Queens. Renewed efforts by the eastern Towns to establish a new county began with a meeting in Mineola on January 28, 1898. Benjamin D. Hicks of North Hempstead, a successful banker who had long hoped to create a new county, was named chairman. Though a few attendees favored alternate plans, including annexation to Suffolk, most of them agreed that a new county, composed of the three towns in rural eastern Queens, should be established. The meeting adopted a motion calling for the citizens of the Towns of North Hempstead, Hempstead and Oyster Bay to withdraw from the County of Queens as it was the "desire of the people to have a county free from entangling alliance with the great city of New York."

On February 5, a draft bill to establish the County of Nassau, a name selected after heated discussion as superior to Matinecock, Norfolk or Bryant, was presented to Assemblyman George Wallace. Despite the strong opposition of Queens Democratic leaders, who didn't want to lose control of nearly half the county they represented, the bill was passed by both houses and signed into law by Governor Frank S.

A typical North Shore Long Island farm-estate as shown in Portrait and Biographical Record of Queens County, published in 1896.

Black. Just a year after New York City annexed western Queens, eastern Queens became Nassau County. This new, 64th county in New York State encompassed 274 square miles and had a population of 54,000.

While the population was small and its county government, based on old English models, was uncomplicated, it nevertheless needed a real courthouse and real jail to run the county effectively. Groundbreaking for a court house in Mineola took place on July 13, 1900. A large crowd gathered to hear Governor Theodore Roosevelt offer remarks at the dedication, saying "all free men are alike in privileges, duties and responsibilities."

North Hempstead leaders saw the formation of Nassau County as an opportunity to protect their way of life, which was still mostly rural, and to have a greater say in their political destiny. Little did they dream that a popular history published in 1974 by Edward Smits, now county historian, would be called *Nassau, Suburbia, U.S.A.*

In 1884, rooms at the Sands Point Hotel cost from $1.00 to $2.00 per day, as shown in this page from an advertising leaflet. (Courtesy, Port Washington Public Library)

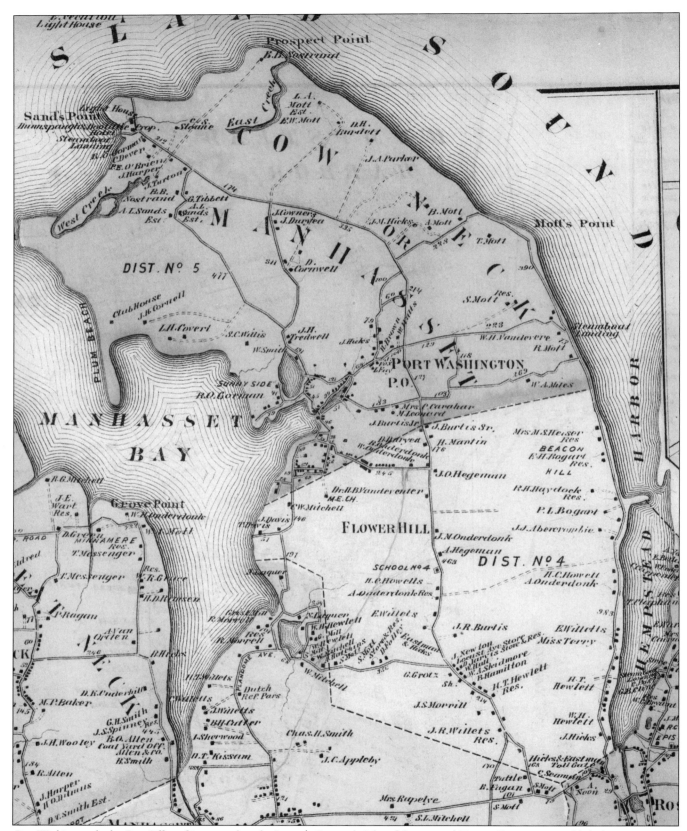

Port Washington had a Post Office of its own when the Beers & Comstock Atlas of Queens and Nassau Counties was published in 1873. (Courtesy, Cow Neck Historical Society)

CHAPTER 7

1900-1920
MOGULS MOVE IN:
THE AGE OF GREAT ESTATES BEGINS

f Thorsten Veblen had waited a few years, he could have found some splendid examples for his best-selling 1892 book, *The Theory of the Leisure Class,* by visiting Sands Point. Polo, golf and yachting had all become fashionable leisure-time pursuits of industrialists and executives, society leaders and society strivers. Many owners of Fifth Avenue mansions and Brooklyn townhouses established Long Island country homes where their families could enjoy those favored activities calling for ownership of lots of land or membership in country and yacht clubs.

Athough a few wealthy businessmen had chosen Sands Point as the location for their summer homes in the late 19th century, it wasn't until Howard Gould purchased more than 200 acres around 1902 that estates on a grand scale were developed in Sands Point. The men who made fortunes in railroads, mining, steel mills and telegraph companies before the days of income taxes built homes in all the New York suburbs. The trip into the city was quick, thanks to the Long Island Railroad. Later, chauffeur-driven automobiles whisked their owners in grand, though dusty, style to the Long Island City ferry or across the Brooklyn Bridge.

The 1906 *Beers and Comstock Atlas of Nassau and Suffolk Counties* lists a who's who of industrial leaders

Watercolor of Hempstead Harbor c. 1900, by Lafayette Olney. (Courtesy, Joan G. Kent)

as Sands Point property owners. Owning parcels of up to 200 acres with frontage on both Hempstead Harbor and Middle Neck Road were William Guggenheim, Howard Gould, Isaac Guggenheim and Bourke Cockran. A. A. Messenger owned a big chunk of property that encompassed today's Messenger Lane and Sycamore Drive. Future Congressman Frederick C. Hicks had a house on Manhasset Bay that was marked at end of the map as "new road" (later named Barkers Point Road). Other holders of substantial properties included Mrs. R. O'Gorman (sand mining), A. G. McDonald, Charles William (attorney who specialized in trademark law and estate management), Mrs. H. Van Wart, William Lippincott (publisher), Amelia Baker, Mrs. W. W. Chapman and Mrs. R. B. Van Nostrand. Peter Gallagher had property on the Bay near Plum Point. Representatives of an earlier era included Walter Cornwall, Thomas Mott, and George W. Tibbits. The Sands Point Hotel was gone, but Seaman's smaller establishment was still down near the edge of Half Moon Beach.

THE GUGGENHEIM FAMILY

William Guggenheim (1868-1941), the first of four brothers to choose Sands Point, built an Italian-style villa in 1900 on 150 acres that once belonged to the

Mott family and called it Waterside Farm. (It later became known as Fountain Hill.) The property was adjacent to Howard Gould's, which was subsequently purchased by Daniel Guggenheim (1856-1930).

While his siblings all married members of distinguished Jewish families, William's first wife, a divorcee named Grace Brown Herbert, was considered so unsuitable by the family that it gave William a choice: divorce her or be disowned. He chose divorce and later married the eminently acceptable Aimée Lillian Steinberger. In 1927, Waterside Farm was sold to Averill Harriman, who used it as a guest house for such notables as George Baker, then publisher of the *New York Post*, and his wife, Dorothy Schiff, owner of the *Post*.

Daniel Guggenheim was one of four multi-millionaire brothers who maintained large and lavish estates in Sands Point. His property of about 200 acres and most of its original buildings is today part of Nassau County's Sands Point Preserve. (Courtesy, Port Washington Public Library)

Explaining who designed and built Daniel and Florence Guggenheim's Hempstead House, showpiece of their estate, is nearly as complicated as explaining the structure of the Guggenheim corporate empire. The land was purchased from a family named Fay by Howard Gould (1871-1959), one of six children of stockbroker and financier Jay Gould, who was famous for cornering the gold market during Grant's administration. In 1892, Howard Gould married

Howard Gould's Castlegould, built in 1910, is featured in this advertisement by its roofer, who supplied "Mottled Purple and Green Roof Slate 1-1/4" thick." Daniel and Florence Guggenheim renamed the mansion Hempstead House when they bought out Gould in 1917. It is 228 feet wide and features a 60-foot tall tower. (Courtesy, Nassau County Museum System)

Katherine Clemmons; she was, according to one account, an actress, and according to another, a circus performer. After a honeymoon trip to Europe aboard Gould's 272-foot yacht, they came home ready to build on the Sands Point property. Katherine wanted a mansion modeled after the castle she had seen in Kilkenny, Ireland. Their architect, Abner J. Haydel, didn't quite share her vision; he allowed for "only" 60 rooms, despite the fact that Katherine wanted 200. Heydal was promptly dismissed, although many of his designs for outbuildings, including the estate's imposing stables, were followed.

The Goulds weren't getting along with each other so well by 1907. Gould sought grounds for divorce, and the story was told in gleeful detail by the *Port Washington News*: "In the hope of securing evidence against his wife to counteract her separation suit, city detectives have been scouring the Tenderloin in the interests of Howard Gould. Private sleuths have been at work for months, but now, Mrs. Gould charges, her husband's millions has induced the municipal police to come to his aid to prove that Katherine Clemmons had a husband living, and that therefore she was guilty of bigamy in marrying him." Gould later named William Cody, better known as Buffalo Bill, as correspondent in his divorce suit.

Despite his marital woes, Gould went ahead with his plans for the estate and in 1909 commissioned New York architects Hunt & Hunt to design a manor

Bank and a director of the Floral Park Bank, the Glen Cove Insurance Co., Sea Coast Realty Co. and Nassau County Trust Co. Hicks was an energetic man who made several trips to Europe during World War I to report back to his constituents on the progress of the troops.

The news of his first wife's death in the 1918 flu epidemic made the front page of the *Port Washington News*. When he became engaged in 1920 to Miss Marie Christie Stevens of Washington, the daughter of an Army officer, it made the front page, too.

Julius Fleischman bought the J. D. Maguire estate in Sands Point for $20,000, the *Port Washington News* reported on July 4, 1919. The property adjoined the estates of Mrs. Ralph R. Thomas and Mrs. August Belmont. Fleischman's money came from the family business founded by his father, Charles Louis Fleischman (1834-1897), an inventor and manufacturer best known for his development of compressed yeast and improved distilling equipment. Fleischman senior also had strong interests in horse racing and art collecting. Julius, one of his three children, at one time operated the Fleischman harness racing stable in Millstone, New Jersey. Julius was also the first man in Sands Point to build his own polo field. With company headquarters in New York City and the popularity of polo and racing on Long Island, it is easy to see why Julius chose Sands Point as a home site.

Alva Smith Vanderbilt Belmont as a young woman. It was as the widowed Mrs. O. H. P. Belmont that she built Beacon Towers (later Hearst Castle) near the Sands Point Light in 1916. (Courtesy, Vanderbilt Museum, Centerport)

MRS. BELMONT BUILDS A CASTLE

For pure color, audacity and flamboyance, it would be hard to beat Mrs. O. H. P. Belmont (1852-1933), who in 1916 built a Norman castle near the Sands Point Light, which she called Beacon Towers. Alva Belmont, who made divorce socially acceptable among the wealthy, was the former wife of William K. Vanderbilt and mother of Consuelo, a famous beauty who became the Duchess of Marlborough. Alva was 46 when she became Belmont's second wife and the builder and chatelaine of fantasy mansions on Long Island, in Newport and Manhattan. She was a widow, free do exactly as she chose, when she built her gothic fantasy on the tip of Sands Point. The money to pay for the masonry came from her $10 million settlement from Vanderbilt and her inheritance from O. H. P. Belmont, one of the three sons of August Belmont. August was a German immigrant who made a fortune as a banker and married Caroline Slidell Perry, daughter of Commodore Oliver Hazzard Perry, the man who opened the door to trade with Japan.

Alva's Beacon House was designed to look like a fortified castle rising from the sea. It had towers and balconies and crenelations (Richard the Lion Hearted would have felt right at home). The interior was in

Built in 1916 and torn down for tax reasons in 1942, the 140-room Beacon Towers is probably the best-known demolished building in Sands Point. The flamboyance of its owners, first Alva Belmont and then William Randolph Hearst, and the extravagance of its design have given it a permanent place in the Sands Point collective memory. (Courtesy, Port Washington Public Library)

medieval style, too, its severity sparsely relieved by somber murals of the life of Joan of Arc covering the walls of the hallways and reception rooms. A hidden, private elevator ran from the owner's bedroom down to the beach. Despite her creation of a home that reflected the Middle Ages, Alva Belmont was an active suffragist leader. Many supporters' meetings were held under the watchful eyes of Saint Joan.

Of course, beach front property had its drawbacks, one of the major ones being the general public's tendency to believe that it had a right to walk on the sandy beaches that Mother Nature had supplied. Mrs. Belmont erected a wall delineating her property, but it didn't do the trick. Eventually, she resorted to buying the lighthouse and its surrounding property to serve as a buffer.

Restless spirit that she was, Alva tired of Sands Point and sold Beacon Towers to William Randolph Hearst in 1927. She went off to Paris to live out the rest of her days. What became known as Hearst's Castle was demolished in 1942. Only segments of the walls and gatehouse survive.

The big estates and all the people who worked on them meant business for Port Washington merchants such as "William V. Nostrand, Groceries, Paints, Oils and Varnishes." In the early part of the 20th century, orders were delivered to Sands Point customers by horse and wagon. (Courtesy, Institute of Long Island Studies at Hofstra)

WAMPAGE SHORES ON PLUM POINT

Even before the first train came hooting into Port Washington, large parcels of land on Cow Neck were being divided for development. In Port Washington, the old Mitchell farm sprouted large Victorian houses on small lots. In another part of town, Oliver Baxter and Charles Hyde were selling off the ancestral acres in 1911-1912 as Baxter Estates, a development that was incorporated as a Village in the 30s.

Reproduced from an old postcard, this shot shows the first house built at Wampage Shores, c. 1910, Sands Point's first luxury home development out at Plum Point. (Courtesy, Cow Neck Historical Society)

It is not surprising that Sands Point got its very own new development around 1912, when S. Osgood Pell & Co. offered building lots in Wampage Shores on Plum Point to what seems to have been a very eager buying public. Advertisements in the Port Washington News promoted a "Perfectly Developed and Unusually Attractive Waterfront Park on Manhasset Bay, Sands Point, L.I.R.R. Station, Port Washington. Quarter-acre plots and larger Waterfront for Residential Purposes." Prospective buyers were assured that a "Private Launch makes regular trips from Port Washington Town Dock to Wampage Shores" and were asked to call Pell's Fifth Avenue, New York, office for "particulars."

Samuel Pell was a prominent real estate broker who sold land to clients who were assembling parcels for large estates as well as to people seeking smaller, though still impressively located, building lots. Pell's own home, a large brick Colonial Revival structure called Inisfree, built some time prior to 1906, is at 5 Pelham Lane (the end of what must have been the original driveway of the Pell estate); in 1998 it was owned by Denis Carey, brother of former New York State Governor, Hugh Carey.

Prospect Lane and Pelham Lane became the principal streets of the Wampage Shores development. Though not quite as wealthy as the Guggenheims, Bourke Cockran or Mrs. Belmont, people of substantial means were attracted to the beautiful waterfront and water view locations. Soon the stockholders in the Wampage Shores Association, which maintained the beach and docks, included such names Robert T. Pell, John H. G. Pell, Charles A. Keit, Harry T. Galpin, Clarence P. Eagle (commander of

John Philip Sousa, his daughter Priscilla and his dog Toby enjoy their Sands Point garden in this undated picture.
(Courtesy, Port Washington Public Library)

the Port Washington Home Guard during WWI), Sarah G. F. Pell, Gertrude Foster Brown and Annette G. Ruhl.

Impressive houses were going up in other sections of Sands Point, too, as other large properties were subdivided. Typical was the 15-room stone, brick and stucco house at 25 Cedar Lane built for Wilkinson DeForest Wright, Esq., who called it "Deephaven." The Landmarks Preservation Committee's survey describes it as "pseudo-Tudor style, two-and-one-half stories high," with several small round windows and two dormers on the facade. It was one of the more popular styles favored in Sands Point at the turn of the century.

THE NEW AND THE OLD

In 1907, A. B. Trowbridge put up a two-and-a-half story stucco house at 24 Hicks Lane on a long, narrow plot overlooking Manhasset Bay. Eight years later it was purchased by America's beloved March King, composer and band leader John Philip Sousa. The family found the house with the help of local realtors. An undated, handwritten letter (c. 1913-1915) to Charles Wysong, attorney, real estate developer and one-time Nassau County District attorney, initiated the search.

The Sousas called the house Wildbank, for the sloping bluff on which it sits was kept in an uncultivated state. They built a two-story addition which housed the dining room and a bedroom. Sousa used the house as his "home base" from 1915 to 1932.

Sousa, whose music is known to almost every American, was director of the United States Marine Corps Band, playing at many historic and ceremonial occasions. Later, he directed his own marching bands. He composed more than 100 marches including still popular, "Stars and Strips Forever." In an undated interview on file at the Port Washington Library, John Philip Sousa III painted an enviable picture of his grandparents' life in Sands Point:

In the early Sousa days of Sands Point, my grandfather stabled several horses at the house....Sousa did a lot of horseback riding over what were then almost totally empty fields....I imagine that the Guggenheims and the Sousas were friends, or at least acquaintances. I do know that John Lagatta, the famous magazine illustrator who lived down Barker's Point Road away, and my family were close friends. Every musical celebrity of that period visited the family...My grandfather composed much of his music from the second period of his career in the library of the house.

Henry Remsen Tibbits lived in the old Benjamin Sands house at 210 Sands Point Road. He was active in real estate matters and one of the founders and first President of the Port Washington National Bank, which opened in May of 1919. Alfred Valentine Fraser was vice President.
(Courtesy, Port Washington Public Library)

Not everyone who lived in Sands Point was nationally famous or made his/her money building international industrial conglomerates or developing sand mines. Some, such as Henry Remsen Tibbits, were successful local businessmen—bankers or real estate developers. Tibbits, a life-long bachelor, lived in the old Benjamin Sands house at 210 Sands Point Road. He was active in real estate matters as well as a founder and first President of the Port Washington National Bank, which opened in May 1919.

ESTABLISHMENT OF AN INCORPORATED VILLAGE

Most Sands Point farms and pastures had long since given way to an "estate village" of forty or so large holdings—but there still weren't very many people in Sands Point in 1910. The first year a separate census count for Sands Point was available, 1920, showed a population of 280. The Town of North Hempstead was delighted to have affluent Sands Point in its tax base…but Sands Point property owners, such as Thomas Mott and James Laidlaw, were not so happy about it.

They felt that incorporating Sands Point would reduce expenses and allow them to establish the stringent zoning laws they needed to preserve their elegantly rustic way of life. The villagers planned to establish their own water and highway departments. Some homeowners hoped to secede from Union Free School District #4 as well, and establish a district just for the village of Sands Point. Since most Sands Point children were not in residence during the school

Sands Point was still essentially rural at the time of incorportion as this photo of a logging operation, probably on Alfred Fraser's property, taken c. 1911 by his son Robert Fraser, demonstrates. Sledge is drawn by oxen. (Courtesy, Peter Fraser)

months, there would be few students and, as a result, a lower tax rate.

Forming the present village was not simple. In 1910, the state permitted new villages to be no larger than one square mile, and three quarters of the property owners in the proposed village had to approve it before the state would grant the incorporation. With those requirements, the formation of one incorporated village would leave two-thirds of the residents at the tip of Cow Neck out of the magic Sands Point circle. So the founding mothers and fathers quickly came up with an ingenious plan. There would be three villages to start with—Barkers Point, Motts Point and Sands Point, which would later be consolidated. The required number of signatories materialized when landholders did a little multiplication, transferring small parcels to their spouses or children. (*Port Washington News* reported 20 land transfers in October, 1910)

Most of the 152 property owners in Sands Point signed the incorporation petition, including Charles and Nina Sloane; W. Irving and Helen I. Van Wart; John and Adeline O'Donohue; Mary, Gertrude and Charles Nelson; Kate and Helen Scheffer; Elizabeth and Elliott Laidlaw; Louise L. and William Judson; John, Harry and Frank Hoffstot; William Guggenheim; and Helen and Howard Gould.

Among the 87 owners of Barkers Point property petitioning for incorporation were Alice and Howard

Though automobiles began to appear on the Cow Neck Peninsula shortly after the turn of the century, a horse drawn sleigh, pictured here in 1903 on Sandy Hollow Road, was still a lot more dependable in snowy weather. (Wittmer Collection. Courtesy, Cow Neck Peninsula Historical Society)

Thayer Kingsbury; James and Harriet Laidlaw; Henry and Hall J. Tibbits; Noah, Howard, Charles, Mary and A. Wright Chapman; Forbes and Alice Hawkes; Frederick and Georgine Hicks; H. A. Messenger; and Osgood Pell. There were 87 property owners in the proposed Motts Point as well; petition signatories included a cross section of old family members—Thomas and Martha Mott; Martha, Robert, Beatrice, Alfred, Kathleen and A. V. Fraser; Caroline, Frances and Gertrude Thayer; Marly, Jessie and Sara Lippincott; Jessie and Carrie Guggenheim; and William, Sarah and Sadie Buckely.

Separate hearings on these proposed villages were held on October 5, 1910, in front of North Hempstead Town Supervisor Philip J. Christ. After all those present approved the establishment of the three villages, James. R. Laidlaw was elected president of the village of Sands Point. Thomas Mott, appropriately, became president of the village of Motts Point.

Village founders hoped to keep things simple, but they soon realized there would be a good deal of "machinery to organize" after the consolidation was

These fourteen men in top hats standing in front of the Port Washington Railroad Station are on their way to Theodore Roosevelt's presidential inaugural in in Washington, DC, in January, 1905. The tall man on the far right may be Congressman Frederick Hicks of Sands Point. Just a few years before they would have taken a stage coach to Great Neck to start their journey. (Courtesy, Port Washington Public Library)

effected. Said Howard Thayer Murphy of Barkers Point, "In short, we have a considerable job on our hands for which we shall doubtless continue to get little thanks and much criticism."

Local political leaders and elected officials, who feared loss of tax revenues, protested the action taken by Sands Point. Civic boosters were concerned about fragmentation of what they saw as the village of Port Washington. A reader wrote to the *Port Washington News* on October 1, 1910, that, "The password should be: 'One great progressive village from Plandome to the light house on the extreme Sands Point.'"

The successful vote to consolidate the villages took place in July of 1912 with Laidlaw continuing as president. Only male property owners could vote according to statewide law. Harbor Acres, which was basically one large estate in 1912, was not originally included in the expanded village; it was annexed in 1932, after development by Vincent Astor and others.

LONG ISLAND'S PRESIDENT

The political attention of the Sands Point residents during the first decade of the new century had a local focus, with the incorporation of their village and the dominance of a Long Islander in national politics. Like most North Shore residents, they were highly

A member of the "Old Guard," Alfred Valentine Fraser, shown in 1912 with two feathered friends, lived with his wife Martha Mott in the 18th-century Mott family "Old House." on Hempstead Harbor. He was mayor of Sands Point from 1927 to 1931. (Courtesy, Peter Fraser)

conscious of (and frequently entertained by) Theodore Roosevelt, their neighbor from Oyster Bay, who was noted for his decisive government reforms, trust-busting actions and colorful personality. The New York governor, who went on to become president, had a major influence during the first decade of the 20th century. Riding on the popularity he gained through his Rough Rider exploits, he was elected vice president on the Republican ticket in 1900.

On September 14, 1901, following the assassination of President William McKinley by anarchist Leon Czolgosz, Vice President Theodore Roosevelt became the 26th president of the United States of America, the first—and so far only—one from Long Island, and the first sworn in during the 20th century. He spent the next seven and one-half years putting the United States' name in larger letters on the world map, and entertaining, enlightening and sometimes startling his constituents with his efforts to make the country do what he thought it should.

SUMMER WHITE HOUSE

When he became President, TR's Oyster Bay home (Sagamore Hill) became the summer White House and the little hamlet of Oyster Bay became the "summer Capitol." Though it took rather a while to get there—automobiles were rare in 1901—folks from Cow Neck were not adverse to a little jaunt to Oyster Bay in hopes of catching a glimpse of the buoyant president or his wife, a woman who sailed serenely above the hubbub surrounding her. Though there are no records showing that Roosevelt visited Sands Point, he did visit Port Washington for Liberty Bond rallies during World War I, and old newspaper clippings show his daughter Alice in attendance at Sands Point weddings and parties However, it is likely that the president enjoyed the hospitality of fellow Republicans such as Congressman Frederick Hicks of Barkers Point or his Bull Moose supporter, Bourke Cockran.

SANDS POINT AND THE BULL MOOSE

Sands Point folks got mixed up with Teddy's political maneuvering in 1912 when the erstwhile Republican ran for President on the Progressive Party ticket. After completing his second term (first elected term), he followed custom and announced that he would not run again. It was a decision that Roosevelt, a man of boundless energy, soon regretted, for his subsequent

life of travel, exploration, hunting and book writing was less satisfying than he had expected. As his dissatisfaction with his personally-selected successor William Howard Taft grew, he began to look back longingly at the White House

Party liners didn't see it Roosevelt's way, however, and blocked him from running on the Republican ticket. Teddy organized the Progressive Party (nicknamed Bull Moose) and ran on a separate line, with Cockran the Progressive Party nominee for the First Congressional District, which then included Nassau and Suffolk Counties and parts of Queens. The regular Republicans nominated the equally popular Frederick Hicks. Roosevelt did not win, but his splinter party grabbed enough votes from traditional Republicans to swing the election to Democratic candidates in many jurisdictions. Nassau County Democrats stuck together and polled 6,900 votes to help elect Woodrow Wilson as president. Roosevelt was close behind with 6,535; incumbent President William Howard Taft received 4,590. In the hotly contested congressional race, Democrat Lathrop Brown defeated Cockran and Hicks. The next time Brown and Hicks ran against each other—in 1914—the results were even closer. It took a year of litigation to determine that Hicks had won the seat by a ten vote plurality.

The Manhasset Bay Yacht Club in 1909.
(Courtesy, Cow Neck Historical Society)

A VERY NICE LIFE

"They had saddle horse. They had picnics on the beach. People came from town by horse and carriage. They went clamming for fun. They had beautiful

Knickerbocker Yacht Club Station around 1910.
(Courtesy, Port Washington Public Library)

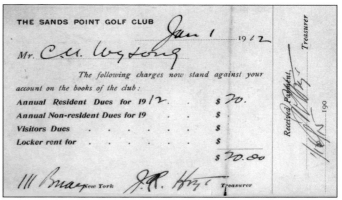

Dues ($20) at the Sands Point Golf Club in 1912 were considerably less than they are today. (Courtesy, Port Washington Public Library)

gardens. It was a very nice life if you were rich," says Fay Fraser of Port Washington, of the old days in Sands Point.

Many of the people who moved to Sands Point did so because they loved salt water—to look at, swim in, walk beside, sail or row upon. By 1910, Manhasset Bay was becoming an important yachting center. The Manhasset Bay Yacht Club, which had moved here from Douglaston in 1902, was the first yacht club in the area. Knickerbocker Yacht Club, which started its existence in 1874 in a small club house on the Harlem River, built a station (a branch yacht club) on the shore of Manhasset Bay sometime before 1910. Early Knickerbocker commodores included Sands Point residents Julius Fleischman and Peter Gallagher (1919).

There were some pretty big boats that called Port Washington home port. Among its data for 1900, *A Centennial History of the Manhasset Bay Yacht Club* lists the steam yacht of Vice Commodore George B. Wilson, the *Anita*, which weighed 232 gross tons and had an length overall of 187 feet. Former Commodore Charles A. Gould owned a 130-foot steel boat.

SPORTS AND CLUBS

Sands Point had (and still has) sports-related clubs within its village limits for many years: a golf club organized in 1918, and its successor founded in 1927; and the Sands Point Casino on the tip of Plum Point, and its successors variously called the Sands Point Bath Club, the Sands Point Bath and Tennis Club, and the Sands Point Bath and Racquet Club.

Most clubs are founded by groups, but a number are the creations of single individuals. Such was the case of the golf club founded in 1918 by New York attorney George L. Reynolds (as in Reynolds Tobacco Company), who bought a chunk of property owned by Walter and William Cornwall off Cow Neck Road. He built what eventually became the back nine of the present Sands Point Golf Club course and operated it for a short time as the Harbor Hills Country Club. Julius Fleischman bought him out in 1922.

Considerably less ambitious was the Bilgewater Yacht Club, formed in 1911 and described by Peter Fraser in a *Cow Neck Historical Society Journal* article as "The Most Exclusive Yacht Club on Cow Neck." It was a very informal organization of neighbors and family members; the club included Alfred Valentine Fraser and his younger brother Robert; Wright Chapman, who had a summer home on Sands Point Road and his older brother Charles H.; and William Lippincott and his brother "JT." Edward Lapham, who married a Willets and lived in the old Sands house in Port Washington, was the seventh member. Both Frasers were directors of the of the New York branch of C. M. Lampson & Co., a London-based fur auction house which became the Hudson's Bay Co. Chapman was treasurer of the Turner Construction Co.

The club house was a two-room boathouse on Lippincott's beach and the fleet consisted of three gaff-rigged sloops about 12 feet long and painted white. Fraser's sister Kathleen Mary provided a perpetual trophy that was won in 1911 by the Lippincott brothers and in 1912 by the Frasers.

Dreams of greater racing glory on the part of Bilgewater members brought about the demise of the Club, as the members joined larger clubs that offered

Book publisher William Lippincott, who bought a large shingled home down on Hempstead Harbor around 1906, is shown here on his beach-house terrace. His son, William Lippincott, Jr., was a member of the Bilgewater Yacht Club along with the Frasers and Motts. (From the Collection of Peter Fraser)

stiffer competition. By 1913, Bob Fraser (who went on to become a commodore of the Manhasset Bay Yacht Club) and Wright Chapman both had much larger boats. The two compiled distinguished racing records over 40-year sailing careers.

PARTIES AND GOOD WORKS

Many people who had dining rooms seating 20 or so used them for more than entertaining family and friends. Often, they were the locale for philanthropic or political endeavors. The Daniel Guggenheims hosted Liberty Bond rallies. Bourke Cockran was known for his staff Christmas Party. Mrs. Belmont and Mrs. Laidlaw entertained members of various groups that supported votes for women.

Congressman Hicks frequently entertained constituents in his home. His Fourth of July party in 1917, billed as a patriotic occasion, included a large cross-section of the then all-male voting public. Among the guests were 40 uniformed members of the Sheriff's Reserve (an auxiliary organized during World War I) and more than 100 members of the Home Defense Corps, which was under Major Clarence Eagle, another Sands Point resident. They all marched up from Port Washington, led by the St. Peter of Alcantara School Band. The Home Defense Corps gave an exhibition drill on the lawn, Hicks delivered a "rousing speech," and Mrs. Hicks and her friends served Cow Bay clam chowder and sandwiches.

The women of Sands Point during the early 1900s

AMERICAN SMELTING & REFINING CO.

120 BROADWAY,

DANIEL GUGGENHEIM,
PRESIDENT.

NEW YORK.

July 16, 1918.

Charles N. Wysong, Esq.,
    Port Washington,
        Long Island, New York.

My dear Mr. Wysong:

I am in receipt of your letter of July 11th and appreciate the situation outlined by you regarding the rector of the Episcopal Church at Port Washington. While I should not care to obligate myself to make regular contributions for the purpose mentioned by you, I take pleasure in enclosing my check to your order for $100.00 as a contribution to the fund which you are raising.

I shall be obliged if you will return the receipted voucher to me at your convenience.

With kind regards,

Sincerely yours,

Daniel Guggenheim

Daniel Guggenheim was a noted philanthropist who supported local endeavors as well as national causes. Though Jewish, he probably chose to contribute to St. Stephens because Charles Wysong, a member of its vestry, was Guggenheim's local lawyer. (Courtesy, Port Washington Public Library)

were as involved with local charitable organizations as their predecessors had been. In a 1961 article in *The Port Mail*, long-time Port Washington resident Eleanor Haffner reminisced about her childhood: "I was in the first Campfire troop in Port Washington. Kathleen Norris, the famous writer, Priscilla Sousa [John Philip Sousa's daughter] and Col. Green's wife were all our leaders. We used to camp at Laidlaw's at Sands Point."

THEY COULDN'T HAVE DONE IT WITHOUT THEM

You can bet that Mrs. Hicks had help in the kitchen and gardeners on hand to repair damages to the lawn caused by all those party guests. A domestic staff was a necessity in the households of the well-off. It was close to impossible to operate a large establishment of that day without help. At the Daniel Guggenheim estate there were 200 or more people working on the grounds, the farm, in the stables and in the house during the summer months. Though a number of the house servants lived on the premises, many of the workers had homes in Port Washington that were close enough that they walked to work. Some, such as Alfred Hults, superintendent of the Howard Gould and the Harry Guggenheim estates from 1910 to 1940, were from old Port Washington families. Many were immigrants who had been in service in Europe and found work on the great estates when they came to this country.

One of the more exciting jobs on the Sands Point estates was that of chauffeur. Many estate owners had been accustomed to coachmen caring for and driving their horses. Naturally, they wanted to hire someone to care for and drive their automobiles. (Many estates had their own gasoline tanks and pumps.) Others thought it was too difficult or dangerous to learn to drive. So having chauffeurs played a vital role in early 20th century Sands Point life and were often provided with pleasant living quarters on the grounds. That way, they were on call whenever they were needed.

It was fortuitous for four-year-old Martha, daughter of A. A. Messenger of Sands Point and his second wife, that Joe Salerno, chauffeur for their neighbor Hawthorne Howard, was nearby on a Monday afternoon in March of 1920. Martha was playing on the ice of a large pond near the house when she broke though and went under. Her initial scream drew the attention of Salerno, who "jumped into the water and, feeling around under the ice, happened to

An employee soccer team at Castlegould c. 1912-1913. (Courtesy, Institute of Long Island Studies at Hofstra)

catch hold of the end of her coat and succeeded in pulling her out…she recovered rapidly…and now seems none the worse for her experience," reported the *Port Washington News.*

RELATING TO LABOR

Estate owners such as Daniel and Florence Guggenheim took a sincere interest in the welfare of their employees. An Athletic Association was formed in 1920 by the employees of Hempstead House and Guggenheim, who supplied a challenge cup, was named honorary president. The club played in a district baseball league; Sunday afternoon home games took place on the Hempstead House grounds and the public was invited. Soccer was another popular sport.

Isaac Guggenheim was also a well-liked owner. He was known for distributing gold coins in amounts of $5 to $75 to his estate staff at Christmas.

Bourke Cockran was generally respected by the people who worked on his estate. Gertrude Crampton Nicoll, a life-long Port Washington resident whose father was superintendent of the estate, described a staff Christmas party in a 1983 interview: "I remember as a little girl, Mr. Cockran taking me by the hand…to see if we could find him (Santa Claus)…We knew what Mr. Cockran meant to us."

The first Mrs. A. A. Messenger took her generosity beyond the bounds of her Sands Point property. When she died in 1905 "after a long and serious illness," the obituary noted that "she was always ready to help those who needed it. There was not a movement for

William Crampton, Supervisor, Cockran Estate (Courtesy, Gertrude Crampton Nicoll Collection, Port Washington Public Library)

the betterment of society or the village that did not have Mrs. Messenger at the head. Her place can never be filled."

THE AUTOMOBILE ARRIVES

Teams of handsome horses pulling elegant carriages filled with well-dressed and wealthy passengers were common sights in Sands Point in 1900. A decade later, horses other than saddle horses used for recreational purposes had all but disappeared from the village roads. Carriages had been replaced by automobiles. Coachmen had become chauffeurs. Auto mechanics and garages were doing a good business. The personal automobile, the vehicle that changed the face of 20th century America, had arrived.

We don't know who was the first person in Sands Point to buy an automobile, but it was probably a Guggenheim, and the car quite likely was a Cadillac. The Cadillac made its debut at the New York Automobile show in 1903, where it received excellent reviews. Cadillac's reputation for quality soon made it one of the best-selling autos in the country despite the fact that it was an expensive vehicle.

Automobiles became more available to the middle class in the next year when Henry Ford, then 40 years old, brought out his first car, which was a two-cylinder model selling for $850.

The Locomobiles, Cadillacs, Packards, Oldsmobiles and Haynes touring cars favored by the estate owners were soon outsold by Ford's mass-produced cars. Soon, chauffeurs could afford their own cars and women were getting behind the wheel. By 1915, the price tag on a Ford Model T was as low as $440.

Nevertheless, big luxury cars continued to traverse the winding roads of estate areas where poor roads made driving quite hazardous. In Cow Neck, only the major roads such as Northern Boulevard or the shore road from Manhasset to Port Washington were paved. Most were dirt-topped with a few crushed oyster shells or stones, and were muddy and rutted in the spring and fall, frozen and rutted in the winter, dusty in the summer. With inexperienced drivers at the helm and unreliable parts in the body, the early autos were extraordinarily accident prone. Crashes were frequent and sometimes fatal.

A crowd of enthusiastic spectators at the foot of Manhasset Hill waits for the big Vanderbilt Cup racers to roar past in 1906. (Wittmer Collection, Courtesy Cow Neck Peninsula Historical Society.)

AUTOMANIACS IN

SANDS POINT AND ABROAD

By 1904, someone had dubbed the drivers of speeding motor cars "Automaniacs," and the law soon went out to get them. Bourke Cockran was given a $10 ticket in 1906 for going 25 mph in Los Angeles—an offense that was duly reported by the *Port Washington News* for the benefit of readers who followed with great interest the activities of the popular congressman.

Automobile collisions and near-collisions on the yacht club driveway between members, who apparently hadn't quite absorbed the concept of keeping to the right, were a concern of the Manhasset Bay Yacht Club Board in 1907. The Trustees ordered the House Committee to seek and implement a solution. What that was is not on record

Howard Gould's driver was involved in a tragic incident in Sands Point when two boys who were sledding on a snowy incline near the road crashed their sled into the rear end of Gould's automobile. Chauffeur William Holland, the shaken but blameless driver, rushed the boys to Dr. Cooke's Chantaclair Sanitorium, but eight-year-old John Reumens was dead on arrival. His friend Sullivan DeMar, 11, was treated and taken to his home.

An accident that was the result of human error—speeding—occurred when Walker Hewitt, who was driving down Middle Neck Road from Sands Point with his guest, George Baldwin, collided with Isaac Guggenheim's car, which was driven by a chauffeur.

The chauffeur "came tearing around the corner en route for the depot," scolded the *Port Washington News*. All but one of the occupants of the two vehicles escaped injury. The renown of the auto owners put the story on the front page of the August 4, 1916 issue.

Though running boards made it easier to climb up into the high-clearance vehicles, and were regarded as a legitimate way to cram more passengers aboard, they were a constant source of early auto accidents. Congressman Hicks suffered a concussion when he fell off on his way to tennis matches at Wampage Shores.

Some of the roads were in truly deplorable condition. Louis Jandorf, who had recently built a new home near Cornwall Road in Sands Point, went before the Town Board in July of 1914 to complain that "it is in very serious condition and it is only a matter of time before a serious accident occurs." The Town Board told Jandorf they had no jurisdiction over the matter and he should to go to the village of Sands Point, which promptly told him the section in question wasn't theirs either.

Despite the ineptitude of some of the early drivers, the quirks of most of the early cars, and the poor condition of many roads, the automobile continued to gain acceptance and soon gave birth to a wildly popular sport—automobile racing.

THE BIGGEST SPECTATOR SPORT OF ALL

The glamour and glory of the automobile got a big assist when millionaire William K. Vanderbilt, an automobile enthusiast, established the Vanderbilt Cup races (1904-1910). Drivers competed for the prestige and prize: a Tiffany-designed silver cup valued at $2,000. Trailing clouds of exhaust and dust, the big cars roared through Long Island's villages and hamlets, jeopardizing the lives of the drivers and the nearly one million spectators who thronged the roadside along the route. (Later races were run on the Vanderbilt Motor Parkway, the first concrete non-stop exclusive automobile road in this country, which ran 35 miles from the Queens border to Ronkonkoma. Vestiges are still in use in Dix Hills.) Crowds came from the city and all over the Island to line the roadside and watch the races, packing local hotels, inns and farmhouses the night before the race. The big cars built here and abroad for speed, driven by racing stars such as

People were fascinated by airplanes, and Long Island's first aviation meet in Mineola on September, 1911, drew thousands of spectators. Sands Point's own Caleb Bragg set altitude records and became a WWI test pilot. (Wittmer Collection Courtesy, Cow Neck Historical Society)

America's Barney Oldfield, attained speeds of up to 100 mph by 1909.

It was that very power that did in those great races. The author of *America On Wheels* summed up the popular race's demise, saying: "Lacking the steering and brakes of today's cars, it's not surprising that far more pedestrians were killed at road races than drivers. At the finish line, for example, crowds had to be hosed off the track in advance of the speeding vehicles."

ROCKING THE CRADLE OF AVIATION

Although the average person did not own an airplane or even hope to do so, the use of aircraft during World War I drew attention to the exploits of skilled and daring flyers, both military and private. Nassau County's flat Hempstead Plains buzzed with overhead activity, causing it to be called the Cradle of Aviation.

Seaplanes, especially, captured the fancy of those who lived near the water. Some Sands Point estates had their own seaplane hangars. Most communities had a local flyer-hero. In Sands Point, he was Caleb Bragg of

A 1906 walking party relaxes at the Cockran's Landing Stage with Hempstead Harbor in the background. (Wittmer Collection, Cow Neck Peninsula Historical Society)

Wampage Shores, who graduated from Yale in 1908 and first made a name for himself as an automobile racer. On September 28,1917, he set an altitude record of 21,500 feet over Mineola in a Wright Martin aircraft. Though not a member of the armed forces at the time, Bragg's experiments in high-altitude flight provided valuable to Army research. Bragg maintained a seaplane hangar on the shores of Manhasset Bay near the Port Washington Yacht Club, as did Harold Vanderbilt (both hangars were destroyed in 1928 in the fire that also ravished the Purdy Shipyard). He added another altitude record to his list in October of 1919, when he flew to 19,100 feet above Port Washington in a Loening seaplane equipped with a Hispano-Suiza motor. It took him 15 minutes to get up there. Bragg also owned a speedboat named *Krazy Kat*.

DOWN WITH THE NEW, UP WITH THE NEWER

Among the first of the "new" houses to change hands was Alfred Fraser's Ashcombe, the large, shingled summer home he built for his sizable family around 1895. After his death in 1915, his son Robert sold the Fraser property to Edgar Luckenbach, the steamship magnet. Luckenbach wanted to use the name Ashcombe, but Fraser would not sell it. The name came from the family estate in England and was one that Fraser used again when he built a new Ashcombe in 1953 on Old House Lane overlooking Hempstead Harbor. (The original Sands Point Ashcombe was located on what is now Shorewood Drive.)

Luckenbach eventually built an Italianate mansion called Elm Court. Either he knew little of country life or his gardener knew little of plant life. Robert Fraser's son Peter passed along a family story that Luckenbach built a fence along Middle Neck Road and instructed his gardener to plant something that would be colorful in the fall. It turned out to be poison ivy.

Robert Fraser, who married Anie Franke from Beacon Hill in 1917, moved his family uptown to a house on Port Washington Boulevard, where the EAB building now stands. It was just a few blocks from the railroad station, simplifying his commute. Fraser's move did not inspire a mass exodus from Sands Point.

Steamship magnate Edgar Luckenbach's mansion later became the Sands Point Country Day School. The building was demolished in the 1980s to make way for new houses. (Courtesy Port Washington Public Library)

On the contrary, affluent individuals and families continued to find the peninsula an appealing place for their country homes and, increasingly, for their all-year residences.

CHAPTER 8

1915-1920
TIME OF MOMENTOUS DECISIONS: WORLD WAR I, VOTES FOR WOMEN, PROHIBITION

hroughout its history, Sands Point has been a village whose residents readily throw themselves into political, social and charitable causes. Men and women of Sands Point fought for independence from Britain and later battled to preserve the union. When the U.S. entered World War I, Sands Point supported the war effort the same as it supported George Washington and his friends at the time of the American Revolution. Sands Point women (and men, too) were leaders in the fight for women's right to vote; others took pivotal roles in temperance crusades. Almost everyone pitched in to help during the virulent flu epidemics of 1918 and the '20s.

The early years of the 20th century were happy and prosperous for most Long Islanders. The few remaining farmers in Cow Neck sold their crops at good prices and their land at even higher ones. The new estates in Sands Point provided jobs for many Port Washington residents and boosted local business. Their owners enjoyed the amenities of Sands Point and shared a busy social life with friends from the city as well as their neighbors in the country.

When Archduke Franz Ferdinand of Austria and his wife were killed in Sarajevo on June 28, 1914 by student nationalists, it's unlikely that it occurred to Cow Neck residents other than historians that the distant political incident would involve the United States in a global conflict, or that the United States, which had tried to stay out of European wars, would soon enter one that would rearrange the balance of power in Europe and set the stage for World War II some 26 years later.

After the assassination, Austria declared war on Serbia. Russia put its troops on alert. Germany went to war with Russia and France. Britain declared war on Germany. And the Germans invaded Belgium on their way to France. Conflicting loyalties and bids for power turned Europe into an especially bloody turmoil.

Leo Forman, who later married his distant cousin Katherine Forman of Sands Point, drove an ambulance for the U.S. Army in Italy. He was decorated for bravery by the Italian Government. (Courtesy, James Forman)

AMERICA WAKES UP

By 1915, Americans had been shocked into awareness of the "horrible slaughter going on in Europe," according to the *Port Washington News* editor, who theorized that, despite prayers for peace by the general public, the profit motive was extending the conflict. Editor Hyde asked, "are numbers of our great factories filling orders for munitions of war and shipping them to the combatants only to prolong the struggle?" And he speculated about the advisability of bringing the war to a halt by ceasing to supply American munitions to the combatants.

The exigencies of war really hit home on May 7, 1915, when a German submarine sank the British liner *Lusitania* off the Irish coast. Of the 1,959 passengers and crew aboard, 1,200 lost their lives, including 128 Americans who had ignored the advertisements published in U.S. newspapers by the German Embassy that warned Americans not to sail on British vessels. The American public was indignant, but the American government, led by President Wilson, remained determined to keep the country out of war. The Germans claimed the *Lusitania* was carrying munitions, an assertion that later was found to be true.

Wilson made neutrality his major goal and campaigned for reelection in 1916 with the slogan "He Kept Us Out of War." Other Americans supported aiding the French—or at least getting ready to do so. Former President Theodore Roosevelt, bored and feeling left out, was one of the moving forces behind the growing Preparedness Movement. On May 13, 1916, a parade of preparedness organizations took place on Fifth Avenue, with Teddy Roosevelt prominent among the dignitaries on the reviewing stand. Among the marchers was a group of 1,200 society women organized by Eleanor Alexander Roosevelt, wife of Theodore Roosevelt, Jr. Marching under the banner of "The Independent Patriotic Women of America" were her normally retiring mother-in-law, Edith Kermit Roosevelt; Mrs. Robert Bacon; Mrs. J. Borden "Daisy" Harriman; and Mrs. Hamilton Fish. It seems quite likely that such Sands Point activists as Harriet Laidlaw and Alva Belmont were marching beside them.

Despite the success of the parade, Roosevelt believed that the country as a whole remained in a stupor of indifference. "I despise Wilson," he wrote, "but I despise still more our foolish, foolish people who partly from ignorance and partly from sheer timidity, and partly from lack of imagination and of sensitive national feeling, support him."

SUBS TORPEDO NEUTRALITY

A year later, Roosevelt's speech might have been more charitable. On February 26, 1917, the man who had hoped to keep America out of war was forced to arm U.S. merchant ships. The German submarine fleet of more than 100, hoping to starve the Allies into

One day in 1917, Port Washington's Home Guard assembled on the field in front of the high school and posed for this group shot. The Guard, commanded by Sands Point's Major Clarence Eagle, is shown with South Washington Street behind it. The house (left) with the flag on the porch still stands. (Courtesy, Bryant Library)

submission, was causing havoc with trans-Atlantic shipping. American ships, which were assumed to be carrying supplies to the French and English, were not spared in the attacks.

Wanting to play an active role, Theodore Roosevelt requested permission to raise a division of reconstituted Rough Riders. Alice Roosevelt's biographer, Carol Felsenthal, writes that Congress "had authorized TR's request to take his volunteers to France, the public loved the idea, and French Prime Minister George Clemenceau wrote an open letter urging him (Wilson) to send TR, but Wilson…said no. TR now called Wilson an 'abject coward' and an 'internal skunk in the White House.'"

Then, in a dreadful nine-day period in March, five American ships were sunk without warning. Wilson finally felt compelled to ask Congress to declare war, saying, "It is a fearful thing to lead this great peaceful people into war, into the most evil and disastrous of all wars, civilization itself seeming to be in the balance." Congressional support was overwhelming. War against Germany was declared on April 6, 1917.

THE HOME GUARD

While waiting for Washington to act, Americans became seriously concerned about preparedness. Harking back to the Revolutionary War's tradition of a citizen militia, Home Guard groups sprang up throughout the state. Port Washington's Home Guard unit was particularly successful due, quite likely, to the military and administrative skills of Major Clarence H. Eagle of Sands Point, a former member of the New York National Guard who was appointed its commander. Able-bodied male residents signed up eagerly; on April 13, 1917 the *Port Washington News* wrote:

> *The citizens meeting at Liberty Hall last week will go down in local history as having been one of the most important gatherings in the way of good and patriotic work well done ever held in the confines of the Port…the forming of the home guard was effective and thorough. Many of Port's citizens enrolled themselves for such future service as would best aid the protection of the hometown and the country at large if stern necessity demanded…."* Two weeks later, the local newspaper was still lauding the Home Guard while berating the uninvolved. "*Many people do not yet realize that our country is at war. May no disaster, sorrow or suffering come through any failure on our part!*

The State of New York established a two-tier Home Guard on a state-wide basis in May of 1917. The First Division was a quasi-military one designed to replace the New York State National Guard when it was called into federal service. In addition to the commanding officer Clarence Eagle, others included writer John Floherty, captain of Company A, who lived in Baxter Estates and had been a member of the Seventh Regiment in New York City; F. T. Lyons, who headed Company B; and Captain Henry Eagle, the major's son, who was in charge of Company C. (Henry Eagle later became mayor of Sands Point from 1931 to 1939).

SANDS POINT'S MAJOR EAGLE

Clarence Eagle, son of Commodore Henry Eagle, United States Navy, and Minerva Smith Eagle, was born in New York City in 1856. He joined the fashionable 7th Regiment in 1875, was commissioned Captain in the 12th regiment in 1883, and later became a Major on the first brigade staff. Eagle was also an active club man and, according to his 1922 obituary in the *Port News*, belonged to Alpha Delta Phi, the Loyal Legion, Sons of the Revolution, the

Patriotism was fashionable during WWI and a frequent design motif. This elaborate silver frame (with photo) was a gift from Captain W. L. Gay, stationed at Camp Mills, to his fiancee Helen Willets Remsen of Roslyn in 1917. (Courtesy, Joan Gay Kent)

Naval Order of the United States, the Aztec Society and the Military Order of Foreign Wars. He was survived by his wife, "a daughter of late Enoch Ketcham, son Henry, and a daughter, Mrs. Herbert A. Fell." (The failure to give the first name of either woman, demonstrates the still-prevalent attitude that women were but accessories to their husbands.)

The Port Washington Home guard, officially the Military Division of the Home Defense League of Port Washington, was the first in Nassau County to take the oath of allegiance to the state and be recognized as Reserve State Militia. The new militia was highly regarded by the people of the community, who saw its mission as essential to the war effort. At the 1917 Memorial Day exercises at the high school (Main Street School) grounds, the Guard was presented with a silk flag by the women of the Village Welfare Society.

In accepting the gift, Major Eagle was reported as saying, "I believe that the battalion is worthy of such a flag. It took some grit and determination for practically every man to take the oath of allegiance, to organize under the laws of the State of New York, and become real soldiers, entitled to wear the uniform and be armed with military rifles...."

The Home Guard of well over 100 members marched and drilled on the high school field, learned to handle firearms in military fashion, and was available for special assignments. According to a member of the unit, the Port Washington Home Guard was so well prepared that members who subsequently entered the service did so with the rank of corporal. The various local Home Guard units were eventually folded into the Home Defense Regiment of Nassau County, with Captain Samuel D. D McAlister of Garden City, a retired regular army officer, appointed as commander by Governor Whitman. Major Eagle retained his rank in the county setup.

The home of Dr. Forbes Hawkes c. 1910-1915. Hawkes and his wife Alice were among the 87 property owners who signed the petition in 1910 requesting incorporation as the Village of Barkers Point. Mrs. Hawkes was one of the founders of the Village Welfare Society. (Courtesy, Port Washington Public Library)

VILLAGE WELFARE SOCIETY

The Village Welfare Society was concerned with health and social welfare activities, which included the Port Washington Visiting Nurse Association. A number of Sands Point residents assisted this worthy organization, which was founded in 1909, including Advisory Board members W. Butler Duncan, Daniel Guggenheim, Howard T. Kingsbury and W. DeForrest Wright. The Executive Committee included Mrs. Forbes Hawkes and Mrs. Isaac Guggenheim. When the

Port Washington Red Cross chapter was organized in 1917, the Village Welfare League pledged its support.

World War I veteran George Bergman, mayor of Sands Point from 1953-1957, at center, marches down Main Street in Port Washington's 1999 Memorial Day Parade. (Courtesy, Port Washington News)

SANDS POINTERS IN SERVICE

General John J. Pershing, who had served with distinction in the Mexican war, was appointed to lead the American Expeditionary Force (AEF) to France. Nearly 1000 people turned up at the Port Washington High School auditorium on the evening of May 11, 1917, to listen to Bourke Cockran laud the 11 young men from Port Washington who had enlisted in the armed services.

Congress backed its declaration of war by passing the Selective Service Act, requiring the registration and drafting of males between the ages of 21 and 30. Registration for the Federal Draft took place on June 3, 1917, and 548 eligible men registered that day from Port Washington (including Sands Point). Training camps were established throughout the country. When Selective Service expanded the age limit in September, 793 Port Washington men between the ages of 18 and 45 "registered their name upon the rolls of the available for the final smashing blow at the Kaiser," reported the ever-chauvinistic *Port Washington News*. By July 13th there were 31 names on Port's Honor Roll. In all, 330 men from Port Washington saw military service in 1917 and 1918. Sands Point was represented by both estate owners and estate workers.

M. Robert Guggenheim (1885-1959), oldest son of Daniel and Florence Guggenheim, who up until

Camp Mills on the fringes of Garden City was truly a tent city that sprang up almost overnight. It served as a staging area for troops, including those from Long Island, who were going overseas. (Courtesy, Institute for Long Island Studies)

then had been a coupon-clipping "gentleman of leisure," joined the 69th regiment as a lieutenant. While overseas he met Lt. Dwight Eisenhower, who became a lifelong friend. This led to his appointment as ambassador to Portugal during Eisenhower's presidency. (Unfortunately, Guggenheim managed to insult a woman from an important Portuguese family and the host country requested his removal.) Though Guggenheim's life ambition seemed to be to marry well (which he did, four times) and amuse himself, he remained in the Army Reserve after the war and attained the rank of Colonel, a title of which he was most proud, and served on the staff of the War Department from 1932 to 1935.

Harry Guggenheim (1890-1971), the son of Daniel Guggenheim, is known locally as the co-founder of *Newsday*. He was also one of Long Island's

early aviators, and had an opportunity to put his favorite pastime to work for his country when he joined the Navy. A graduate of England's Cambridge University, he had learned to fly shortly before the U.S. entered the war. He was commissioned in the U.S. Naval Reserve on September 14, 1917, and sent to bombing and gunnery school in France. By the end of the war he had attained the rank of lieutenant commander and was permanently committed to furthering the development of aviation.

Airman Caleb Bragg, a man who really helped aviation get off the ground by setting altitude records, was one of Sands Point's more adventurous residents. A member of the Yale class of 1908 who did graduate work at MIT, he was described in his *New York Times* obituary of October 26, 1943, as a "pioneer automobile racing driver, an Army test pilot during the first World War, a champion altitude flier, aviation manufacturing company officer, consulting engineer and amateur sportsman." He was also an inventor. So it was no surprise that by the time America entered the fray, Bragg was already in Florida training a Yale aviation unit. He was soon commissioned as a captain in the Army and assigned to Cook Field in Dayton, Ohio. In 1918, he set a speed record of two hours and fifty minutes flying from Dayton to Washington, D.C.

After the war, Bragg continued to set speed and altitude records. He served in executive positions and as director of several aviation-related firms. It is presumed he was a bachelor; his only known survivor was a sister who lived in Syosset. At the time of his death, at age 56, Bragg had residences on Park Avenue in Manhattan and at Montauk.

Major Frederick Greene, a civil engineering graduate of Virginia Military Institute in 1890, had had an extensive career in construction work when he was commissioned shortly after the U.S. entered the war. He directed road construction at Camp Upton, the huge training camp in Suffolk County, and was subsequently sent to France, charged with reconstructing roads destroyed by artillery or mines. He faced the dangers of combat at the Battle of the Argonne Forest. Governor Alfred E. Smith drew on the major's expertise in March of 1919, when he appointed Greene New York State Commissioner of Highways. Greene was an active supporter of the Port Washington Public Library. Grace was a local leader in the women's suffrage movement, an activity that had her husband's support.

The childhood home of William W. Douglas was the Sands Point lighthouse, of which his father was keeper. Young Douglas was working on the Sands Point estate of Mrs. C. D. Welch when he was called to service. Enrolled in the 310th Infantry, he arrived in France in June and subsequently was wounded by machine gun fire, from which he recovered. However, he later contracted lumbar pneumonia and died on February 12, 1918.

Leo Forman wasn't yet a Sands Pointer when he joined the U.S. Army Ambulance Service with the Italian Army (an ally in that war) in 1916. He was a member of the class of 1917 at Oberlin College that volunteered en mass to serve, even though their country had not entered the fighting. Most of his service was spent driving the rugged mountains behind Venice, the territory described by Ernest Hemingway, a fellow ambulance driver, in a *Farewell to Arms*. Private First Class Leo I. Forman was awarded a Distinguished Service Medal by the Italian government for his rescue of an Italian soldier pinned beneath a burning ambulance. The medal was presented by King Victor Emanuel at a ceremony in the Pantheon in Rome.

THE YALE BOYS

Even before the Home Guard was organized, a group of 12 Yale college students were learning to fly over Manhasset Bay as the First Unit of the Aerial Coast Patrol. They were led by Trubee Davison of Locust Valley, son of H. P. Davison of J. P. Morgan & Co., and Robert Lovett, son of Robert Lovett of the Union Pacific Railway. Financed entirely out of their families' large pockets, the "Rich Men," as they were called by the *Port Washington News*, were housed at the Davison family estate, "Peacock Point," and commuted daily by auto to Manhasset Bay.

The intrepid group used a floating hangar at the Town Dock belonging to the Trans-Oceanic Company, founded by Rodman Wanamaker, who had hoped to develop and build a flying boat large and

This Burgess-Dunne Seaplane afloat on Manhasset Bay near Port Washington Yacht Club in 1917, may have been flown by the Yale students who trained in Port the previous summer. Caleb S. Bragg, who lived in Sands Point, kept his own plane in the hangar shown in the background. (Courtesy, Nassau County Museum collection)

powerful enough to cross the Atlantic. The Yale Unit later added two more flying boats at its own expense. The seriousness of their intent, and the dazzle of their exploits, captured the fancy of Cow Neck residents. By September, when Trubee Davison's plane lost an engine over the East River and he and passenger Robert Lovett plunged 1,000 feet to land the flying boat on the water, the Yale boys were referred to as "Port Washington Aviators."

In the fall, the Yale contingent left Long Island for New Haven with their planes, and training continued. When the U.S. entered the war, the Yale boys were ready to transfer their skills to aerial warfare. With few planes available for instruction, trained flyers such as the members of the Yale Unit must have been welcome recruits.

THE FLU AND OTHER EPIDEMICS

In all, 330 men from Port Washington and Sands Point saw military service in 1917 and 1918. Eight of those young men lost their lives in the conflict. Half of the deaths, such as that of William Douglas, were due to respiratory ailments, no doubt exacerbated by crowded conditions in the camps and bivouac. In those pre-penicillin days, disease took a toll as heavy as bullets.

The 1918 Spanish influenza epidemic killed more than 500,000 Americans. The sometimes-deadly and easily-transmitted disease gained momentum in

September. The New York State Health Commission issued a warning detailing the all too-familiar symptoms. Emergency hospitals were soon set up all over the country to isolate and treat the victims. One was established at Barkers Point under Red Cross auspices, with Mrs. Allen Walker in charge.

By the end of the month, the hospital had discharged all of its patients and was closed. Over at the Camp Mills embarkation center in Mineola, the severity was such that County Officials decided to cancel the popular exhibition at the Mineola Fair Grounds set for the end of October.

It was typhoid that killed Georgiana Strong Hicks, wife of the Congressman Frederick Hicks of Sands Point. She died on the first day of 1918 at the couple's Washington home after a few days of illness. Active in local and national philanthropies, she was a well-known figure in Port Washington and her death was reported on the front page of the community newspaper.

Americans had to contend not only with the flu in 1918, but the return of infantile paralysis (polio) as well. The New York epidemic that started in 1916 began in the tenement districts of Brooklyn, rapidly spread to other parts of the city, and then expanded out into the suburbs with the aid of the subway and train systems. The situation was sufficiently serious for the New York State Department of Health to issue instructions on "how to Prevent Infant Paralysis," which appeared in newspapers throughout the state. Ten thousand leaflets were distributed door-to-door in North Hempstead by volunteers from Nassau County women's suffrage groups. One Sands Point family fought the threat by buying farms in the hills of Vermont, to which they retired for the hottest summer days.

LIBERTY BOND SALES EXCEED QUOTAS

Selling Liberty Bonds was one way the government raised the money needed to expand the American arsenal. The people of Cow Neck backed their "boys" with their pocketbooks, consistently going over the top in their purchase of Liberty Bonds and strong support of the American Red Cross with money and volunteer hours. A typical fund-raiser, promoting the Fourth Liberty Bond Drive, was billed as a "Big Patriotic Meeting." It took place in the high school auditorium on October 8, 1917 and featured Clarence Buddington Kelland—a Port Washington resident and nationally known author who, according to the advertising, had just returned from France where he had "been in every principal fight of the American Forces since May 25th."

A more informal bond rally took place on the broad lawns of Hempstead House when Mr. and Mrs. Daniel Guggenheim hosted a gathering of "patriotic people" in 1917. After the close of the requisite speeches, Mrs. Guggenheim announced that $375,000 had already been subscribed. She then dispatched 20 members of the Young Woman's Recreation League to circulate amongst the crowd and distribute application blanks. After one hour, the total had grown to $400,000. "Let's make it a half a million," Daniel Guggenheim is alleged to have said, and "the most patriotic millionaire Port has yet had," according to the *Port Washington News*, went down on the list for $100,000.

RED CROSS VOLUNTEERS HARD AT WORK

The people of Cow Neck also backed their "boys" with energy. The local chapter of the American Red Cross was inaugurated in February, 1917, at a meeting of 25 women. They listened attentively as Port Washington's Allen Walker, an executive of the Chamber of Commerce of the United States and husband of one of the group's organizers, talked to them about the spirit and purpose of the American Red Cross. It was "the surgical and medical angel of military and naval preparedness and after all, the most Christian part of it." The Port Washington Chapter attracted such strong support that it reached 200% of its membership quota.

The Red Cross was expected to produce medical and hospital supplies. The Port Washington chapter offered training in first aid and turned out supplies in its Main Street workroom. A description of the comfort supplies assembled in one week says: "28 knitted sets, 4 helmets and 10 extra sweaters were delivered at the Red Cross chapter's house for the Aviation men, a total of 19 sets over and above the quota of 93 allotted to Port Washington."

The Red Cross also raised money for medical supplies through direct solicitation and fund-raising events. So involved was the community in Red Cross activities that the *Port Washington News* devoted front page space to a regular column entitled "Red Cross Notes." Items from just one week's column indicate the extent of the involvement of Sands Pointers. (Sands Point didn't have a chapter of its own because there weren't enough people in the village.)

> *"Mrs. Isaac Guggenheim has sent 150 books to be distributed among the soldiers at Camp Mills, a thoughtful and generous contribution.*

> *"Through the kindness of Mesdames Wm. Cornell and Noon, two sewing machines have been secured for additional Red Cross work.*

> *"Mrs. Montrose has donated a quantity of writing pads which will be presented to the soldiers in the Camp Mills hospital."*

Camp Mills in Mineola was established in 1917 as a point of embarkation. Hazelhurst Field in Carle Place trained U.S. aviators such as Quentin Roosevelt, son of the former president. After he was shot down and killed over Germany, the airfield was renamed Roosevelt Field. (The name remains though the "field" is now a giant parking lot for the largest shopping mall on Long Island.)

This World War I Victory Parade made its way up East Broadway in Roslyn in 1919. (Photo by W. R. Pickering. Courtesy, Bryant Library)

SANDS POINT WOMEN, SUFFRAGIST LEADERS

Some of the women rolling bandages no doubt took the opportunity to further the cause of women's suffrage. By the 1900s, the cause had become both fashionable and politically popular on Long Island, and the movement towards voting rights for women continued to gain momentum around the country and on Long Island after 1910. It involved such Sands Point notables as Harriet Burton Laidlaw (1873-1949), who was ably assisted and supported by her husband, James Lees Laidlaw (1858-1923); Mrs. Frederick Greene; Grace E. Clapp; and Alva Vanderbilt Belmont.

Mr. and Mrs. Laidlaw are among the five Long Islanders whose names appear on the New York State Suffrage Memorial plaque in Albany. She was one of a number of educated women who had the talent and leisure time to devote themselves to the increasingly popular cause of votes for women. She had the additional advantage of firmly-demonstrated support from her husband. He often appeared on the platform with her when she had a speaking engagement, adding an air of respectability to her efforts that was not always accorded to other female other women's suffrage advocates.

The Laidlaws had homes in Manhattan and Sands Point and were active on national, state and local levels. Harriet was an officer in the North American Woman Suffrage Association (1911-1920, a member of the New York State Woman's Suffrage Party, and a leader in the Nassau County suffrage campaign in 1917. She also hosted benefit tea parties on her front lawn, marched in suffrage parades and attended benefit balls. James Laidlaw organized the New York Men's League for Woman's Suffrage in 1910 and was president of the national Men's League for Woman's Suffrage from 1912 to 1920. Laidlaw also backed his moral support with dollars; a newspaper account tells of his matching gift of $1,000 to a Nassau County fund-raising effort.

Grace Greene was particularly effective on the local level. She was chairman of the Nassau County Suffrage Party for five years, resigning in 1920 when the appointment of her husband as State Highway Commissioner brought their move to Albany in 1919.

Alva Belmont could have been sufficiently busy simply managing her five households. In addition to Beacon Towers in Sands Point, she owned a Manhattan town house, an estate in East Meadow, and two Newport mansions. Instead, she chose to use her time, considerable energy and financial resources to work for the cause of women's suffrage. Alva organized one of the first suffrage clubs on Long Island, in East Meadow in 1911. The following year, she took fellow suffragists on a hike from New York to Albany to publicize the cause, and followed it up in 1913 with a "march on Washington," a feat that led the media to call her "General."

She also held meetings at her Sands Point home and was right out in front, marching, whenever there was a suffragist parade.

Sands Point was well represented at the New York State Woman Suffrage Party convention in 1916, held in the resort City of Long Beach. Long Island leaders in attendance included the indomitable Mrs. Laidlaw, novelist Kathleen Norris of Port Washington, Mrs. Charles L. Tiffany of Oyster Bay, and the hard-working Mrs. Greene, who was re-elected Vice Chairman of the group. Another Sands Point resident attending one of the largest gatherings of its kind ever on Long Island was Mrs. George A. Thayer.

On January 12, 1915, a resolution to enfranchise women was debated on the floor of the House of Representatives. It was very first time this subject had been considered. Though the resolution was defeated 204 to 174, due to overwhelming opposition from southern congressmen, the very fact that the issue got as far as the House floor heartened the suffragists. Carrie Chapman Catt, chairman of the Empire State Campaign Committee, proclaimed that "It was the threshold of victory."

By the time the United States broke off relations with Germany, the New York State Woman's Suffrage Party boasted 500,000 members, with representation in each of the 150 assembly districts. With its excellent instinct for attention-getting publicity, the party adopted a resolution offering its services to Governor Whitman. The suffragist' strategy—to show the valuable assistance women could provide in time of crisis—resulted in useful civilian war service as well as new respect and admiration for the determined women suffragists. In August of 1917, Mrs. Laidlaw was named chairman of food conservation for the Suffrage Party. Her job, supporting the national program run by U. S. Food Administrator Herbert Hoover, was to ensure the distribution of 100,000 food conservation pledge cards.

Harriet Burton Laidlaw was Manhattan Borough Chairwoman of the Woman Suffrage Party when this photo was taken around 1915. (Courtesy, Mary Backus Rankin)

MRS. LAIDLAW LED THE WAY

In her later years, Harriet Laidlaw was known to her family as the beloved grandmother of a boisterous crew of tennis players and horseback riders. During her early years in Sands Point, however, she was a vocal and industrious suffragist. She felt strongly about women's rights and expressed those thoughts loudly and sometimes dramatically. Laidlaw publicly heaped her scorn on women who opposed voting rights, calling them "ultra society women." She proclaimed, "We are not afraid of the opposition of these society women but what we are afraid of, what we have to overcome is the opposition of corrupt politicians." The Laidlaws were never afraid to show where they stood. In covering the 1913 Votes-for-Women Ball, the New York Times wrote, "There were tired, shabby little cash girls, waltzing in shirt waists. There were boys in worn, well-brushed sack coats, and there were Mrs. Herbert Carpenter and Mrs. James Lees Laidlaw in glittering ball gowns and their husbands in correct evening dress."

In July of 1913, she was the keynote speaker when a "large number of ladies met at the home of Mrs. A. A. Kilduff" to discuss the help "women could give towards bettering the conditions of the world" when they got the vote. Evidently, she was persuasive, as the North Hempstead Equal Suffrage League was formed at that very meeting. Officers elected included Sands Point residents: Mrs George Thayer, Treasurer, and Corresponding Secretary, Mrs. Frederick S. Greene.

James Laidlaw, Sands Point's first mayor (then called "president") was the grand marshal of a Suffrage Party Parade (c. 1912-1915). He is with Frederick S. Greene, also of Sands Point, whose wife was as active in the suffrage movement as Laidlaw's. (Courtesy, Harriet Backus Todd)

MEN IN THE SUFFRAGE MOVEMENT

James Laidlaw became president of the New York State Men's League for Woman Suffrage. In April 1914 he claimed that "men were joining by the hundreds." The Port Washington Suffrage League was reaching out to men, with Frederick S. Greene leading a meeting devoted to women's suffrage from the businessman's point of view. Both men were photographed mounted on horseback, riding at the head of a New York suffragist parade.

W. Bourke Cockran spoke in favor of the enfranchisement of women at a meeting held at the Academy of Music in Brooklyn, declaring that the "right of the ballot…was the proper function of a true democracy." Other men were picking up the women's suffrage banner. Politicians of both parties supported the movement and the newspapers gave it tremendous coverage, reports Ed Smits, the author of *Nassau, Suburbia, USA.*

However, when New York State put a suffrage amendment before the voters in 1915, it was defeated. (But we must remember, all of the voters were men.) In Nassau County, despite media support, the proposal went down 8,338 to 7,079. Undaunted by defeat, the suffragists just worked harder. By 1917, politicians were taking strong stands in favor of giving voting rights to women. Congressman Frederick Hicks, the Republican from Sands Point, was an advocate, as were all "the Long Island men" in the Albany Legislature.

WOMEN VOTE, AT LAST

Seeing that the tide of opinion in 1917 was turning in favor women's suffrage, Mrs. Greene enlisted the assistance of a group of energetic women who gathered 13,635 women's signatures and petitioned the Nassau County Board of Supervisors to support voting rights for women. The Supervisors endorsed a suffrage amendment to the New York State Constitution, which was approved. New York was thus added to North Dakota, Ohio, Indiana, Rhode Island, Nebraska and Michigan as states where women won the vote in 1917. Two years later, Congress adopted a joint resolution calling for the 19th amendment to the U. S. Constitution granting women the right to vote. Tennessee became the 36th state to ratify the amendment in 1920, making women's right to vote the law of the land.

TEMPERANCE AND PROHIBITION

The success of the woman's suffrage movement demonstrated what organized and determined women could accomplish. So did the temperance movement. The National Women's Christian Temperance Union of the United States (WCTU), founded in 1874 in the midwest where the temperance movement was already strong, doggedly carried the message to the rest of the country. Women believed that they and their children were the primary victims of alcoholism and drunkenness. Vaudeville performers sang, with appropriately doleful looks, "Father, dear father, come home with me now."

Though the WCTU was the most powerful force in the temperance movement, the organization (primarily composed of educated, church-going women) took a temporary back seat to the male-dominated Anti-Saloon League when its young women turned their energies to gaining the right to vote. The Anti-Saloon League, representing a number of temperance societies and evangelical Protestant churches, played a big part in the passage of the 18th Amendment.

Little is recorded about the involvement of Sands Pointers in the temperance movement at this time, probably because, like many easterners, they thought moderation to be a much more desirable goal than prohibition. And, of course, there were no saloons in the neighborhood to oppose. The *Port Washington News* reflected the prevailing Cow Neck attitude in a 1916 editorial: "the individual should be his own judge; to stake his manhood against a possible evil. Coercion, therefore, by the law, enacted by a minority, may not, after all be the best, and surest way to abate or correct the evil of drunkenness."

Secluded Sands Point beaches along Hempstead Harbor made ideal landing spots for daring rum runners during the Prohibition Era. (Watercolor by Dorothy Butterfield. Photo by Will Wright)

"BEER IS NOT INTOXICATING"

The alcoholic beverage manufacturers were adamantly opposed to prohibition of any kind and ill-disposed towards undue regulation. In 1917, the New York State Brewers' Association decided to do something about the distressing prohitionists by publishing a series of advertisements, extolling the virtues of beer, in newspapers. The *Port Washington News* printed the following: "Beer, on account of its small percent of alcohol is no more a dangerous intoxicant than coffee, with its small per cent of caffeine is a dangerous drug." Professor Chandler of Columbia University was quoted as saying, "Beer is not intoxicating in ordinary quantities and is one of the few foods that is free from bacteria."

It was obvious why the liquor distillers and brewers were opposed to prohibition—their industries would be obliterated and hundreds of thousands of men and women thrown out of work. Those involved with the shipping, distribution and retail sales of alcoholic beverages were equally concerned. Chairman Hurley of the Shipping Board used patriotism as his platform when he spoke before the Senate Agricultural Committee in 1918: "We've got to put all the smash and drive we've got into this war…taking away beer from working men would be a practical interference with labor."

Despite the implied threat of work slowdowns, the prohibitionists remained firm and the moderates seemed apathetic. The movement continued to gain momentum and clout until the forces of abstinence won and Congress proposed the 18th Amendment to the Constitution prohibiting the "manufacture, sale, or transportation" of liquors, beer and wine. In January, 1919, with Nebraska's ratification, it became law. The only states that didn't approve the 18th Amendment were Rhode Island and Connecticut. Maybe their voters knew something the rest of the country did not!

The WCTU and and Anti-Saloon League and their supporters had triumphed, but in the long run, the people who said it would never work were proved right. And Sands Point, which had had few, if any, problems stemming from the consumption of alcohol prior to the advent of Prohibition, got its share—and a bit more—once the new law took effect.

The E. Belcher Hyde map published in 1923 clearly shows Sands Point's largest property holders and the extent of Cow Neck sound mining activities at their peak. (Courtesy, Cow Neck Historical Society)

CHAPTER 9

1920-1929
GOLD COAST DAYS:
WHY F. SCOTT FITZGERALD
LOVED EAST EGG

In the decade from 1919 to 1929, so many prominent people came to live in Sands Point that the Village tax roll looked like a page of Who's Who. Celebrities were commonplace and millionaires, both newly minted and "old money," could be found on the polo field, golf course or picking up mail at the Port Washington Post Office. As large properties continued to be subdivided, enough new people moved in that the village government had to increase its police force. There was one policeman in 1923, Arthur Miller, who received $1,800 annually, plus one special policeman (who, we assume, worked on Miller's days off) at $300. By 1927, the force consisted of an acting sergeant, William Borer, and two officers. The Village Board minutes reported that it was becoming difficult to keep the Village Police with the existing salaries of $125 per month, as nearby villages and police districts were paying a minimum salary of $150 per month. Accordingly, the sergeant's pay went up to $150 monthly and the other officers received an increase to $140 per month.

In 1928 the New York State Association of Chiefs of Police profiled Borer in its annual Convention *Journal*. Now a Lieutenant and "Commanding Officer of the Sands Point Police Department," he had six patrolmen in his command. The village was described as "an exclusive residential community with many large and beautiful estates, the home of the very wealthy citizens. It has no business district. It is governed by a mayor, Mr. A. Valentine Fraser and Board of Trustees. Population about 400."

THE OLD GUARD, AND THE NEW

Who were the people the policemen were sworn to protect? Obviously, they included the old, established

A favorite landmark of yachtsmen since the turn of the century, Lands End was built for attorney C. D. Sloane and later owned by celebrity editor and public relations man Herbert Bayard Swope. The poolhouse was added sometime after Swope's death in 1958. (Courtesy, Port Washington Public Library).

families whose names continued to reappear on the village board and the boards of local charities and institutions. In 1923, the village board members were Howard Thayer Kingsbury, president, and Henry B. Anderson and Francis E. Thayer, trustees. The collector of taxes was Hall J. Tibbits. In 1928, the mayor was A. Valentine Fraser (sometime along the way it had been decided that president was too grand a title for so small a government body) and the trustees were Henry Eagle and Donald B. Cowl.

There were many outstanding newcomers, too, such as Mrs. Christian Holmes (nee Bettie Fleischman), who became an ardent advocate for prohibition reform; Dale Marker, a partner in the Harriman Brothers investment bank, with a seat on the New York Stock Exchange; Herbert Bayard Swope (1882-1958), the Pulitzer Prize-winning editor and publisher, who filled his Sands Point dining room with publishing and theatrical figures; Mr. and Mrs. Charles Rumsey, whose house was designed by McKim, Mead and White; Henry A. Alker,

Vincent Astor (1891-1959), became a Sands Point taxpayer in 1922 when he bought the 35-acre William Butler Duncan estate on Hempstead Harbor. (Courtesy, Port Washington Public Library)

construction company president; and publisher Condé Nast, who brought the glamour of *Vanity Fair* to the Gold Coast. And, not to be forgotten, were Averill Harriman and Tommy Hitchcock; they, along with John Hay "Jock" Whitney, were the wealthy players responsible for bringing polo to Sands Point. And it was Vincent Astor, who initiated the development of Harbor Acres.

Everybody in Sands Point wasn't rich, of course. There was John Duryea, still working his farm on Cow Neck Road when he died at the age of 93 in 1927; Mrs. Annie Seaman, who was driven from her property near the lighthouse by government connivance; and the local horseradish king, farmer Mahoney, an immigrant from County Cork whose grandsons made pocket money as caddies for Daniel and Solomon Guggenheim.

Donald Cowl was a valuable addition to the Village and its Board, which he served for several years. He also ran for trustee of Union Free School District No. 4 (Port Washington-Sands Point area) in 1928, sponsored by the Sands Point Association. Cowl and his backers believed that Sands Point, with an assessed valuation of more than $5 million, deserved representation on the School Board that spent its tax money. Cowl, of James A. Hearn and Son Co., a department store in New York City, came to Sands Point in 1923. His purchase of 13.5 acres from the estate of Susan Reynolds Cornwall, including 700 feet of waterfront in the "finest Sands Point Section," made the front page of the *Port Washington News* on April 27. The paper speculated that the price was between $8,000 to $10,000 per acre and predicted that Cowl

would "build a magnificent home on the highest point."

Francis Thayer, a securities broker, and his family lived in a large Colonial Revival house built by his father and mother, Kendall and Kanny. His cousin, A. Valentine Fraser (1869-1931), whose father, Alfred, had chosen Sands Point for his summer home in 1895, lived with his wife, Martha Mott Fraser, in the Mott family home near the shore. It was known as the Old House, to distinguish it from the more recent construction by Tom Fraser. Fraser was in the fur brokerage business with his brother Robert, who lived in Port Washington.

Martha Fraser had a reputation in the family as a no-nonsense person with little tolerance for trespassers on her beach, as the Sands Point police blotter for 1928 attests, as well as a tendency for frugality. According to her nephew Peter Fraser, she was known to recycle presents and put a stiff price on the fresh eggs she sold to her relatives. She was also a hard-working community volunteer, a founder of the Village Welfare Society, an organizer of the Port Washington Needlework Guild, a member of the Port Washington Library Board and a leader of the Manhasset Quaker Meeting. She was a member of the Manhasset Bay Yacht Club, the Colonial Dames, the Women's National Republican Club and a director of the Long Island Historical Society.

NEWCOMERS MAKE THEIR MARK

Henry A. Alker's entry in the *National Cyclopedia of American Biography* could be headed "Ideal Sands Point Resident c. 1925." He descended from a family that came to the United States from France in 1825. Born in Great Neck, he graduated from Yale in 1907 and went into construction work. One of his more spectacular assignments was working as the assistant engineer on the building of the Hudson and Manhattan railroad tunnel under the Hudson River. He married Charity Rose, daughter of a mining engineer, in 1908. The family moved to Sands Point in 1921 when he bought the large Mediterranean-style house at 248 Middle Neck Road, built by J. B. Donohue in 1914. He served as treasurer of the Village for 25 years.

Using the financial expertise he gained as officer of large construction firms, Alker organized the Harbor

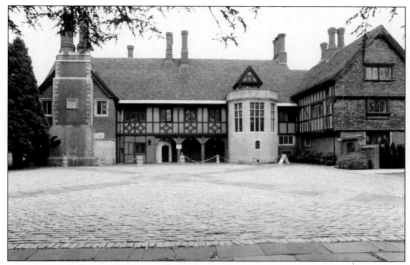

The Chimneys on Middle Neck Road, now the home of the Community Synagogue, is little changed on the exterior since it was built by Mrs. Christian Holmes in 1928. (Photo by Will Wright)

pantry and serving rooms, 11 master bedrooms, eight baths, 10 servants' rooms with four baths and a studio. Named after six of its major features, the Chimneys is one of the few important Sands Point estate houses that is clearly visible from a major roadway. Mrs. Holmes, her two sons and their families occupied the house until her death in 1941. She was described in the *Port Washington News* philanthropic person with a deep interest in human nature—and a thorough American." The property on Middle Neck Road in Sands Point, surrounded by a well-preserved serpentine brick wall, is now owned by the Community Synagogue. The exterior of the mansion, designed by Edgar I. William, looks the same as it did when Mrs. Holmes was in residence.

National Bank in Port Washington in 1929 and became its president. (Eventually it was merged with two other local banks to become the Port Washington-Manhasset National Trust Company in 1937.) The bank vice president was Alfred C. Bayles, a Port Washington pharmacist and real estate investor. In his capacity as Village treasurer, Alker distributed Sands Point's funds between his own bank, Harbor National, and the Roslyn Savings Bank. He was a member of many clubs including the Manhasset Bay Yacht Club, where his father had been Commodore from 1903 to 1907; the Lions Club of Port Washington; and the American Legion. He was also a member of St. Stephens Episcopal Church and took his turn as Sands Point's member of the Port Washington School Board.

THE CHIMNEYS

Bettie Fleischman Holmes built one of Sands Point's most handsome houses, the Chimneys, in 1928 after the death of her husband, C. R. Holmes. (He was dean of the Medical School at the University of Cincinnati in Ohio.) Her brother Max already owned a summer estate, The Lindens, at 225 Middle Neck Road. Proximity to the nearby Sands Point Golf Club as well as to her brother was said to be the reason she chose that particular site, which required 17 separate purchases to amass the approximately 40 acres. The neo-Tudor house had 42 rooms including a living room, great hall, gallery, library, dining room, breakfast room, kitchen, flower room, pressing room,

The Lindens, at 225 Middle Neck Road, shown in a 1999 photo, was built sometime prior to 1914. It was the home of Mrs. Christian Holmes' brother Max Fleischman in the 1920s. (Photo by Will Wright)

Alexander Aberdeen Forman, a real estate developer, came to Sands Point c.1921-22. He purchased some 200 acres south of Middle Neck Road, running from what is now Hilldale Lane to what is now Sousa Drive, and about 120 additional acres north of Middle Neck Road. According to his grandson, Jay Forman, whose own grandchildren are the fifth generation of the family to live in Sands Point, A. A. first built a little beach house/summer cottage down on the shore for week-end use, but it was pilfered so often that he gave up on it. He then built a very large house further back from Hempstead Harbor and laid out plans, which never saw fruition, for an extensive subdivision. In the spring of 1939, the main

Real estate developer A. A. Forman moved his family to Sands Point in the early '20s. Shown (l. to r.) in this c. 1927 photo are his children: Robert, who as an adult served for many years as Village attorney, Aberdeen and Katherine. (Courtesy of James Forman)

Editor Howard Bayard Swope introduced big-time croquet to Sands Point, entertained theatrical and literary celebrities at his waterfront home and served as a serious-minded member of the Sands Point Village Board. (Courtesy, Port Washington Public Library)

house burned down in a fire so spectacular that it made the front page of *The New York Times*. The family then built a house at the end of Hilldale Lane later occupied by their youngest son, Robert Forman, a long-time Village attorney, and owned in 1999 by Barbara and Oscar Lewnoski.

Alexander Forman's daughter Katherine married a cousin from Ohio, Leo Forman, in 1928. The young couple moved into a spacious colonial revival, a wedding present, which was built next door to her parents. For many years, Leo and Kay Forman conducted a Great Books Program in conjunction with the Port Washington Library, which frequently met at the Forman home. After World War II, taxes went up and the Formans sold off most of the rest of the property, although Katherine and her brother continued to live side by side until his death in 1990.

THE GLAMOUR GUYS AND GALS

Herbert Bayard Swope made two momentous decisions in 1928. First, he resigned as Executive Editor of Joseph Pulitzer's *New York World*. (The front-page banner headline of the *World* for December 23, 1928 read, in letters that filled the width of the paper, "SWOPE QUITS.") Then, a month later, he paid $325,000 for a 15-acre estate in Sands Point overlooking Long Island Sound, which he called Lands End. The house was built in 1900 by C. D. Sloane and subsequently sold by his son, Malcolm, to the Swopes. Alfred Allan Lewis, author of a Swope biography published in 1978, credits Stanford White as architect of the stately colonial revival house. However, there

seems to be considerable doubt about that popular assumption. The Society for the Preservation of Long Island Antiquities, in its 1998 book *Long Island Country Houses*, states that the architect is unknown. In any event, no matter who the architect was, the house now owned by Virginia Payson is a splendid sight, as splendid a sight to sailors passing by today as it was the day the Swopes completed their extensive renovations.

According to Lewis, Swope, who was a shrewd investor worth anywhere from $4 million to $15 million, spent close to $1 million making the place "habitable." Margaret Swope was equally extravagant as an interior designer. In addition to decorating her home lavishly with the help of leading decorators, she engaged two complete sets of household servants—a day shift and a night shift. Guests could get suits pressed or dine on steak and champagne at any hour it struck their fancy.

Swope was interested in horses and maintained a stable on his estate. (He spent $100,000 in 1929 on racing stock.) He didn't care much for riding, but his children did. According to tales that the head trainer, Tom Spratt, told his daughter, Fay Fraser of Port Washington, working for Swope required flexibility. Prior to his marriage in 1932, Spratt lived in an apartment above the Swope garage. It was not unusual for Swope to wake him up at 1 a.m. and have him come take the place of a croquet player who had become too drunk to finish a match or a poker player who had fallen asleep over his cards.

The Swope guest list read like a celebrity gossip column come to life. There were old friends such as writer Dorothy Parker, critic Alexander Woollcott, columnist Heywood Broun; Broadway types such as George F. Kaufman and Moss Hart; and movie people, including the fabled Harpo Marx, who played croquet with the intensity he usually reserved for his namesake instrument. In later years, the Swopes got to know their neighbors—Margaret Vanderbilt Emerson, Averill Harriman, Condé Nast and Jock Whitney and his sister, Joan Payson—who lived in Manhasset.

Despite his celebrity status and lavish spending on creature comforts, Swope was civic-minded and cared about the community in which he lived, serving several terms as a Sands Point Village trustee. One of his duties was to write laudatory tributes about deceased Board members.

Neysa McMein, a popular illustrator, magazine cover artist and noted hostess, and her husband, architect John Baragwanath, were good friends of the Swopes; they preceded the Swopes in Sands Point by two years, buying a country home at 34 Barkers Point Road. Publicist and lyric writer Howard Dietz, another a member of the Swope group, wrote in his autobiography, *Dancing in the Dark*, that Neysa was "queen of party games." In the '30s, theatrical director and producer George Abbott became a co-owner of the Baragwanath house.

If the chauffeur was late, one could always take a taxi. Here is Crowley's Service Station and taxi service as it looked in 1922. (Courtesy, Cow Neck Historical Society)

Vincent Astor owned one of the largest yachts registered in North America. For a short time he also owned the former Bourke Cockran estate and launched its development as Harbor Acres. (Courtesy, Port Washington Public Library)

THE VERY RICH MEN

Averill Harriman (1891-1986), a multi-millionaire whose money originally came from railroads, maintained a country home in Sands Point for many years. He developed a taste for Democratic politics and public service and become wartime ambassador to Russia, Governor of New York State from 1954 to 1962, and advisor to presidents from FDR to LBJ. As a dapper sportsman in his thirties, he almost single-handedly started the Sands Point Club in May, 1927. The *Port Washington News* described it as an "Exclusive Sports Club…Controlled by Group of Millionaires on Pleasure Bent" The club was indeed exclusive. It opened with just four polo-playing members: Harriman, J. Cheever Cowdin, Thomas Hitchcock, Jr. and A. Charles Schwartz. (It did, however, propose to let in 50 additional members that year.) The group took over the field built by the late Julius Fleischman near Middle Neck Road and planned a new 18-hole championship golf course, swimming pool and tennis courts. A Sands Point Golf Club history, published in 1979, paints Harriman as an autocrat who more or less dictated the membership and management of the club, "its founding father and guardian angel to a degree rare in the annals of clubs." Harriman made good use of his own 150 Sands Point acres in his polo-playing years, although the rambling waterfront house was primarily a summer home and hardly compared in

Vincent Astor's Nourmahal is sailing through the North Sea in this oil painting, c. 1930-40. The 264-foot ocean-going yacht was his favorite "residence." The present owner of the painting purchased it from a former captain of the vessel. (Courtesy, Joan G. Kent. Photo by Will Wright)

Vincent Astor was happiest aboard his yacht, the *Nourmahal*—both the first version, built for his grandfather in the 1880s, and the one he had built for himself in the '20s. He financed the latter, in part, with $300,000, he made as a backer of the first movie version of *Ben Hur*. The craft was 264 feet long, cruised at 16 knots and had a range of 20,000 miles without refueling. There were 11 staterooms with baths and a lounge with open fireplace. She carried a crew of 42 and was maintained in "ready to sail" condition all year long at an annual cost of $125,000. One of the most famous guests to come aboard was Franklin D. Roosevelt, a friend who often visited Astor's Rhinecliff estate when he was in Hyde Park. Roosevelt used the luxury yacht for a 10-day cruise just prior to his inauguration in 1933.

In addition to the steel-hulled *Nourmahal*, on which he traveled the world (until he gave it to the government at the onset of WWII), Astor owned, at least for a short time, another equally impressive vessel, the *Winchester*, built by Cox and Stephens. The *Port Washington News* of June 3, 1927, headlined a short item, "Astor Buys New Boat." It was "the fasted steam yacht afloat" with a speed of 33 knots and, at 225 feet in length and a beam of 21 feet at the water line, it had "the general contour of a destroyer." At the time of the report, the boat was being overhauled and repaired. There is no further mention of this yacht in the *Port News*, so she might have been purchased for

grandeur or size to Arden in Orange County, the Harriman family compound 12 miles west of the Hudson that once included 20,000 wooded acres in the Ramapo Mountains and boasted a main house with 30 bedrooms.

Another rich man, William Vincent Astor (1891-1959), whose passion was yachting, not polo, became a Sands Point taxpayer in 1922 when he bought the 35-acre William Butler Duncan estate on Hempstead Harbor. This Astor was the son of John Jacob Astor IV, who went down with the *Titanic* in 1912, and his first wife Ava. Vincent Astor paid around $175,000 for the estate, which he planned to use as his residence. However, given Astor's reputation as a real estate investor and developer, it wasn't too much of a surprise when readers of the *Port Washington News* learned, on February 19, 1926, that Astor had purchased the Cosden (formerly Cockran) property for $1,550,000 in cash and planned to divide its 310 acres into plots for medium-priced homes.

Astor built a very nice house near Hempstead Harbor, since demolished, for himself and his first wife Helen Dinsmore Huntington. Astor's second wife, Minnie Cushing, was the sister of Babe Paley and Betsey Whitney. His third and last wife was Brooke Marshall. As his widow, she became an important philanthropist and society figure.

Flamboyant Gothic was the decorative motif of Mrs. O. H. P. Belmont's Beacon Towers shown c. 1925. There was also a somewhat forbidding mural of Joan of Arc in the foyer. (Courtesy, Nassau County Museum Collection, Long Island Studies Institute at Hofstra)

THE LONE EAGLE
LANDS IN SANDS POINT

The '20s was an era of glamour and glitz for Sands Point, with celebrities commonplace and many important political and business figures in residence. No one in 1927 eclipsed Charles Lindbergh for sheer star power. His daring Atlantic flight, good looks and modest manner captivated the world—especially the American world. A. Scott Berg, in his 1998 biography of Lindbergh, said, "People acted as though he had walked on water, not flown over it."

News of Lindbergh's record-breaking New York-to-Paris flight made the front page all over the United States on May 21, 1929.
(Courtesy, Cow Neck Historical Society)

Following his dramatic exploit, Lindbergh signed a book contract with George Putnam, who engaged a professional ghost writer. When Lindbergh saw the finished product in galley proofs, he was appalled with the inaccuracies and florid prose and decided to write the book himself. Before he could start, he had to complete a three-month, 48-state tour in his plane, the *Spirit of St. Louis.* (He visited 82 cities on the tour and returned to Mitchel Field on October 23, 1927.) Lindbergh set a goal of writing 10,000 words a week, a pace that would make a seasoned professional writer shudder. He met that goal by moving into Harry Guggenheim's Norman manor-style mansion, Falaise. With Guggenheim keeping visitors and adulators at bay, Lindbergh achieved his goal in three weeks, writing his book in longhand.

Harry Guggenheim is, according to Berg, "perhaps the most important but least known figure in the development of American aviation." Harry's father, Daniel, established the Fund for the Promotion of Aviation in 1926 with $500,000, putting Harry, who had served in WWI as a naval aviator, in charge. That family fund sponsored Lindbergh's tour. In later years the friendship between Guggenheim and Lindbergh was sorely tested by Lindbergh's support of the isolationist America First movement.

THE POLICEMAN'S LOT

On the surface it appears that a great and wonderful party was continuously celebrated in Sands Point during the years 1920 to 1929. But of course, life wasn't all great and wonderful. There were disasters, accidents, fires, and problems generated by Prohibition. In the typical summer of 1928, the Sands Point Police did many of the same things they did in the summer of 1998: They chased speeders, broke up unauthorized beach parties, questioned strangers in strange places, sorted out automobile accidents, settled minor disputes, and looked for lost boats and lost dogs. True, the force was much smaller in 1928. Only five names signed the entries in the "blotter," or log book, that is so carefully preserved at the present-day headquarters.

There were serious occurrences as well, including several drownings, a domestic dispute where the husband threatened to shoot his wife, and a bellicose butler who refused to leave the premises after being fired. Two Sands Point Police officers caused a minor scandal when they became drunk on duty. (The gift of a bottle of liquor in the middle of Prohibition had proved too great a temptation.) Burglaries, especially of closed summer homes, were common in those days before alarm systems.

When W. H. Rosenstein, of West End Avenue, Manhattan, came out from the city in December, 1924, to check on his property, he found about $1,000 worth of linens, silver, clothing—and suitcases to put the loot in—missing. A week later, thieves made off with $5,000 in linens and carpets from the home of William Guggenheim.

Port Washington's Protection Engine Co. displays its equipment in this 1923 photo. The Village paid the Port Washington Fire Department $300 for coverage in 1924, a fee that was increased to $4,500 by 1931. The PWFD earned every penny of it. (Photo by Earl Markham. Courtesy, Port Washington Public Library)

FIRES AND FIRE HAZARDS

Although the Village contracted with the Port Washington Volunteer Fire Department for protection, and the volunteers undoubtedly did their best, fighting a fire in Sands Point was difficult and often frustrating due to the scarcity of a water supply from fire hydrants or ponds. A building could be well on its way to ashes by the time a hose was strung to reach a water source that could be as far as a quarter mile or more away.

One of the most spectacular fires occurred in 1925; it demolished the Sands Point Casino at Plum Point that had opened just two years before to the applause of an enthusiastic membership. The stucco clubhouse, which had a huge verandah with a view of the Sound, could accommodate 300 guests at dinner. After a waiter spotted flames in the Casino from his room in another building, everything that could go wrong did. The waiter had trouble waking the manager. It took 16 minutes to rouse the central telephone operator to call for help. When the fire fighters finally arrived they had to contend with changing winds and the lack of water pressure. The Casino burned to the ground in an hour and the loss was estimated to be $100,000 by Howard T. Kingsbury, club president, who was president of the Village at that same time. In another spectacular blaze,

the J. T. McNulty house was destroyed in June, 1927. Again, an inadequate water supply created a problem. It took 2,100 feet of hose and 20 minutes to obtain water from the nearest hydrant. The Village's cost for protection by the Port Washington Fire Department rose from $300 in 1924 to $4,500 in 1931—and judging by local newspaper accounts, the PWFD earned every penny of it.

PROHIBITION WASN'T WORKING

Long-time residents of Sands Point and Port Washington tell tales of rum runners who landed their cargoes on the shores of deserted beaches on moonless nights, but there is little in the local press or police reports to support that romantic notion. However, the *Port Washington News* columnist Ernie Simon, who was around at the time, wrote in a 1970's column: "Long Island Sound was full of rum runners in those days. Several of them landed at Isaac Guggenheim's shorefront on Hempstead Harbor. However the Port Washington Police Department always seemed to be on the spot to apprehend the 'boys.'"

While there were no speakeasies in Sands Point, drink was readily available in Port Washington and Roslyn. People made gin in garage stills and brewed beer in basements. The hip pocket flask accompanied sportsmen into duck blinds and partying

Mrs. Christian Holmes (nee Bettie Fleischman) was an active advocate of Prohibition Reform. She is shown here (in black dress) with two guests at a meeting (c. 1930) to further the cause at her Sands Point Home. (Mason Studios Collection, Port Washington Public Library)

Cover of a sales brochure issued around 1928. The house on the left remains as it appears in the photo.
(Courtesy, Port Washington Public Library)

couples into the Sands Point Casino. Relying on illegal means, well-stocked pre-Prohibition cellars, or a grandmother who knew how to make dandelion wine, those who wanted to drink managed to do so. "On my father's frequent business trips to Canada," recalls Peter Fraser, "he always smuggled bottled scotch in his luggage on the labels of which he had written, 'for medicinal purposes only.'" An April 2, 1926, local newspaper article tells of three individuals in the Valley Road area of Port Washington who were arrested and fined for operating stills in their homes. The disregard for the law that was generated by Prohibition caused many thoughtful people to feel that the 18th Amendment was a failure and should be repealed before the country degenerated into a state of further lawlessness.

WAY OF THE FUTURE

The large estates were beginning to break up by the mid-1920s. The 53-acre estate of Congressman Frederick Hicks, who died unexpectedly of a heart

attack in 1925, was sold a year later to the Lewis Development Company, which already held 100 adjacent acres that had been purchased from the Susan Cornwall estate. Plans were announced to develop the land, with five-acre plots and winding roads following the contours of the land.

While Prohibition, universal suffrage, and the stock market crash of 1929 all had an impact on the social fabric of Sands Point, it was the sale by Vincent Astor of his 284 acres in Cow Neck to the Harbor Acres Realty Company in 1926 that determined the course of Sands Point's development. Astor's original plan, which was more or less followed by Harbor Acres Realty, called for a country community of large houses on plots averaging five acres with community tennis courts, a beach house and bridle paths. The architecture of the mini-estates was eclectic, but tended to favor Tudor and Colonial Revival styles. Astor's advertising brochure boasted, "Among the various sites are locations suitable both for the most imposing and elaborate summer homes, as well as for those of modest proportions intended for occupancy during the entire year."

One of the first houses built was the entrance lodge at 1 Harbor Road, designed by the well-known architect Aymar Embury II (who also prepared plans for various other sites). The clapboard and shingle residence is typical of the smaller houses within the

Built in 1922, this brick and slate house shown in 1925 is still standing at the end of Astor Lane on the edge of Hempstead Harbor in Sands Point. It is believed to have been designed by Delano and Aldrich, a firm responsible for nearly as many Gold Coast mansions as McKim, Mead and White. (Courtesy, Institute for Long Island Studies)

development. John Freeman, who lives on Cornwell's Beach Road today (1999), remembers living in that house as a child. When his father, who was a friend of Vincent Astor, suffered financial reverses, Astor invited the family to live in the house rent free in return for his father acting as caretaker and real estate salesman. When their situation improved, the Freemans moved to Bayview Colony, built in Port Washington by Carl Fisher, the developer of Miami Beach.

Harbor Acres at the beginning of the twenty-first century is not exactly as it was planned—but close to it. Some of the larger plots have been subdivided, but the roads still wind, a heavily-wooded landscape still prevails and the Harbor Acres beach house, which has a French-Norman roof on a Mediterranean stucco building, looks about the same as it did when the Harbor Acres Association held its first beach party.

The development of Harbor Acres, approximately 300 acres that had once been the country home of one man, brought the end of the estate era. The proximity of Cow Neck Peninsula to Manhattan drove land prices up, encouraging subdivision and attracting prosperous business men and professionals. Sands Point was growing…and even a stock market crash and Depression didn't stop the momentum.

CHAPTER 10

1930-1940
A TROUBLED DECADE:
DEPRESSION AT HOME,
WAR CLOUDS ABROAD

In the summer of 1929, Sands Point was the second home of some immensely rich families and the first home of many substantial ones. New areas were under development; the neighboring community of Port Washington, which the Village depended upon for shopping, labor, transportation and schools, was thriving. The population of Port Washington (including Sands Point) was 10,000, second only to Great Neck in the Town of North Hempstead.

Then came the October stock market crash, when U.S. securities lost $26 billion and triggered a world-wide economic crisis. The post-World War I boom was abruptly over. By 1930, the good times had ceased rolling. Although not a single Sands Point owner of a great estate was reduced to living in the gate house (like Clarence Mackay, owner of the 500-acre Harbor Hill in Roslyn), many of them had to reduce their expenses after the crash turned into a world-wide depression. Some closed their houses, some cut back on staff and others sold portions of their property.

Federal, state and local governments struggled to cope with pressing economic problems and, most critical, unemployment on a scale greater than anyone had ever seen before. President Herbert Hoover, who had served with distinction as chairman of the American Relief Committee in London during World War I, tried without success to use his organizational skills to solve the country's economic woes. Because they were so immersed in their own economic problems, Americans paid little attention to the economic difficulties in Europe that eventually gave rise to the Nazi party in Germany.

PUTTING THE COUNTRY BACK TO WORK

It took time for the ripple effect of the woeful national economic situation to touch the average American, but it eventually affected every strata of the citizenry.

The formidable Mrs. Christian Holmes (in black), opened her home, The Chimneys, to charitable and social welfare causes. During the Depression she provided jobs for unemployed Port Washington men by financing the construction of a stadium at the high school. (Mason Studio Collection, Port Washington Public Library)

As the Depression progressed ever further, hitting its nadir in 1932, it became obvious that towns and villages could not wait for help from the states and federal government; they had to help themselves. Many American towns heeded President Hoover's suggestion that they seek local solutions.

Cow Neck came up with one long before Hoover's successor, Franklin Roosevelt, instituted the WPA (Works Progress Administration) in 1933. The Citizens Unemployment Committee for Port Washington was formed in November of 1931. Henry A. Alker, Sands Point Village treasurer and president of the Harbor National Bank, was named one of the five trustees. The Committee embarked on a drive to raise $25,000 that would be used to provide wages for work projects such as clearing land for a new elementary school. Mrs. Christian Holmes (Bettie Fleischman) and her son Jay pledged money to build a stadium at the new (c. 1919) Port Washington High School (later Weber Junior High) on Port Washington Boulevard, and financed temporary jobs for seven people at the

Holmes' estate in Sands Point. The Water Board hired 52 men to construct a large water main. By the time the Committee's fund drive goal was met on December 18, after more than 100 volunteers had collected donations from homeowners and businessmen, it was able to boast that it had found jobs for 67 unemployed men. However, as many as 320 people still needed work.

Courtyard at Mille Fleurs. The comfortable French country manor house was built for Florence Guggenheim, widow of Daniel, in 1932. Its construction during the middle of the Depression provided welcome jobs for local unemployed workers. (Courtesy, Port Washington Public Library)

Some of them may well have found work at Mille Fleurs. One of the most attractive houses to go up in 1932, the livable French country manor house was built for Florence Guggenheim (whose husband Daniel had died two years previously). After 15 years of living in the drafts and discomforts of the palatial Hempstead House, Mrs. Guggenheim sought the comfort and easy management of a traditional upper-middle-class home. Constructed of brick with a tile roof, the two-story Mille Fleurs faced the water and, with its extensive gardens, was appropriately named. The house is now part of the Sands Point Preserve and, in recent years, has occasionally been used as a Designer Showcase to raise money for the maintenance of Hempstead House.

The seriousness of the Great Depression is evident in two side-by-side articles in the *Port Washington News*, one announcing the formation of the Unemployment Committee, the other cautioning readers to be wary of professional beggars going door to door. Homeowners were told that if "they are local people who are in need, their wants will be taken care of by the Village Welfare Society, if they are worthy."

Built sometime prior to 1914, this stucco mansion on Cedar Knoll became the Long Island Bath & Tennis Club in 1926 and later the home of Margaret Vanderbilt Emerson. It was destroyed in 1942 by a fire. (Courtesy, Port Washington Public Library)

A major cause of local unemployment was the reduction in staff by the hardest-hit Sands Point estate owners. One was Condé Nast, publisher of *Vanity Fair*, *Vogue* and *House and Garden*. Nast maintained a country home in Sands Point as well as a 30-room penthouse on Park Avenue, where he entertained as many as 350 people in lavish style. The parties came to a halt when Nast's personal fortune was severely reduced by the crash. During the 1920s he had invested heavily in his publishing empire, which included French and British editions of *Vogue*, and in the stock market. The annual income from Nast's publications fell from $10 million to half that, and the company stock dropped from $90 to $5 per share. With the aid of Lord Camrose, the British press owner, Nast was able to keep his company afloat—though he was forced to fold the unprofitable *Vanity Fair* in 1936. (The magazine was successfully revived almost a half century later.) Condé Nast's Sands Point house, a colonial revival, burned down in the 1950s, but its two-story garage, converted to a residence, remains on Sands Point Road near the corner of Middle Neck Rd.

THE BANK COLLAPSES

The event that, more than anything else, drove the reality of the economic crisis home to those living and working in Sands Point was the collapse of the Bank of North Hempstead, which closed its doors on December 24, 1931. (If you couldn't trust your bank, what could you trust?) Bank failures had occurred in other parts of the country, but this was a first for Cow

The Bank of North Hempstead (right foreground) was thriving when this photo of lower Main St., Port Washington, was taken in 1910. The Depression caused its failure in 1931. (Photo by Henry Otto Korten, courtesy of Nassau County Museum)

Neck. The Bank of North Hempstead, founded in 1902, was the oldest bank in town—and the only one until the Port Washington Bank & Trust Co. was founded in 1919. Run by a board of respected local citizens, The Bank of North Hempstead prospered during the 1920s and moved into large, new quarters—the substantial stone building (which still bears its name) on the corner of Main Street and Central Drive.

The bank board's resolution authorizing the closure stated that its action was due to "depreciation of the bond account and steady withdrawals occasioned by malicious rumors." The bank was said to have had 7,500 depositors at the time it closed, including Town of North Hempstead and Nassau County agencies—a prodigious feat when you consider that the population of Port Washington/

"Hilltop," on Middle Neck Road, was the home of Sands Point Village Treasurer Henry A. Alker, founder of the Port Washington National Bank and Trust Co., which successfully weathered the national epidemic of bank failures during the Depression. (Courtesy, Robert L. Harding, Jr. Real Estate)

Sands Point was around 10,000. Depositors eventually received about 55% of their money. Despite later efforts by the board and chamber of commerce, the bank was never reorganized.

Fortunately for community morale, the two other banks in town weathered the financial storm nicely. These were Harbor National Bank, founded in 1929 by Henry A. Alker, and Port Washington Bank & Trust Co., with Henry Remsen Tibbits at the helm. Bank failures in the rest of the nation became so bad that one of Franklin Roosevelt's first acts after his election to the presidency was to declare a nationwide bank holiday on March 5, 1933, and an embargo on the exportation of gold. Congress soon passed stricter banking regulations that helped reduce the number of failures.

REPEAL, THE NEW CAUSE

While banks were failing and unemployment spreading, Prohibition was proving unworkable and an expensive, unpopular fiasco. Making wine at home, which was a long-standing family tradition in some ethnic groups, took on new dimensions under Prohibition. Saloon keepers went underground; speakeasies were born and became popular. So was beer-brewing in the basement—though the mixture did tend to explode. People who had used up their stock of wine and liquor before Prohibition, or had never had one to begin with, relied on illegal distillers and importers. When speakeasies weren't handy, men and women brought their own supplies to parties and sporting events, some carrying their liquor in sterling silver flasks from Tiffany's. (Bootlegging was one business that prospered during the depths of the Depression.) With vast numbers of otherwise law-abiding citizens blithely ignoring the law, treasury agents had difficulty with enforcement.

Many solid citizens thought that Prohibition wasn't working, and Mrs. Christian Holmes was one of them. The indomitable Mrs. Holmes, who led the local Repeal of Prohibition movement, hosted a meeting of 300 women at her Sands Point estate in July of 1930 and urged the group to join the National Prohibition Reform Organization. The next month, she garnered front-page headlines in the *Port Washington News* after she testified in front of the grand jury about the prevalence of speakeasies in

Nassau County. Mrs. Holmes submitted a list of places in the vicinity of Port Washington where it was rumored that liquor might be purchased. However, the paper added, "the society matron had no personal knowledge of the existence of any such places…."

Most Nassau County residents agreed with Mrs. Holmes' viewpoint. The Republican Committee of the Town of North Hempstead adopted a resolution in July, 1931, calling for the repeal of the 18th Amendment. The snowball was rolling in Sands Point and elsewhere in the country. Bettie Fleischman Holmes kept up the fight right to the end, hosting a garden tour of her estate (admission $1) in the summer of 1933 to help the Women's Organization for National Prohibition Reform in its campaign to secure the ratification of repeal in states where the vote was in doubt. Later that year, on December 5, 1933, the 21st amendment to the United States Constitution was ratified.

Howard Dietz, shown holding paws with "Lassie", was MGM Studios' publicist and a song lyricist, who commuted between Hollywood, Broadway and Long Island. He brought home a host of celebrity guests to his beloved Sands Point country house.
(Courtesy, Port Washington Public Library.)

Crowds line up at Port Washington's Beacon Theatre in 1937 to see the double feature presentation of The Great Garrick and Breakfast for Two. (Courtesy, Port Washington Public Library)

BROADWAY BY THE BAY

As the Depression crawled on, movies became a popular escape from the harsh realities of joblessness, bank failures and mortgage foreclosures. It didn't cost much to enter the glittering celluloid world, and those who had been forced to take a salary cut and forego vacations could still manage to take their families to the movies once a week. Free dishes, double features, and continuous shows were added inducements.

The people who made those motion pictures became rich, and some of them chose to live in Sands Point. It was a natural extension of Port Washington's long-time popularity with theater people. The first theatrical personality to move to Sands Point was Katherine Clemmons, a sometime actress who married Howard Gould in 1906 (she lost her Mrs. when he divorced her a few years later over her affair with William "Buffalo Bill" Cody). In 1915, bandmaster John Phillip Sousa took up residence at 24 Hicks Lane, and his death in March of 1932 was mourned by the nation as well as his friends here. John Lagatta, the illustrator and a Sands Point neighbor of Sousa, was an honorary pallbearer at the musician's elaborate military funeral in Washington, DC, as was Henry Eagle, a one-time Village mayor.

In the late 1920s, Herbert Bayard Swope invited his Broadway and Hollywood friends to his home at Lands End. One of them was Howard Dietz, publicist for MGM studios and lyric writer for hundreds of songs (including "Dancing in the Dark," a title he used for his 1974 autobiography). Dietz loved Sands Point and purchased a rambling old farm house on Cow Neck Road. At first it was a summer home (he maintained an apartment on 11th Street in Manhattan); later, it became the full-time home of Dietz and his third wife Lucinda Ballard, a theatrical costume designer. The couple entertained such film notables as Laurence Olivier and Vivian Leigh, and international figures including Randolph Churchill (son of Britain's prime minister, Winston Churchill), who was a friend of Dietz' second wife, Tanis Guiness.

George Abbott, shown in this undated photo, summered in Sands Point in the '30s and '40s and made Broadway history by writing and directing more plays than anybody since Shakespeare. (Courtesy, Port Washington Public Library)

Churchill, a large, florid, heavy-drinking journalist, was a frequent visitor to the Dietz household, and when he felt lucky, Churchill could be counted on to keep Swope's poker-playing friends at the game table until 4 am.

In addition to enjoying parties and poker, Dietz developed a late-blooming love of boating. He described his first boat, which was black and gold, as a "craft that looked like an ocean liner." Called *L'Apache*, it had previously been sailed in southern waters by Carl Fisher, the developer of Miami Beach and the person who tried to create a deep water port in Montauk. Dietz kept his boat, which had a crew of five and "drank up 75 gallons a day," moored off the Sands Point Bath and Tennis Club. Then he added two speed boats to his "fleet," for commuting to his New York City office (one had a top for rainy days). Later, as war approached and gasoline became more difficult to obtain, Dietz sold his boats to the U.S. Coast Guard.

George Abbott, the playwright, director and producer, became co-owner in 1933 of the house at 34 Barkers Point Road which had been used as a country home by illustrator Neysa McMein and her husband Jack Baragwanath. (Abbott bought them out in 1944.) Abbott was responsible for an enormous number of theater hits, and his extraordinary career lasted nearly to the day of his death at age 107. Every year for close to 30 years (1935 to 1961) there was at least one play running on Broadway that George Abbott had written or directed, or done both.

THE INDUSTRIAL DESIGNER

Newcomers to Sands Point came from other walks of life as well. Industrial Designer Raymond Loewy must have startled his friends when he purchased the 18th century Sands House at 195 Sands Point Road in 1937. Even more surprising, he kept nearly the entire house the way it was. (He did add a modern kitchen, but retained the old open hearth.) Loewy had been born in Paris in 1893 and migrated to the United States in 1919, later becoming an America citizen. He designed a great many notable American products, from the Lucky Strike cigarette package to locomotive exteriors to the interior of an Air Force One plane. A lover of fast cars and boats, he made such diverse vehicles as the 1929 Hupmobile, the 1945 Studebaker and the 1961 Avanti look like they could fly off the highways.

He and his wife Viola, who was active in his business, frequently entertained at Sands House. In his 1979 book about his work, Loewy looked back fondly

Louise Laidlaw, shown here in the early '30s, was the daughter of Sands Point's first mayor James Laidlaw and his wife Harriet, a well-known suffragist. Louise, a published poet, married attorney Dana Backus in 1933 and took over the Laidlaw house in Sands Point. She later became President of the New York City Chapter of the United Nations Association. (Mason Studio Collection, Port Washington Public Library)

on their life at Sands House: "Those were elegant days, and I still see us playing badminton at night on a floodlit court. The chef was excellent, the bar well stocked (mint juleps were the specialty), plenty of popular music in the background. The weekends raced by." Loewy liked racing by on other days, too.

Unfortunately, his fast driving habits brought him to the attention of the "tough Long Island motorcycle cops" too often. So he designed a 40-foot, 42-knot, twin-screw power boat for himself called *Media Luz*, which he said could go "back and forth to New York in about fifteen minutes, usually with a drink close at hand."

Society figures of the mid '30s took up residence in Sands Point, which was now dubbed "The Newport of Long Island" by the *Port Washington News*. One was Alfred Gwynne Vanderbilt, who bought The Lindens at 225 Middle Neck Road, former home of Max Fleischman.

THE PUBLISHERS

Alicia Patterson, daughter of Joseph Medill Patterson, the Chicago-based North American newspaper tycoon, came to Sands Point when she became Harry Guggenheim's third wife in July, 1939, and moved into Falaise, the Norman manor house overlooking Hempstead Harbor that Harry had built in 1923 on 90 acres given to him by his father, Daniel. Some people might have viewed her as just another trophy wife—but they would have been wrong. Alicia had ambition, perseverance and an idea: to start a tabloid newspaper on Long Island modeled after her father's *New York Daily News*. Although her father advised her that a tabloid would never work on Long Island, her

One might say that Newsday was Harry Guggenheim's wedding present to his third wife, Alicia Patterson, whom he married in July, 1939. He supported her emotionally and financially when she began publication of the Long Island daily newspaper in January of 1940. (Courtesy, Port Washington Public Library)

This converted barn, shown in 1999, is all that is left of the 58-acre estate in Harbor Acres that belonged to Cissy Patterson, editor and publisher of the Washington Herald and aunt of Newsday founder Alicia Patterson Guggenheim. (Photo by Will Wright)

forward-looking husband felt that it would, and he backed her financially. The first issue of their little paper, which they called *Newsday*, came out in January of 1940. The rest, as they say, is history.

There was another Patterson who had a home in Sands Point during the '30s. That was Eleanor "Cissy" Patterson, Joseph's sister and Alicia's aunt, who was also a successful editor and publisher. The view from her country home was not as spectacular as the one from Alicia's cliff top manor, but Cissy's location in the midst of 58 wooded acres, in what is now Harbor Acres, must have been quite nice. An estate barn, converted to a residence, is still in use today. After a ten-year career of novel-writing, reporting and marriage to two husbands, Cissy was hired in 1930 as editor and publisher of the *Washington Herald*. There, according to *American National Biography*, "she built a newspaper that had appeal for Washington's working class as well as for the members of the high society in which she was born and raised." Though she was on the outs with most family members, she joined their vehement opposition to President Roosevelt and the New Deal. Her political position didn't seem to bother her readers one bit. By 1937 she had doubled the paper's circulation.

Still another publisher summering in Sands Point in the 1930s was Raoul Fleischman, backer of the *New Yorker*, the favorite magazine of Sands Point's more sophisticated and literary residents.

Another of the Village's distinguished summer residents was Bernard M. Baruch, who maintained a home in Sands Point in 1939. Baruch, a financier, advisor to presidents, and very likely the only person in Sands Point to have a college named after him, was born in South Carolina in 1870. As a result of speculation in the stock market, he became wealthy before he reached age 30. During World War I, he was chairman of the War Industries Board; during World War II, he was special advisor to Secretary of State James F. Brynes and later, U. S. Representative to the United Nations Atomic Energy Commission.

Private airplane hangars were to be found on both sides of Manhasset Bay. Here, members of the Aviation Country Club meet in Sands Point in 1934 to discuss "plans for a cruise to the Thousand Islands." Shown are (l. to r.) Mr. and Mrs. Grover C. Loening, Rudolph Loening, Mrs. Richard P. Hoyt, George B. Post, Miss Frances Maddux, Mrs. Post and Richard Hoyt. (Courtesy, Nassau County Museum Collection, Institute for Long Island Studies, Hofstra)

A LIVELY LIFESTYLE

Despite the Depression, Sands Point in the 1930s was a very pleasant place to live. There was still a great deal of open space, thanks to the large estates of the Guggenheims and Mrs. Holmes, the golf course, and miles of beach. New housing with traditional architecture was going up in Wampage Shores and Harbor Acres as well as along Cornwells Beach Road. If you liked horseback riding, you could stable your horse at the Sands Point Club and ride the many trails that looped through the remaining estate land. Despite harder times and higher taxes, impressive yachts were still afloat. The *Nourmahal,* owned by former resident Vincent Astor, measured 263.10 feet in length overall and was the largest yacht in the

Manhasset Bay Yacht Club fleet. (The next one down the list was only 114 feet in length overall.) Porch-sitters with binoculars could often get a glimpse of J. P. Morgan's *Corsair,* anchored off Glen Cove.

As the Depression diminished, many family fortunes began to mend. Membership in the yacht and country clubs was climbing back to pre-crash highs. And a new club opened in Port Washington in 1938 when New York's Columbia Yacht Club leased property at Orchard Beach from Manorhaven developer Charles W. Copp. It must have seemed a daring move by the membership, as three other clubs—Sands Point Yacht Club, North Hempstead Yacht Club and North Shore Beach and Yacht Club—had unsuccessfully occupied the premises during the previous ten years. Colonel M. Robert Guggenheim was named commodore. His yacht *Firenze* was so large that it required a crew of 24 and cost $250,000 per year to maintain.

During winter months, Sands Point residents still enjoyed skating and sledding. During the very cold winter of 1936, when Manhasset Bay froze solid, a group of sailors and boaters, including Thomas Fraser, fostered a revival of ice boating. In a race for a silver trophy put up by Jack Aron of the Knickerbocker Yacht Club, Fraser had the fastest time for an individual lap of 25.53 miles per hour. The ice was so thick, the foolhardy even drove their cars across the ice to Kings Point.

On shore, two annual benefit events, the Polo Match and Horse Show, gave participants a good time and excellent competition while raising funds for

Port News editor, Ernie Simon (l.), at the Knickerbocker Yacht Club in the early '30s with fellow members James Horton, Henry Loweree and Frederick Kraemer. (Courtesy, Port Washington Public Library)

Polo Matches at the Sands Point Club drew large crowds and benefited local charities such as the Village Welfare Society and benevolent funds of the Port Washington and Sands Point Police Departments. (Old Westbury Gardens photo. Courtesy, Port Washington Public Library)

Margaret Emerson, widow of Alfred Gwynne Vanderbilt who went down on the Titanic, lived on a 17-acre Sands Point estate. She was a member of the serious croquet-playing crowd led by editor Herbert Bayard Swope. (Courtesy, Port Washington Public Library)

worthy charities. Both were popular spectator sports. Polo matches at the Sands Point Club, featuring Sands Point's own world-famous Tommy Hitchcock and other internationally-known players, drew traffic-snarling crowds and raised money for the local police departments and other causes. The Sands Point Horse Show, inaugurated in 1934, raised money for the Village Welfare Society. The Second Annual Sands Point Horse show, which took place on the grounds of the Luckenbach estate (off Middle Neck Road) on Sunday, June 21, 1935, made the front page of the *Port Washington News*. Following the journalistic style of the time, it listed the participants' names. They came from Sands Point, of course, and Locust Valley, Westbury, Huntington, and as far as West Stockbridge, Massachusetts. Those who showed their horses included Miss Nancy Guggenheim, Mrs. Vanderbilt Smith, Mrs. Edward C. Stout, Jay Holmes, Walter Ericson and Master Peter Holmes. Sponsors included Mrs. W. Averill Harriman and Mrs. William Randolph Hearst. Though the top winner came from Huntington, Nancy Guggenheim's Lady Johren took first prize in the lightweight class.

INDOOR SPORTS

Cocktail parties and card games were increasingly popular, and some poker parties, including the Swope's and Margaret Emerson's, made the gossip columns. The repeal of Prohibition caused cocktail parties to flourish. They were a wonderful way to entertain with a minimum of fuss and fewer servants. Bridge, the game that offered respectable women a socially acceptable way to use their brains, was popular, too, with games in the afternoon for women at homes such as Neysa McMein's. In the evenings, both sexes played. A refinement of the ancient game of whist, bridge was the invention of Harold Vanderbilt, son of Alva Smith Vanderbilt Belmont. While Harold never owned a Sands Point house (as far as we know), it is reasonable to assume that he was a frequent guest of his mother when she resided at Beacon Towers. He wrote two books on his favorite subject: *Contract Bridge* (1929) and *New Contract Bridge* (1930). Society chronicler Louis Auchincloss wrote, "Some may find it distasteful to contemplate the enormous role that this game plays on social occasions and in the lives of the elderly, retired, and ill, or that it formerly played in the long days of middle and upper-income women before work became the prerogative of both sexes but one could argue that Harold, for better or worse, was a major force in American social history." Vanderbilt was also one of America's leading yachtsman during the 1920s and 1930s. He won 11 major races between 1922 and 1938 and defended the America's Cup in 1930, 1934 and 1937. Not surprisingly, it was on a non-competitive voyage in 1926 that he developed contract bridge. The rules by

The Famous Dorsey Brothers Orchestra

AT SANDS POINT BATH and TENNIS CLUB, SUMMER, 1934

The Dorsey Brothers Orchestra played at the Sands Point Bath and Tennis Club in the summer of 1934. Shown are Glen Miller (far left) and Tommy (left) and Jimmy Dorsey flanking singer Kay Webber. Miller left soon after to form his own orchestra. (Photo from Bath Club Collection. Courtesy, Edward A. K. Adler)

which the game is played today remain basically the same rules that Vanderbilt established.

Almost every American home had at least one radio, and it played a major role in family life. Little children learned about the 21st century from Buck Rogers and listened eagerly to the squeaky-clean exploits of high school star athlete Jack Armstrong, the "All American Boy" (who supposedly got that way because he ate Wheaties cereal). At 6:45 p.m. their parents tuned in to hear the original news pundit, Lowell Thomas, bring them up-to-date on national and world affairs. And the whole family laughed uproariously at the comic adventures of Amos and

Peter (seated) and Robert W. Fraser, Jr., of Port Washington, were frequent visitors to the Sands Point home of their Aunt Martha Mott Fraser, who lived in the original Mott homestead at the end of what is now Old House Lane. (Collection of Peter Fraser)

Andy (they didn't know it would one day be politically incorrect for two white men to write, produce and star in a show about black people, most of whom were stereotypes — lazy, scheming and lascivious). Live broadcasts of the big swing bands enlivened late nights and you could dance to Benny Goodman or Tommy Dorsey without leaving the house. Serious radio enthusiasts could be found in their living rooms at 2 a.m., trying to bring in London or Moscow on their short wave bands.

AFTERMATH OF THE LINDBERGH KIDNAPPING

Life in Sands Point wasn't always pleasant. There were robberies and burglaries, suicides and murders, fires that burned houses to the ground, an airplane crash off of Barkers Point that killed two New Yorkers (the pilot kept his plane in a hangar on Manhasset Bay), and the far-reaching impact of the Lindbergh baby kidnapping in 1932. Although the crime took place in New Jersey, where they lived, Lindbergh and his wife Anne Morrow Lindbergh were frequent visitors to Harry Guggenheim's Sands Point home. Many Village residents knew them, and they were highly regarded by all. George Mahoney, who caddied for Lindbergh, recalled that he, "Just played for the fun of it. He was one nice guy."

The shocking abduction and subsequent murder of the Lindbergh infant frightened many wealthy residents, who hired guards and put up higher, stronger fences. After the kidnapping, Mahoney's brother Tom became a watchman on Sands Point estates. At one time he worked for George Vanderbilt, who purchased the 32-acre Sloane estate fronting on Long Island Sound in 1935, not far from his mother Margaret Emerson's house on Middle Neck Road. Tom Mahoney served as a children's bodyguard in Sands Point and in South Carolina, where the family lived during the winter. "Every estate had guards on 'em. That was up until the War. The War changed a lot of things," George Mahoney recalled. (The house that Vanderbilt built, which was considered daringly modern for the time, is still standing at 5 Vanderbilt Drive.)

GRIM MOMENTS

Though Sands Point was presented by the media as a carefree playground for the rich, the famous and the theatrical, its residents did not escape the whims of the gods of Fire, Storm and Accident. Fires destroyed 200-year-old-houses; accidents destroyed the lives of homeowners and servants alike; storms wrecked havoc with boats and waterfront property.

The indiscriminate use of volatile gas and fuel caused explosions in the most up-to-date homes. The biggest problem in putting out fires remained the difficulty in bringing water to remote dwellings. The 200-year-old Treadwell homestead, home of Colonel Dwight Cushing, was severely damaged when a fire broke out in 1936 after a kerosene lamp exploded in the kitchen. (There had been a storm-caused power outage.) Mrs. Kathryn Knowles Jandorf, wife of automobile accessory dealer Louis Jandorf, died in August, 1933, following a propane gas tank explosion in the kitchen of her Sands Point home, which was sandwiched between the estates of Mrs. Clarence Eagle and A. C. Lordly. The Jandorf butler and maid were severely burned.

The Port Washington Volunteer Fire Department had difficulty fighting the November, 1936 fire at the Sands Point Bath Club because of 75-mile-an-hour winds and the problem of a lack of hydrants near by. As it was, an estimated $5,000 in damage was caused by the blaze, which was started by two men who tried using a blow torch to clean the kitchen range!

The Port Washington firemen had a three-alarm day on May 19,1939, when they had to deal with a trio of major fires in succession. The volunteers were already pouring water on a house fire in Manorhaven when they were notified of a fire at Alexander A. Forman's house in Sands Point. "Grandmother was having a luncheon party at the time," recalls grandson Jay Forman. "The roof was cedar shakes. That caught first." The fire department was short of men, as some had been left behind in Manorhaven. Those fighting the fire in Sands Point were hampered by a lack of water. They ran a hose 1,800 feet to a pond on the nearby Van Wart estate and the Manhasset Lakeville and Great Neck fire companies joined the battle, but the two-story house, built in 1928 at a cost of $150,000, was doomed. There were 24 rooms and 20 baths in the big house, which was considered "one

of the most beautiful on the North Shore." Mr. Forman also quoted a loss of $200,000 in furnishings. Then, while the firemen were still battling the Forman fire, another alarm sent a contingent to the Port Washington home of Admiral Craven, U.S.N., retired, and Mrs. Craven, who were away on a world cruise. A recently-installed oil burner had started a blaze. Fortunately, no one was living in the house at the time.

The owner of Marino's Castle on Port Washington Blvd. was surprised when police found three men operating an unlicensed still on his property in 1934. After all, Prohibition had been repealed the previous year. This photo shows the house in a neglected state in the '50s. It was demolished for a shopping center in the 1970s.

SANDS POINT FIGHTS CRIMINALS

Crime prevention was not advanced by the local newspaper's questionable custom of printing the comings and goings of estate owners, thereby alerting literate burglars to safe hunting grounds. Even if a caretaker was in residence or a watchman on hand, he could not be everywhere. The rambling wooded nature of Sands Point and the extensive shoreline made access and escape easy, as it had been since the days of the whaleboat raiders.

The Sands Point Police faced a challenge in August, 1933 when $7,000 in jewels was stolen from the guest room of Mrs. R. Wagner's home on Barkers Point Road, apparently when the guest was asleep. The next year, cash and jewels valued at $6,000 were stolen from the Harvey Cushman estate in Harbor Acres. Golf balls worth over $300 were taken in a break-in at the caddie shack of the Sands Point Club in August of 1935. The May 31, 1936, burglary of the home of Seymour Johnson, a wealthy stockbroker, was solved through the combined efforts of Lieutenant Borer of the Sands Point Police, Nassau County detectives and private investigators hired by the Johnson's insurer. A good part of the stolen $1,500 in flat silver and linens was recovered.

Some habits die hard—and the operation of illegal distilleries was one of them. James Marino, sand mine operator and owner-builder of an eye-catching stone house (c. 1900) on Port Washington Blvd., called popularly Marino's Castle, claimed to have no knowledge of the still being operated by three New York City men in a garage on the back of his property. Nevertheless, he was arrested by raiding police on October, 1934, and charged with being the owner of property on which an unlicensed still was found. Some of his surprise at the raid may have been due to the fact that Prohibition had been repealed the previous year.

GROWTH BY ANNEXATION

When Sands Point residents awoke on the morning of May 24, 1932, they did so in a village that had grown overnight in size by one-third. It went from a population of around 440 to a population of close to 600, and increased by an additional 450 acres. This occurred because the Village Board had approved "petitions for annexation, with written consent from the Board of the Town of North Hempstead" of the "so-called Lordly, Barkers Point, Sands Point Club and Harbor Acres areas" at its meeting held on the previous evening.

Undeveloped Harbor Acres land as shown in the 1930s advertising booklet. (Courtesy, Port Washington Public Library)

The Harbor Acres Beach House in 1930. (Courtesy, Port Washington Public Library)

Of course, those who read the local papers and took in the gossip at the Bath Club and the Sands Point Club had been well aware that the process of annexation was underway. The proposal was a subject of great concern to Town and special district officials as well as civic leaders who nursed the hope of combining greater Port Washington, including Sands Point, into a city. The first time the petitions were presented to the Town Board in March of 1931, they were turned down. The reason was the same as the one later given to the Hicksville District of Port Washington, when its request for annexation to Manorhaven was denied. Speaking for the Board, Justice Arthur W. Jones of Port Washington explained that annexation would affect every special district in Port Washington outside of the Sewer District and would involve nearly one and one-half million dollars of assessed valuation. (Ironically, Jones was one of the founders of the Village of Port Washington North after the city of Port Washington movement fell apart.)

BY POPULAR DEMAND

However, determined signers of the petitions persisted, among them Bettie Fleischman Holmes and Ada F. Lordly, who owned an estate just south of the old Cornwell homestead on Manhasset Bay, Henry Remsen Tibbits and John and Florence Lagatta (Barkers Point), Theodore Roosevelt Pell (Wampage Shores) and Cissy Patterson (Harbor Acres). By the time petitions were resubmitted, changes in state law had removed the ability of the Town Board to block such requests.

As required by law, the petitions were signed by "the owners of a majority in value of the property to be annexed." Their objective was not simply a save-taxes scheme for the wealthy; being part of an incorporated village was viewed as an advantage by such qualified voters of more modest means as Harry Crampton, whose father had been Bourke Cockran's estate superintendent, and Lawrence Kehoe, who had also worked for Cockran. John Duryea, whose farm was adjacent to the Sands Point Club and whose board and batten house still stands on Cow Neck Road, was another petition-signer, as was Police Chief Borer, who lived on Seamans Road.

Upwards of 400 boats were torn from their moorings, sunk or smashed against the shore of Manhasset Bay and Hempstead Harbor as the result of The Hurricane of 1938 and its ensuing tidal wave. (Courtesy, Port Washington Public Library.)

Though there might have been loftier reasons, the driving force behind the movement of Harbor Acres to join the Incorporated Village of Sands Point was to escape the taxes of the Port Washington Water District—and, eventually, to leave the local school district. In becoming part of Sands Point, the petitioning homeowners were, for the most part, successful in reaching their goal. Although the Sands Point residents never managed to exit from the school district, they were able to keep their taxes down either by doing without (such as relying on cesspools rather than sewers) or by providing their own services, including water and police. Taxes in the Incorporated Village of Sands Point remained somewhat lower than those on similarly-assessed properties in Port Washington until the purchase of The Village Club in 1994.

The areas brought into Sands Point in 1932 included Wampage Shores (a development on and near Plum Point), acreage including Arcadia Drive, and old Cornwall property bordered in part by Manorhaven and Manhasset Bay, the property of Mrs. Holmes adjacent to the Sands Point Club and 100 or so acres of the Club itself, plus the 284 (plus or minus) acres of Harbor Acres.

DEFENDING THE BEACHES

Perhaps in retaliation for taking all of the taxable Harbor Acres property from the Port Washington special districts, the quarrel about "who owns the waterfront" rose again in June of 1932 when a taxpayers' group complained to the Town Board of the "high-handed tactics of upland owners" in putting up a fence along the beach that had long been used by townspeople (we assume this was in the area of the Sands Point Light). The Town retaliated by cutting holes in the fence. Sands Point came back, in turn, with "no parking" signs on the road alongside the beach. (The Village, it should be pointed out, had originally closed the beach the previous year "Upon the advice of the health officer to prevent the spread of this terrible disease...." The terrible disease cited was polio, which was epidemic that year.) Pressure to open its beaches to Port Washington residents let up later in the year when the Town purchased Orchard Beach (now Manorhaven Park), which provided a convenient bathing beach for Town residents and ample parking. The Sands Point waterfront still continues to attract illicit beach-goers, and chasing the unauthorized off private beaches remains a summer-time activity of the Sands Point Police Department.

THE HURRICANE OF 1938

Port Washington felt the fury of the "Hurricane of 1938" on September 21. For nearly a century, there hadn't been any storm in the area that could truly be called a hurricane. At the time, tracking hurricanes was still in its infancy, and when the storm came ashore, most people literally didn't know what had hit them. The *Port Washington News* reported: "After five days of steady rain, a tornado struck Port Washington with all its fury late Wednesday afternoon bringing with it a tidal surge that left a million and a half dollars of damage in its wake."

The hurricane uprooted trees and flooded yacht clubhouses and other waterfront properties. Upwards of 400 boats were torn from their moorings, sunk or smashed against the shore. At the Port Washington Yacht Club alone, 100 boats were washed up onto the club beach or the nearby Manhasset Bay Estates Beach. The Sands Point Bath Club weathered the storm far better, losing only four cabanas. Nearly 100 trees went down in Sands Point and most homes along the northwest side of the peninsula were inundated by high tides, as was the Sands Point Police Station, which established temporary headquarters at the nearby Hitchcock Estate. For days afterwards, volunteer firemen were busy pumping out cellars, county road crews were removing fallen trees, Long Island Lighting was restoring power to blacked-out Manorhaven and Sands Point, and insurance agents were wrestling with a myriad of claims from people who never thought a hurricane would hit Long Island.

CLIPPER SHIPS WITH WINGS

Sands Pointers who liked to get places in a hurry had opportunities to get there a great deal faster after 1937, when Pan American Airline's flying boats began to take off from Manhasset Bay, first to Bermuda and later to Europe. Former Sands Point Mayor (1982-89) Edward Madison had the distinction of being the first unaccompanied child to fly the route when he was sent to spend a vacation with his grandmother, who lived on the island. People had been looking for commercially feasible ways to cross oceans in something faster than a steamship ever since Lt. Commander Albert C. Read and Lt. (j.g.) Walter Hinton flew a Navy NC 4 from Newfoundland to the Azores in 1919, guided by a "bridge of lights" from Navy destroyers that shot flares off above the water.

The Germans thought they had the answer to transatlantic flight when they introduced giant zeppelins, which sailed silently and gracefully through the sky in the early 1930s. A company brochure rhapsodized: "the Zeppelin Airship reduces the time in transit over trans-ocean voyages from weeks to days. The prophetic vision of Jules Verne has been realized." Zeppelin-spotting became a favorite outdoor activity for New Yorkers. In August, 1934, the *Port Washington News* reported: "Many Port Residents had a glimpse of the *Hindenburg*, giant zeppelin [on] Wednesday at 4

Probably the most famous flying boat of them all was Pan American Airline's Dixie Clipper, a giant Boeing 314 which took off June 28, 1939, from Port Washington and flew the first passenger trip to Marseilles with stops in the Azores and at Lisbon. She carried a crew of 10 and 74 passengers, had a range of 4,175 miles and a top speed of 190 mph. (Courtesy, Cow Neck Historical Society.)

Pan Am did not have a monopoly on Manhasset Bay. This Air France plane is shown just before it took off from Port Washington on July 16, 1939, on the first non-stop commercial flight across the Atlantic between the United States and France. The plane was a Latecoere 521. (Courtesy, the Cow Neck Historical Society)

p.m. when she floated majestically over Sands Point." Unfortunately, the rigid steel construction of the cigar-shaped airship required highly flammable hydrogen gas as a lifting agent (soft-sided blimps use nonflammable helium). The tragic fire that destroyed the great ship at its mooring in Lakehurst, New Jersey, killing 35 people, put an end to commercial airship travel.

Pan Am filled the air-travel-to-Europe gap on June 28, 1939, when the *Dixie Clipper*, a giant Boeing 314 flying boat, took off from Port Washington using most of Manhasset Bay as a "runway," and flew to Marseilles. She carried a crew of 10 and 74 passengers,

Manhasset Bay was a center for international travel when Pan American Airlines used it as a base for commercial flights to Europe in 1939. Hangar in background, on the shore near Sands Point, was used for aircraft parts manufacture during World War II. (Courtesy, Port Washington Public Library)

had a range of 4,175 miles and flew at a top speed of 190 mph. With stops in the Azores and Lisbon, the flight took 29 hours and 20 minutes.

Travel by clipper proved to be wildly popular with government officials, celebrities, media personalities, movie stars and anyone else who could afford a ticket. Hangars and terminals on Manhasset Isle buzzed with activities and local residents lined the shores to see the great planes take off and land. This boost to the local economy (which included a tidy profit made by some local agents selling insurance in case the craft fell) did not last long. In 1941, Pan Am moved its operations to the Marine Air Terminal in Flushing, which was considerably closer to Manhattan. Later, during World War II, the abandoned Pan Am hangers in Manorhaven were put to use for the manufacture of aircraft parts. Thousands of flying boats were employed in World War II to reach otherwise inaccessible spots, but the development of long-range land planes made them obsolete after the war.

RUMBLINGS OF WAR

Although Pan Am was making it easier to get to Europe from the East coast, and China from the West coast, an increasing number of Americans avoided traveling abroad in the late 1930s. Hitler's Nazi party had taken over the Reichstag (parliament) in 1932, winning 230 seats, and Hitler himself was made

Chancellor the next year. Germany annexed the Saar in 1934 and the Rhineland in 1935, while Italy grabbed Ethiopia. By 1938, Hitler and his storm troopers were on the march, taking over Austria and conquering Poland.

Inside their own country, the Nazis stepped up the anti-Semitic activities that eventually resulted in the Holocaust. Some Jews, who wisely but sadly recognized the direction that the party in power was heading, fled to the United States and other neutral countries. After German troops overran Poland in 1939, Britain and France declared war on Germany. World War II had begun. Although President Roosevelt still publicly proclaimed the neutrality of the United States, when the newly-elected British Prime Minister Winston Churchill ordered the evacuation of children from the cities in 1940, some of the children were sent to the U.S. The 50-room Hempstead House in Sands Point was converted to house up to 75 refugee children from Europe.

The U.S. population was less aware of Japanese activities in the East until two events—the sinking of the U.S. gunboat *Panay* in the Yangtze River in 1937 and Japan's subsequent invasion of China—underscored Japan's desire to be the dominate Asian power. Still, most Americans (including the military) regarded Japan as a quaint, small and backward country without sufficient resources to wage large-scale warfare. Perhaps they were not aware of the large quantities of scrap metal shipped to Japan.

Although most Americans saw little threat from the Far East, by 1939 many of them supported aid—and even intervention—in the European conflict, despite the isolationist stances of such prominent Americans as Joseph Kennedy, Ambassador to Britain, and Charles A .Lindbergh. As the 1940s dawned, it seemed almost certain that the United States would become involved in another European conflict.

Despite the war clouds, the decade ended on a positive note for Village taxpayers. In July, 1939, the Village Board announced that the tax rate would be four cents lower than the previous year. This meant that the average owner paid 6% less, even though the assessed valuation had gone from $12,352,430 the previous year to $14,194,370. Credit for the tax reduction was given to the efficient operation of the Village government.

CHAPTER 11

1940-1950
WORLD WAR II:
THE HOME FRONT AND COMING HOME

By mid-1940, far-reaching national and world events drew the United States inexorably into the European conflict. The disappearance of friends and relatives living in Germany, Austria or Poland, the "loan" of 50 destroyers to Great Britain by President Roosevelt and the passage of the Selective Service Act all brought America to the brink of war. Significant portents appeared on the home front and support of isolationism waned as young men joined Allied military units and the American Field Service. Defend America Committees were established and children evacuated from Britain arrived in America for "the duration."

The Port Washington Reserve Police marching down Main Street on Memorial Day, May 30, 1942. Many of their members would soon be marching to military bands. (Courtesy, Cow Neck Historical Society)

A WELCOME TO REFUGEES

In July of 1940, a group of eight British children ranging in age from 11 months to nine years came from a country town "somewhere in England" to live in Sands Point. They resided at Mrs. Daniel Guggenheim's Hempstead House, which had been refitted for up to 75 youngsters. The British boys and girls were, no doubt, astonished to find themselves living in a castle. The first floor had a playroom filled with books and there were slides, seesaws and wagons in the garden. The owners of other North Shore estates opened their doors, as did many people with fewer rooms than Florence Guggenheim.

Katherine and Leo Forman took in a British teenager who lived with them for two years. The teen extended the Forman's hospitality to her cousins and friends serving in the British merchant marine whenever their ships came to New York. "I could see the dark silhouettes of their convoys making up on the Sound," recalls the Forman's son Jay, who was seven when the war started.

Other, more permanent refugees came to these shores as a result of WWII—European Jews and Christians who had opposed Nazism and somehow managed to survive persecution. Some had sufficient wealth or were prescient enough to leave their homes and country before the war. Others arrived after the war, following years of hiding or incarceration in concentration camps. Emily and Frank Ullman and their sons Leo and Hank came to Port Washington in 1947 after hiding in Holland for five years of German occupation. Why hadn't the Ullmans left before the war? For the same sort of reasons that caused so many others to stay behind, says Emily Ullman in *A Story of Survival*, written for her family in 1978. "We knew that war was inevitable. We should have left Holland already in 1939. How many times we asked this of ourselves! And I do not know the answer. I think we lulled ourselves into thinking that all would be well because we were so happy in Amsterdam living with many dear family members and friends who lived close by." In 1994, four generations of the Ullman family were living in Port Washington, including Sands Point residents Leo and Kay Marbut Ullman, a couple who met in 1951 when they were seventh grade students at the junior high school, which at that time occupied the top two floors of the Main Street School.

DUNKERQUE

The event that truly brought home the realities of war and captured popular sympathy for the British was the evacuation of 335,000 of the 400,000 British troops in the Low Countries who retreated before the Nazi Blitzkrieg of the Low Countries in May of 1940. Thousands of boats—from ferries, coastal steamers and tug boats to pleasure boats of all sizes crewed by civilian volunteers—crossed the English Channel to Dunkerque in Belgium to participate in the rescue effort and aid the hard-pressed British Navy. Front page photographs, showing soldiers wading from shore to get aboard small, bobbing boats, were imprinted on the minds of those who saw the newspapers and magazines. American boaters and sailors in particular appreciated the difficulty of the rescue effort.

STAYING OUT OF WAR (SORT OF)

The isolationists remained active, but they were losing popular support as more and more people favored aid to Britain, particularly after the fall of France in June 1940. In August, a meeting of the Port Washington Chapter of the Committee to Defend America by Aiding the Allies was held at Shorewood, the Sands Point home of Mrs. Robert McNeil, who headed the group. The 37 members present voted to send a telegram to President Roosevelt urging him "to use your great power toward the immediate release of as many old destroyers as we can possibly spare for Great

Charles O'Neil, Vice Commander of the Port Washington American Legion Post, directs traffic during a 1941 air raid drill. Harry Guggenheim and H. B. Swope directed traffic in Sands Point. (Courtesy, Port Washington Public Library)

Britain, our last line of defense." Sands Pointers at the meeting included Mr. and Mrs. Henry A. Alker (banker and Village treasurer), Martha Mott Fraser, Mrs. Forbes Hawkes (the doctor's wife) and Harriet Laidlaw. Mrs. Laidlaw pointed out that the "only way we can save France is by helping Great Britain."

While their petition might not have been the direct cause of Roosevelt's subsequent action, the Defend America Committee nevertheless had the satisfaction of being right when, shortly after it sent the telegram, President Roosevelt signed the agreement swapping U.S. destroyers for leases on British bases in the Western Hemisphere (Lend Lease). Though most Americans (at least those in the east) saw this as a positive action, staunch Republicans such as the editor of the *Port Washington News* viewed the move as the act of a dictator. In a front page editorial on September 6, the editor fumed: "We are witnesses to the method by which a nation which is overwhelmingly opposed to war and overwhelmingly opposed to dictatorship, is being pushed steadily and inexorably on the way to both." Roosevelt-hatred was considered a moral obligation on the part of those who considered him a "traitor to his class" (i.e., the man responsible for higher taxes on the income of the middle and upper classes).

Unfortunately, the destroyers didn't deter Hitler's next major move—the takeover of Greece in early

1941—or the German leader's invasion of Russia. Here in America, the possibility of air raids and/or submarine attacks became a major concern. A preparedness effort promoted by President Roosevelt led to the organization of the Port Washington Defense Council in July, 1941. Two months later, the Council had 65 individual organizations participating in a full-scale blackout defense demonstration, which simulated the effects of dropping of a bomb on the Sands Point School.

Though the Sands Point School wasn't located in Sands Point, the Village was an active participant in the community-wide demonstration. According to the *Port Washington News*, Harry F. Guggenheim and Herbert Bayard Swope (then State Racing Commissioner), along with Baron Robert de Rothschild, a refugee from Great Britain, directed traffic near the "bombed" area. Mayor Clifton S. Thompson guarded the reservoir that served the Village. (We assume this referred to the water tower—Ed.) Samuel Knox and Charles Bomer patrolled the water main line; John F. MacEnulty and Seth Thayer guarded the electric power facilities.

PEARL HARBOR CHANGES EVERYTHING

The Japanese attack on Pearl Harbor wiped out any lingering doubts about entering the war. Americans were angry and ready to fight Japan and Germany. The Japanese and the Germans were the bad guys, the Americans and the British were the good guys, and now it was time to get organized and get rid of the bad guys. After the surrender of the Philippines, no one doubted the need to put Japan in its place. The men and women going to war felt they had good reasons for doing so.

"The Port Washington Honor Roll," a large sign on Main Street sponsored by the Kiwanis Club, listed 341 names of men and women in service by May 25, 1942. At the end of the war, the names of more than 1,600 men and women were inscribed. (The population of Port was around 12,000 at the time.)

Port's Honor roll had close to 1600 names on it when this photo was taken in the spring of 1945. The sign was located on Main Street across from the Main Street School. (Courtesy, Port Washington Public Library)

SANDS POINTERS SERVE THEIR COUNTRY

Captain Herbert Nelson Fell, Jr., whose parents lived in the old Cornwall homestead, was one of those Sands Pointers on the Honor Roll. Born in Port Washington and educated at Friends Academy, Fell was among the first of the local men to enlist. He spent four years and seven months in the Army, starting out in the infantry at Fort Dix and then transferring to the Army Air Force, earning a commission. He was commanding officer of the 236th PAAF Squadron E, Pyote, Texas, at the time of his death (which, ironically, was the result of injuries he

Robert Forman and his first wife Mary on their 1942 wedding day. He served with the Army Engineers from 1942 to 1945, receiving Battle Stars in the Normandy and Northern France campaigns. Mrs. Forman died in a boating accident in 1974. (Courtesy, Guy Forman)

sustained in an automobile accident on North Hempstead Turnpike [25A] when he was home on leave).

Harry Guggenheim once again donned a naval uniform, emerging at the war's end with the rank of captain. Robert Forman served with the Army Engineers from 1942 to 1945, receiving Battle Stars in the Normandy and Northern France campaigns. He remained in the reserves, retiring with the rank of colonel in 1949. Dana Backus, an attorney, entered the Army as a captain, rose to lieutenant colonel, and was assigned to the Judge Advocate General's office in Washington. He moved to Washington with his wife, the former Louise Laidlaw, and their daughters. He, too, remained in the active reserves and retired with the rank of colonel.

Oliver A. Messenger, the son of Albert A. Messenger, for whom Messenger Lane was named, was born in Sands Point in 1913. He attended Port Washington schools and Emory University in Atlanta, and was an employee of Mobil Oil when he left in 1943 to join the Army. Messenger saw combat in France and Germany. He returned to Mobil after the war and later established his own company, Oil Associates, in Amityville.

Perhaps inspired by stories of Sands Point's rustic past, Messenger and his wife Elizabeth moved upstate to Columbia County in the 1950s and took up residence as a gentleman farmer. He spent a good deal of his time studying and writing about the American Revolution and the Civil War, and maintained a collection of antique weapons. When he died in 1998, his survivors included two people with the Messenger surname, one of them a resident of Port Washington.

SEARCHING THE SKIES

Noncombatants jumped with alacrity into wartime positions. By December 12, the Defense Council was designated the Port Washington War Council and became the umbrella organization overseeing community support efforts. After the military asked Port Washington American Legion Post 509 to staff

The tower (right) of Hempstead House in Sands Point was used as a 24-hour-a-day Aircraft Observation Site. Many of the spotters (left) were members of the Port Washington and Manhasset American Legion Posts. (Courtesy, Port Washington Public Library)

the local Aircraft Warning Observation Post for 24-hour duty, observation posts were set up on Cow Neck's high spots, particularly those overlooking the Sound. The hilltop houses and barns of Sands Point were the obvious choices. Among those used were the de Rothchild estate, Belcaro, out on Prospect Point; the cupola of a barn on the Holmes' estate; and best known, the tower of Hempstead House, with its

Robert Fraser, Sr., who grew up in Sands Point and served in the State Militia during World War I, was one of many local men who acted as Aircraft Observers during World War II. (Courtesy, Peter Fraser)

commanding views of the Sound. *Port Washington News* editor Ernie Simon wrote in 1970, "The Sands Point tower was probably one of the best observation posts throughout the country. Its commanding view of the surrounding skyline was not to be excelled by any post in the nation. The long line of cargo ships, with their convoys heading out to the Atlantic, bound for Europe, was something you would not forget in a hurry."

The observation posts were staffed by volunteers, both male and female (nationally, there were 600,000 volunteers). Many were veterans of World War I, and some brought their sons with them. Thomas Fraser, who had served in the Navy, was a spotter; so was his brother Robert. Another volunteer was Leo Forman, a decorated veteran of WWI, who also served on the local draft board, as did Francis K. Thayer, who had been in Port Washington's Home Guard during World War I. Robert Mitchell, who lived for 30 years on Tudor Lane in a house that was part of the Holmes Estate, was in a group of teenage aircraft spotters who took advantage of the opportunity and thoroughly explored Hempstead House, which had been deserted for several years. He remembers a "haunted-house" atmosphere with fabric wall covering hanging in shreds.

Aircraft spotting was serious business. The Army Air Force took pains to train volunteers such as Assistant Chief Observer William Guggenheim II (Harry's cousin), who, by February, 1943, had spent 600 hours searching the skies. He was rewarded for his diligence with a one-week course at the New York City Aircraft Recognition School for Ground Observers, with an obligation to go back and train his fellow aircraft and submarine spotters. Guggenheim and other volunteers spent hours and hours of their time standing out in the cold, peering through binoculars for planes that never came and submarines that didn't go this far up the Sound. Many submarines roamed the seas up and down both coasts, and one submarine did land a small band of spies on the South Shore, who were quickly captured.

WOMEN AT WAR

Working right along with the War Council were the American Women's Volunteer Service and the American Red Cross. Red Cross activities grew to such

The Port Washington Unit of the American Women's Voluntary Services, which was active from May 1, 1941, until disbanded in October, 1945, numbered many Sands Point women among its ranks. (Courtesy, Port Washington Public Library)

an extent that there was a need to name additional branch officers. Surgical dressings were rolled under the direction of Miss Harriet Littig, whose workers met four mornings, two afternoons and three evenings a week in the Flower Hill Hose Company fire house on Haven Avenue.

Young women volunteers offered friendship and assistance to Merchant Seaman convalescing at The Chimneys. (Courtesy, Cow Neck Historical Society)

Despite the small population of Sands Point, which was only 628 according to the 1940 U.S. census, the citizenry made a noticeable contribution to the war effort. Among the members of the AWVS were Mrs. Robert W. Fraser, Mrs. F. Wright, Mrs. Seth Thayer, Mrs. Leo Forman and Mrs. Hamilton Abert (Sousa's daughter, Helen). The motor transport group of AWVS to which Kay Forman belonged drove patients to clinics and hospitals, providing a valuable service in times of gas and tire rationing. The Mobile Kitchen unit served meals to large groups. The Salvage Group collected used clothing, scrap metal and paper. Other members staffed the local Coast Guard offices and the War Council Control Center.

The Chimneys, with its swimming pool and bowling alley, was turned into a Merchant Marine Rest Center under the aegis of the U.S. War Shipping Administration. The Girls Volunteer Group, Port Washington's answer to the U.S.O., entertained the young seamen—playing games, dancing with them, talking, and hosting holiday parties.

Mothers, fathers, siblings, spouses and friends brought photographs of their personal service man or woman to the Port Washington News for recognition in print and installation in the front window of the newspaper's Main Street Office, Port Washington. (Courtesy, Cow Neck Peninsula Historical Society)

THE DEFENSE INDUSTRY RIGHT NEXT DOOR

Nobody in Sands Point could forget there was a war, for Port Washington had a highly visible war industry. Purdy Shipyard on the east shore of Manhasset Bay turned out small power boats for the Navy—98 in all —and the sleek and speedy craft were tested in Manhasset Bay and Hempstead Harbor. Marcia Forman remembers with a shudder that recreational sailors in their small craft were often threatened, and sometimes swamped, by the huge wakes of the fast boats as they were tested by Purdy in Hempstead Harbor.

The honor of christening the boats was usually given to young women in the community. The *Spirit of Sands Point* was launched in August, 1943, and christened by Victoria Thompson, daughter of Sands Point Mayor Clifton Thompson. The cost of the boat was met by War Bonds that were purchased by residents of Sands Point and sold through the First Federal Savings Bank of Port Washington. In September, 1943, *Miss Harbor Acres* was named at the Purdy Shipyard by Jane Priscilla Abert of Harbor Acres. Peterson's Shipyard, next to the Manhasset Bay Yacht Club also built small craft for the Navy, as did other yards in the area.

YACHTS AND YACHTSMEN GO TO WAR

Just as the shipyards put yacht production aside, yachtsmen formed a "picket patrol" composed of civilian sailors and private yachts that had been donated by owners. Some sailed out of Greenport under the aegis of the U.S. Coast Guard, looking for German submarines. The offshore patrol yachts, primarily sailboats of 60 to 75 feet, searched the seas and were prepared to radio for naval support if they spotted the enemy. According to Harman Hawkins (past commodore of Manhasset Bay Yacht Club), who was one of the young club members serving in the picket patrol, not one of the eager volunteers sailing out of Greenport saw a submarine. One of those picket patrol sailors was the late Robert Fraser, Jr., from Manhasset Bay Yacht Club. Bobby's cousin Richard Fraser, who was a child at the time, says, "the offshore patrol involved some of our finest yachtsmen."

CHANGES ON THE HOME FRONT

Rationing and sporadic food shortages motivated residents to garden and fish for provisions. William Guggenheim had a large Victory Garden, the

Mahoneys grew produce on the Van Wart Estate, and Jay Forman's extended family collaborated on a "gigantic victory garden," located where the tennis courts are now. They also had about 100 chickens. At one point, says Jay, "Father and I tried to become fishermen" to supplement the family rations. "We got a little fishing boat," he explains, and took it out into the Sound. Along came a "large destroyer or maybe a cruiser" going at high speed, which overturned their boat and dozens of others. The Formans returned to eating mussels that they could gather easily on the beach at low tide.

Horace Hagedorn, who remembers when the only traffic light in town was a blinker at the intersection of Port Washigton Blvd. and Main Street, and his first wife, the late Margaret Hagedorn, moved to Luquer Road in Port Washington in 1942. Due to gasoline rationing, Horace rode his bicycle to the station to commute to NYC. Due to food rationing, he and some of his neighbors kept chickens and formed the amblitionoiusly-named Luquer Road Poultry Association. (Not all of the neighbors appreciated the chicken project, complaining about odors.) There was still a feed and grain store in town, near the railroad station, that was run by Mr. Mitchell, great uncle of Robert Mitchell, a onetime member of the Sands Point Village Board.

The large aircraft hangers on Manhasset Isle, which had been built in the '20s as the American Aeronautical Engineering Corp. and later was the headquarters of Pan American Airlines' clipper flying boat service to Europe, were converted to factories that made wings for the Grumman "Wildcat." Jay's wife Marcia remembers being a child and watching in wonder as airplane wings on flat bed trucks made their way up Main Street.

The army of servants who had been keeping Sands Point households running began to march off to war, entering the armed forces or taking jobs at such Long Island defense plants as Grumman, Sperry Gyroscope, Fairchild, Republic and a host of subcontracting firms. Some men and women left the state to pursue high-paying war work near military installations. The operation of the large houses they had tended became increasingly difficult. Entertaining was curtailed and, in some homes, sections were closed to conserve fuel oil. A number of homes were leased or donated to the war effort.

R-1148A (ZONE R-1) SERIAL **G** 990534

UNITED STATES OF AMERICA
OFFICE OF PRICE ADMINISTRATION

FUEL OIL RATION
Class 5A Consumer Coupons

Issued to *Port Washington News*
For use only at *166 Main St*
(Number and street)
Port Washington NY
(City and State)
For the heating year ending August 31, 1945.
This sheet issued for *1300* gallons.
War Price and Rationing Board number and address:
War Price & Rationing Board
No. 2530-7
443 Plandome Road.
Manhasset, Nassau Co., N.Y.

GAS RATIONING COUPON from World War II.

The military had priority when it came to gasoline and fuel oil. Consumer supplies were strictly rationed. This coupon was reprinted in the Port Washington News in a 1974 Ernie Simon column.

Gasoline rationing affected daily living. Former Mayor George Bergman (1953-57), who moved to Sands Point in 1940, recalled that, "We all had pools for everything…the mothers of children that went to dancing school pooled, when they went to school they pooled, went down to the Bath Club, they pooled. Of course nobody had more than one car in those days."

Gasoline quotas were allotted so strictly, in fact, that in July of 1943 it was reported that the Port Washington Fire Department, which had nine trucks, had already used its quota through October 25. There was just enough gas left for one more run, according to the *Brooklyn Eagle*.

But Childhood Pleasures Go On

Despite rationing and car pools, the few children in Sands Point had near-idyllic childhoods, with woods to ramble, broad beaches to explore, and some very interesting neighbors. Jay Forman's nearest neighborhood friend was Peter Powell, nephew of Herbert Bayard Swope, who lived with his family in a house on the grounds of the Swope estate. Swope had a "huge official croquet field where they played for lots of money," says Jay. Once, Swope took the two boys to the movies in Glen Cove—which was a big treat because the new movies played in Glen Cove first. "We were there for about a half an hour and he announced we were going home. He didn't like the movie," Jay relates. One day, Howard Hughes flew in on his seaplane to visit Swope. Another time, the two boys saw many *Vogue* models on the beach. They liked that.

Horse trails meandered through the woods. Pansy Schenck's daughters "used to ride through these different estates, horseback riding, and they used to go through the Guggenheim property and Thayer property and other properties that had not been broken up." George Bergman's family had two horses and "there was a lot of empty space. Of course, they had miles and miles and miles of bridle paths through here. Everybody, every family that had girls, the girls all rode, all had horses." Most people, even those such as the Schencks who had lots of acres, stabled their horses at the Sands Point Golf Club, thus eliminating the fuss and bother of maintaining their own stables.

The Backus family, however, kept their three horses and one Sicilian donkey in the old barn (since moved to the Cow Neck Historical Society property) on Backus Farm. Though they had a "most wonderful apartment at 97th and Fifth Avenue with a striking view across Central Park," according to the Backus daughters, "We went to Sands Point about every weekend where father taught us to ride horses, swim, canoe and play tennis, touch football and baseball."

Younger Sands Point children participated in the Annual Sands Point Pet Show. In 1944 the event was a benefit for the U.S.O., held at George Marshal Field, which was opposite the home of Mrs. Forbes Hawkes on Cedar Lane. There were some prizes in serious categories, such as the saddle horse class, but most were open to children under 12 who competed in such fanciful categories as the best educated dog, best educated horse, most comical, most useful and enough other categories to insure that almost every child received a prize. Admission was 25¢ and the public was invited.

PUTTING UP THEIR MONEY

Taxpayers were encouraged to invest in their country by purchasing War Bonds. From the first War Bond Drive in 1942 to the last one in 1945, the residents of Cow Neck were enthusiastic supporters of the program. By the close of World War II, the grand total for all eight local war loan drives was nearly $20 million, reported John F. Shields, Chairman of the Port Washington War Finance Committee. Much of the money was raised through War Bond Rallies. These were not just opportunities for patriotic speeches and polite applause—they were also

The popular and dapper ex Mayor of New York City, Jimmy Walker, was one of the many celebrities to visit Port Washington to promote War Bond sales. (Courtesy, Ernie Simon Collection, Port Washington Public Library)

"happenings." Former New York City Mayor James J. Walker, always a popular personality on the North Shore, was guest speaker at a War Bond show at Beacon Theater, which also featured a group of radio personalities.

At the request of the Treasury Department, Sands Point's Howard Dietz took on Bond promotion on the national level. He convinced comedian Fred Allen to give him air time on his radio show and asked Irving Berlin to write a theme song, which Berlin did, calling it "Any Bonds Today." Dietz also recruited movie stars and sent them on war bond sales tours. Stars such as Dorothy Lamour, of the Bob Hope and Bing Crosby Road movies, made pitches in places like Waterville, Maine.

Those who couldn't afford to buy bonds were encouraged to purchase Defense Stamps. Frani Lauda of Tudor Lane, who was a Port Washington High School student at the time, recalls, "The buying of Defense Stamps was highly competitive, with one high school homeroom pitted against the other. After we bought $18.75 worth of stamps, we would trade the book for a $25 E Bond. We also collected scrap metal from tin cans to anvils and the results, expressed in pounds, then tons, were frequently announced."

Kids were also competitive about collecting scrap metal. Peter Fraser, high school class of 1944, remembers that he "collected something like a ton and a half," which included large animal food cans collected from "my cousin's 'ranch' at the top of lane" in Sands Point. (The cousin was Tom Fraser and the ranch was an experiment in raising minks on Long

Island. "The mink ranch never amounted to anything, but he supplied a lot of big cans," Peter added. John Freeman was somewhat more impressed with the venture when he visited it as a fourth-grader at the Main Street School in 1936. He remembers being shown pelts and carcasses ready to be ground up for fertilizer.)

THAT'S ENTERTAINMENT

Nicholas Schenck, head of MGM studios and a major figure in the entertainment world, and his wife Pansy, a former singer and talented amateur artist, were not deterred by the servant problem or gasoline rationing when they settled in Sands Point. The Schencks had been evicted from their Kings Point home by their government landlord on a short two-weeks notice, and were seeking other quarters. The Schencks purchased a magnificent Norman chateau on 20 waterfront acres on Hempstead Harbor that had been built for W. Butler Duncan in 1906 and was once owned by Vincent Astor. According to Pansy, who was interviewed some 40 years later by the Sands Point 75th Anniversary Committee, she and her husband "fell in love with Sands Point and of course, this house. William Delano was the architect—it was so beautiful."

A Sotheby's brochure that is included in the Sands Point Intensive Level Survey of Historic Homes in 1998 gives architectural credit to Gram, Ferguson & Goodhue, designers of the Cathedral of Saint John the Divine in Manhattan. Mrs. Schenck's contention that it was designed by Delano and Aldrich is backed by her story of meeting Delano at a party and discussing his plan of her home. But no matter who designed it, Coverly Manor, as the mansion was sometimes called, today retains all of the touches that caused Sotheby's copywriter to state that "the craftsmanship of the house also denotes the zenith of the golden era."

The Schencks did little to change the original decor of the house, which had chandeliers that once hung in European castles, but they did remodel Astor's kennel into a private movie theater. The theater proved to be a great attraction to their guests, whether these were friends from Hollywood and Sands Point or heads of state, such as Winston Churchill. Pansy mentioned visits by Norma Shearer and Irving Thalberg, Spencer Tracy, Clark Gable ("here many

times"), Greer Garson, New York City Mayor William O'Dwyer, and Ginger Rogers. "The most adorable visitors," Mrs. Schenck continued, "were little Judy Garland and Mickey Rooney. They were so darling together because they were both so very talented and so full of energy and vitality and they used to argue over the beat of the music."

William Shea, a New York attorney and Sands Point resident, was an enthusiastic member of the Sands Point Bath Club. He became a national figure when he founded the New York Mets baseball team in 1957. (Courtesy, Port Washington Public Library)

Nicholas Schenck's life was "sort of like a Horatio Alger story," according to his wife. Nick was nine and his brother Joe was 11 when the family emigrated from Russia to New York. The boys started out selling newspapers, saved up enough money to open a refreshment stand and then moved on to manage a small amusement park in New Jersey. Nick eventually arrived at MGM and became its president in 1927, a position he held until his retirement in 1956. According to his widow, his goal as head of the company was to make "pictures that the whole family could see." After his death, Pansy lived on in the house she loved, entertaining her children and grand-children. The vast kitchen, designed for a staff of six, with a giant coal-burning range, was modernized by her grandchildren. They went to Sears and bought her a four-burner electric stove that she could manage by herself on her one maid's day off.

There are some who consider baseball to be not only a great national sport, but a great national entertainment as well. One of Sands Point's premier baseball fans was Attorney William Shea, who in 1957 created the most entertaining team of all—the New

Industrial designer Raymond Loewy, who was known for his forward-looking design of autos, trains and planes, lived in the Sands-Nostrand House on Sands Point Road, one of the oldest dwellings in the Village. (Courtesy, Washington Public Library)

York Mets, when he was chairman of the commission to bring national baseball back to New York. William and his wife May Nora "Nori" Shea came to Port Washington in the late 1930s and then moved to Sands Point. Shea was a founding partner of the prestigious law firm of Shea and Gould and an adviser to mayors and governors. (The Long Island Lighting Company was one of the firm's bigger clients.) Former Israeli Defense Minister Ariel Sharon, whom Shea and Gould represented in a successful libel action against *Time, Inc.,* was one of the firm's most famous clients. The Sheas took to Sands Point immediately. Their daughter Patricia Shea Ryan wrote in a 1994 tribute to her mother: "they were members of the famous Sands Point Bath and Tennis Club and spent many nights in the 1930s and 1940s dancing to the music of the Tommy Dorsey Band and Eddie Duchin." Shea was also a member of the Sands Point Golf Club. In later years, Nori Shea was involved in such causes as the National Center for Disability Services, Catholic Charities and Little League Baseball, and was a member of the Board of Visitors of Georgetown University, her husband's alma mater.

Some of the famous residents offered welcome touches of glamor. Raymond Loewy designed the original Lincoln Continental automobile and owned three of the cars. Harvey Levine of West Creek Farm Road, a teenager at the time, remembers that each one had a different color scheme…and Loewy dressed his chauffeur to match. The classy cars also bore a large RL monogram on the back. Women's sportswear designer Tina Lesser, who made her summer home in a converted barn off Middle Neck Road, provided added excitement. Models wearing clothes from her new line were periodically photographed on the grounds of her property.

THE END OF THE WAR

President Roosevelt's death on April 12, 1945, was a source of profound national grief—and concern. Could the relatively unknown Harry Truman, a product of midwestern machine politics, take over the command of the world's greatest fighting machine? Could he bring hostilities to a close? When the time came, would he be able to engineer a lasting peace?

Truman proved his ability to lead when he ordered the controversial use of atomic bombs over Japan. The move saved thousands of lives, it was widely believed, and soon brought the war to an end. One Sands Point example: Army Officer Robert Forman was in San Francisco, on his way to the Pacific, when the U.S. dropped the bomb on Hiroshima. He never had to board his scheduled transport.

On V-J Day, August 8, 1945, sirens all over Port Washington blew in celebration; citizens climbed to the top of the taller buildings on Main Street to release a storm of shredded paper and streamers; the fire department got out its engines and put on an impromptu parade. Blackout curtains went into the rag bag. And the aircraft spotters climbed down from the Hempstead House tower for the last time. The war was officially over on September 2 when members of the Japanese government signed surrender documents aboard the battleship *Missouri.*

Port Washington's War Council disbanded. The AWVS gave its station wagon to the Village Welfare Society. War maps were folded and put away, and people started worrying about peacekeeping and the care of displaced persons and victims of the concentration camps. They wondered if the proposed new world organization would fly—the post-World War I League of Nations certainly had not.

Dana Backus and his wife Louise were in a better position than most Sands Point residents to answer that last question. In 1945, the army detailed Backus to serve on the Secretariat at the San Francisco United Nations Conference. He wrote in 1973, "Louise also attended as a member of the press, thereby rating a very scarce airplane seat to the west coast. We had a delightful ride back east together on the State Department train."

After the war, Louise (and her mother Harriet Laidlaw) became very active in the American Association for the United Nations, working to educate high school and college students about the United Nations and testifying before Congress in favor of the international organization.

A BIG HURRICANE AND A MONSTER BLIZZARD

Thoughts about the war and its repercussions were temporarily blown aside by the 100-mile-per-hour winds of a hurricane that struck Long Island on September 14, 1944. More than 1,000 trees went down in the Port Washington/Sands Point area and, despite frantic efforts to secure moorings prior to the storm's arrival, numerous yachts were washed ashore. Along the relatively short stretch from Louie's restaurant to the border of Plandome, 100 craft were smashed on rocks or beached on the shore. (The yacht loss was estimated at around $1 million.) Power was out for a week. In Sands Point, several boats were washed ashore and streets and lawns of the homes were littered with fallen branches, leaves and other debris. Twenty-five trees were reported down on the K.R. Owens estate.

A blizzard to rival the one in 1888 stormed in the day after Christmas in 1947, when 25.8" of snow fell on the metropolitan area, breaking all records. Lights went out, trains didn't run, sales of snow shovels rocketed, and the people who lived at the end of private roads in Sands Point had strong doubts about the virtues of exclusivity and seclusion.

THE CHINESE DELEGATION PAYS A VISIT

When the fledgling United Nations organization set up temporary headquarters in the former Sperry Gyroscope manufacturing plant in Lake Success, the Chinese Military Delegation to the Untied Nations set up headquarters in Cissie Patterson's Harbor Acres home. Lora O'Reilly Bolte, then a 23-year-old resident of Manhasset, wrote in a 1997 family history about her adventures as assistant to Captain Wen, a recent graduate of VMI and the administrator of the delegation: "There never were such perks in a job! The chauffeur picked me up every morning, the estate had a beautiful pool, at lunch time I ordered my meal sent up from the kitchen and on and on!"

Lora's job was, in essence, that of a social secretary, helping the wives find apartments, arranging parties for the delegation, and trying to avoid embarrassing cultural conflicts—such as explaining to a general's wife (through an interpreter) that one does not bargain with R. H. Macy over the price of a rug. The Delegation's stay in Sands Point was not long. As soon as the UN set up temporary headquarters in New York City, it departed Long Island for 42nd Street.

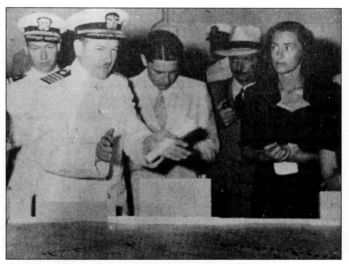

Hempstead House became the U.S. Navy's Special Devices Center in 1946. The former Holmes Estate was used as an officers' club. (Courtesy, Ernie Simon Collection, Port Washington Public Library)

THE NAVY TAKES OVER HEMPSTEAD HOUSE

Three hundred very interesting people came to work (and some to live) in Sands Point in May, 1946 when the Special Devices Division of the Navy's Office of Research and Invention was moved from Washington, DC, to Hempstead House. (The reason why Sands Point was chosen is not clear, but most likely it was the result of Harry Guggenheim's long involvement with the Navy plus the Guggenheim Foundation's interest

When the Navy took over Hempstead House, historic preservation was not one of its major concerns. Note the switch plate mounted on the carved mantel surround. And it is highly unlikely that Daniel Guggenheim would have approved of the grungy steel typing desk placed in front of his marble fireplace. (Courtesy, Port Washington Public Library)

in aeronautical development). Special Devices, as the facility was soon known locally, also took over the Holmes estate. The main house was used as an officers club, and Commanding Officer Captain Donald L. Hibbard and his family resided elsewhere on the property. The Division was engaged in designing devices used for training fleet personnel and reservists in the use of new weapons.

Harvey Levine remembers the day in 1948 when Sands Point residents were startled by the sound and sight of a low-flying helicopter. Leaflets dropped onto lawns, inviting the populace to an Open House at the Naval Special Devices Center on Navy Day. (Harvey, a prep school student, came on his blue motor scooter and was delighted to see that the Navy had 35 scooters just like his, except theirs were painted gray.) Visitors could see and try out equipment designed to help teach seamanship. The most spectacular of all was a 350-degree moving panorama of the ocean and ships at sea, which was viewed through a periscope.

TAXES AND THE TAXED

One way that the rich stay rich is by keeping a very, very sharp eye on the vagaries of tax jurisdictions and tax laws. Sands Point estate owners frequently sought reassessment as a means of reducing their property taxes. Isaac and Daniel Guggenheim did it as far back

as 1918. Edgar Luckenbach regularly appeared before the Village Board asking for assessment reductions. In February, 1948, W. Averill Harriman, a multi-millionaire known for his thrifty ways, sent his attorneys to the Village Board to request that his property be re-valued from $380,650 to $170,000. On that same grievance day, Enrico A. Stein, who must have owned fewer than Harriman's 86 acres, applied for a reduction of assessed valuation from $49,000 to $35,000. When Harriman's application was turned down, he requested a review from the County Board of Assessors and filed again in the Village the next year. Unfortunately, no record is on hand as to the final outcome, but odds favor the Village. The result of Stein's application is also unknown.

In 1946, when the Town of North Hempstead Housing Authority proposed a slum clearance project of 28 acres on the edge of Sands Point off Harbor Road, Dana Backus directed the attention of the Village Board to the potential negative tax effects on the Village residents. The Board in turn directed Village Attorney Herman J. McCarthy "to cooperate as much as possible with the resistance to this proposed multiple dwelling…[as it] would tend to create an economic disadvantage to the school area in which the Village of Sands Point is located." In other words, the project would add children to the school system without adding to its tax base.

Sands Point was not alone in this stance. New Salem, Monfort Hills and Beacon Hill all had strong objections—mostly that the 100 new dwellings would lead to congestion—which they voiced loudly at a Town of North Hempstead board meeting. There were also strong objections on the part of the Estate of Solomon Guggenheim, owner of 200 acres directly opposite the proposed development. Represented by Backus, the Guggenheim heirs maintained that there were other properties available on which it would be more economical to build low-cost housing.

Not surprisingly, the Port Washington Business Association, which anticipated construction jobs and new customers, favored the project; so did the Henderson-Marino Post of the VFW, which supported the development as a means to provide homes for returning veterans. The Town won out and attractive garden apartments replaced the shacks. The apartment tenants did not overwhelm the school system and whatever congestion they produced was quickly absorbed into the local traffic patterns. A few years later, the existence of the development did not deter IBM from buying the Guggenheim property.

Sands Point voters had another way to keep an eye on school taxes. That was to get a resident elected to the School Board. The Sands Point Association made no bones about why it endorsed the candidacy of Henry Wendt, Jr., c. 1950 to replace Fred H. Johnson, also of Sands Point, who had served for six years. J. F. MacEnulty, president of the Association, stated that "the Village of Sands Point pays approximately one-third of the school taxes for the school district with very few of their children attending the schools, and in all fairness they should be entitled to at least one member on the School Board." (One wonders how Sands Point hopefuls of that era got anyone from outside the Village to vote for them.)

But most school board candidates from Sands Point felt differently. Those who have been elected in the last half of the century have had children in the public schools and/or served because of their commitment to excellence in public education. They were, according to district records: Mary Porter (1956-62 & 1965-71), George Graf (1960-61), William R. Perdue (1962-68), Eugene Luntey 1963-1966), Seymour Udell (1967-1970), Leo Ullman (1970-73), Joseph Marro (1972-73), James Hassett (1976-79), Joseph Betz (1976-79), Antoinette Coffee (1973-79), Mina Weiner (1979-85), Katharine Ullman (1979-91), Robert Higgins (1988-91), Bryan McFadden (1989-91), Carol Rossettie (1992-1998), Sandra Erlich (1997-00) and Alan Baer (1998-). Porter, Perdue, both Ullmans, Hassett, Coffee, Weiner and Rossettie also served, at various times, as School Board Presidents. Former Mayor David Kane and longtime Village Treasurer Henry Alker also were school board members.

A GOOD TIME TO BE A TEENAGER

Despite the decline of the large estates, it was possible to live very, very comfortably in Sands Point in the '40s, especially after the end of the war and its wartime shortages. Affluent (as opposed to immensely wealthy) homeowners who had put their boats in storage and hadn't maintained their tennis courts now set out to

The Sands Point Bath Club had a superb location and a special charm of its own. (Courtesy, Institute for Long Island Studies)

enjoy the recreational advantages of their Village. New people, including many veterans of World War II, began to move in as new homes were built after nearly five years of no construction. Adults appreciated the convenience of the community and its proximity to yacht clubs and golf courses. They felt that Sands Point, with its woods, fields, beaches and not much traffic, would be a good place to raise their children. And so it was.

Harvey Levine, who moved with his family to Sands Point in 1944 when he was 14, believes that his was the first Jewish family to live in Sands Point, aside from the owners of large estates such as the Guggenheims. Harvey received his driver's license at age 16 and bought a motor scooter. Soon he knew every road on the peninsula, which he explored with

Mr. and Mrs. Robert Lehman summered in Wampage Shores. (Courtesy, Port Washington Public Library)

A Plum Beach Road home photographed in 1999 looks much as it did in the 1940s. (Photo by Will Wright)

fellow scooter owner and future independent film maker John Cassavetes, who lived at the corner of Barkers Point Road and Sands Point Road. One of Harvey's best teenage buddies was William Ginsberg, now a law professor at Hofstra. (Ginsberg's father was Morris Ginsberg, head of Empire Millworks.) The Ginsberg house had "a wonderful library that was built to resemble the stern of a ship. It even had a column inside that looked like a mast," says Harvey. The house is still standing at the bottom of the hill leading to Plum Point.

Another of Harvey's teenage friends was Katherine Windsor "Kaywin" Lehman, daughter of financier Robert Lehman and his wife Kitty Owen. Her great-grandfather was William Jennings Bryan, whose "Cross of Gold" speech nearly got him elected president of the United States. Kaywin's grandmother was Ruth Bryan Owen, the first woman U.S. ambassador. Kaywin's father Robert Lehman was an art collector of note who donated an entire wing to the Metropolitan Museum of Art. When Harvey visited Kaywin at her family's Manhattan apartment, he was startled to see a Van Gogh painting hanging on the wall—the same one that his mother had hung in his own room. But his was a reproduction—Lehman's was the original.

The young friends Harvey, Bill and Kaywin had "three or four wonderful summers" together. Kaywin had a tennis court, swimming pool and two horses, which were stabled at the Sands Point Golf Club. (The Levines did not belong to the Sands Point Golf Club or the Bath Club, says Harvey, as Jews were not accepted as members at that time.) Lehman, who had business interests in Hollywood, built a 50-seat movie theater (no longer standing) on his grounds, which adults and young people alike enjoyed. On Saturday nights, Lehman would entertain his friends by showing a triple feature of films that had not yet been released. After a newsreel and one feature, the guests would go to the main house for dinner. Afterwards, the older people would remain at the main house while most of the younger ones returned to the theater for two more films.

Harvey's parents bought their house at 18 Plum Beach Road from George Trommer, owner of Trommer's Beer. It was a 17- or 18-room house, probably built around 1912 when Wampage Shores was getting started. Edward Levine was the founder of The Brass Rail food service corporation. Judging by the people that the senior Levines knew, they must have enjoyed Sands Point as much as their son did. Edward became good friends of a summer resident, attorney Arthur Hays, who had supported Clarence Darrow in the famous Scopes Trial in Dayton, Ohio. Other family friends included Rob and Sadye Weinstein and the art-collecting Louis Rabinowitz.

The Weinsteins, parents of former Town Councilman and Village Mayor Jerry Weinstein (1970-71), moved into Sands Point two years after the Levines. Sadye Weinstein was a generous woman, and she showed it after Harvey, his father and his sister made a welcome-to-the-neighborhood visit. Two days later, to Harvey's delight, a 10 pound box of candy from Loft's arrived for his family.

TINTORETTO ON THE CEILING

Among the Levines' friends was the colorful Louis Rabinowitz, who lived at the end of Cornwall Lane near the exit from Dunes Lane in Manorhaven. Rabinowitz made his fortune in manufacturing; his company, Lamar (from his initials, L-M-R) made hooks and eyes for women's and children's garments. He was an art collector and dazzled the neighbors with a painting on his dining room ceiling by Tintoretto, the 16th century Italian master. Rabinowitz was a leading benefactor of Yale University and left his art collection to the school, although he had never attended the institution.

While Rabinowitz was very enthusiastic about collecting, he was rather casual and not one bit neurotic. According to Harvey, his parents and the Rabinowitzes were playing bridge one evening, and Harvey's wife Marcia came to their table. When she accidentally knocked a piece of paper to the floor, Rabinowitz merely said, "Careful." Then he told her that the piece of paper was a new acquisition he was showing his guests—an original Da Vinci drawing,.

Rabinowitz also had a 77-foot yacht and, as his neighbors were astonished to discover at his death, two "wives." Friends who read the obituary and memorial notices in the *Times* were puzzled to see that his widow was identified as "Rose." But the nice lady they played bridge and gin with was Hannah…what did it mean? Well, it seems that Hannah was his "weekend wife"; week days, he lived modestly in a Brooklyn apartment with his legal wife Rose, an Orthodox Jew who did not believe in divorce.

CULTURE SHOCKS

During the postwar years, socio-economic changes taking place right next door in Port Washington and beyond the confines of the peninsula had a marked effect on the Sands Point lifestyle. Families who wanted to see a film could do it locally, without getting into cars. Television, that prewar novelty, was becoming commonplace. (Long Islanders had seen it first at the 1939 World's Fair, held in nearby Flushing Meadows. In fact, with the introduction of table models, many homeowners had multiple TVs. A full page ad in the Port Washington News in the late 1940s, placed by the Motorola dealer, proclaimed that at $179.95. "The Miracle of Television Can Now Be Enjoyed by All the People." (Elaborate console models in a wooden cabinet that enclosed a television, record player and radio cost over $500.)

Fifth Avenue came to the North Shore when a branch of Lord & Taylor moved into Manhasset in 1940. As stores such as B. Altman also opened branches here, shoppers no longer had to travel into Manhattan to keep abreast of current styles in clothing. And parents could take their children to see Santa without having to deal with train sickness.

Now that gas rationing was a thing of the past, two cars in every garage became the norm: one for mom to drive herself around, and to chauffeur the kids, and one for dad to leave at the train station. Sands Pointers and other Long Islanders greeted the opening of the Roslyn viaduct in 1949 with enthusiasm. This road, which crossed the bottom of Hempstead Harbor, meant that motorists traveling east on Northern Boulevard no longer had to spend one-half hour to an hour creeping and crawling through Roslyn Village on a two lane road. Another bonus: once traffic was diverted from the center of Roslyn, the character of the old village, with its historic houses and old stores, remained unchanged from earlier days, and much of it was saved for present and future generations to appreciate.

Something that did not change was the Republican's hold on the Town of North Hempstead. Although the Democrats did well nationally in 1948, especially with the unexpected victory of Harry Truman over New York State Republican Governor Thomas E. Dewey in the presidential election, they did not fare well locally. Voters returned Republicans incumbents to Town Hall, including Supervisor Hartford N. Gunn (a job he held from 1938 to 1950).

By 1950, developers were rolling out plans for ranch houses such as this one that was built on Sycamore Drive in 1951. (Courtesy, Joan G. Kent)

THE BUILDING BOOM BEGINS

1948 was the year the postwar housing boom hit Cow Neck peninsula with near hurricane force. In the ten months between August, 1948, and May, 1949, there were announcements for developments that would add close to 500 houses and a 156-unit apartment complex (Dolphin Green) in Port Washington. New schools, new school taxes and added traffic congestion were sure to follow.

This construction included approximately 100 homes across from St. Peter's Church on Port Washington Boulevard, 75 in the Terrace area, 50 homes near the Sands Point School and 150 to the north of New Salem. Most of the homes would be on 75 foot lots and sell in the $22,000 range, although the 30 custom-built houses planned for Monfort Hills were priced from $25,000 to $30,000.

Sands Point was not exempt from building fever. Fifteen houses—with beach rights—were built in 1948 on a 23 acre tract near Prospect Point. The houses were priced at $45,000 to $50,000, and the first house was to be "a modern ranch-type." The deal was handled by "L.E. and R.S. Forman, Mineola attorneys," said the *Port Washington News*. To satisfy the needs of all these new residents who traveled up and down Port Washington Boulevard, new stores and offices were planned for a large tract of open land that ran south from the Post Office, leased by the developers for 42 years from Burtis Monfort, descendant of the old Dutch family which once had farmed 200 or so acres in the area.

Head-counting provided evidence of significant growth in population. The 1947 school census showed a population increase of 2,500 since the end of 1946. With that information, plus rumors of real estate development, the School Board knew it had space problems well before the official announcements of all those new developments. In anticipation of further growth, the School Board purchased two building sites in early 1948.

THE END OF THE ESTATE ERA

Conspicuous consumption was difficult to maintain during the Depression and did not suit the mood during the war that followed. Very large private estates disappeared when World War II produced a "servant problem" and accelerated again with higher income taxes and ever-rising land values. The Daniel Guggenheim Estate was now occupied by the Navy. The Sands Point Club had long since absorbed Julius Fleishman's golf course.

Though the exact date on which this aerial view of the Daniel Guggenheim estate was taken is unknown (probably 1930s or early 1940s), it shows part of what could be seen from the top of Hempstead House (left) by WWII Aircraft Observers. The stables are to the right and the house on the shore is Harry Guggenheim's Falaise. One could see down Hempstead Harbor (background) and out to the Long Island Sound (left). (Courtesy, Nassau County Museum Services)

When the widowed Mrs. Guggenheim died in May, 1944, the *Port Washington News* reported that she left her 182-acre Sands Point estate and all her paintings to the Daniel and Florence Guggenheim Foundation, and her son Harry was named executor. Although it was not obvious at the time, this bequest indirectly ensured the preservation of her estate for the enjoyment of future generations.

In November of 1949, the last of the estate-owning Guggenheim brothers, Solomon R. Guggenheim, died at his Sands Point home at the age of 88. For a short while there was speculation about the future of his 200-plus acres, and Village officials were concerned. However, after a building project by private developers was unsuccessful, IBM came up with a proposal in the early 1950s that pleased everyone: a country club and conference center for IBM employees.

Sands Point was still a very nice place to live, but it was no longer accurate to call Sands Point an estate village—unless you counted two-acre lots as estates.

CHAPTER 12

1950-1970
POST-WWII SANDS POINT: VETERANS, RANCH HOUSES AND RELIGIOUS INSTITUTIONS

A different Sands Point emerged after World War II. It remained a grand place to live—but most of the living was on one and two-acre plots, not 200-acre estates. Houses that required extensive staffs to run them gave way to homes that could be cared for easily with the assistance of landscape services and weekly housekeepers. World War II veterans, who were now upwardly mobile businessmen, moved with their young families into a community that offered exceptional recreational facilities, an easy commute to the city and good public schools for those who could not afford to send their children to private schools—or chose not to.

This house on Messenger Lane, shown in 1999, is typical of the ranch houses so popular in Sands Point during the early postwar years. The convenient one-floor layouts and ease of maintenance had great appeal to the young families. (Photo by Will Wright)

WORLD WAR II VETERANS MOVE IN

One young veteran who came to Sands Point was future Mayor Leonard Wurzel, who lived in Manhattan with his wife Elaine and two small children until he purchased his first Sands Point home on Sycamore Drive in 1951. The Wurzels had decided they were ready to move to the suburbs. "This was at a time when suburbs were springing up all over and the papers were full of ads for new homes," Wurzel explains. The couple had seen an ad in *The New York Times* for the Country Estates development in Flower Hill and drove out to investigate. The friend who came with them "suggested that we also look at a new development in Sands Point," Wurzel reminisces. "I'm from Philadelphia and I'd never heard of it." The house hunters headed further north on the peninsula. "The trees along Middle Neck Road were beautiful, arching over the road. We went to the corner of Sands Point Road, past the wetlands, and turned into Sycamore where there were two model houses. The two-story and a ranch house." The Wurzels selected a ranch house in the middle of the block. The price was $33,500 plus options. (The only two-story ever built on the street was the model home.)

SANDS POINT'S OWN "GREATEST GENERATION"

William and Lorraine Perdue, who moved into Sands Point about the same time the Wurzels did, met in wartime Washington, DC, when they were both with the Military Intelligence Service. William Perdue, a native of Macon, Georgia, had graduated from Emory University in 1934 with honors and then attended Duke University School of Law (where Richard Nixon was a classmate). He graduated first in his law class of 1937. Perdue began his military career as an enlisted man in the Coast Artillery and Signal Corps and soon transferred to the Cryptanalytic School in Monmouth, New Jersey.

Somewhere along the line, his superiors recognized that the best way to utilize this Phi Beta Kappa in the war was to transfer him to the Military Intelligence Service. Purdue was subsequently commissioned as a second lieutenant and reassigned to develop intelligence from decoded Japanese messages. He later became deputy chief, Pacific Order of Battle Section, and picked up the U.S. Legion of Merit and the Order of the British Empire. He was a lieutenant colonel at his discharge. Lorraine Perdue's wartime service was also noteworthy; she developed intelligence about

Publisher Theodore M. Black, who attained the rank of Lt. Colonel, served with the OSS (Office of Strategic Services) during World War II. Active in Republican politics, he became Chairman of the New York State Board of Regents. (Courtesy, Beverly Pavlek)

Japanese tanker fleet deployment by studying intercepted Japanese military messages.

Bill went on to a distinguished career that included serving as vice president, treasurer and executive vice president of Ethyl Corporation, and later vice president of Inmont Corporation. Lorraine, a graduate of Mount Holyoke College, chaired the Mount Holyoke Alumnae Development Committee and raised alumnae donations to record levels.

After moving to Sands Point, both Purdues became active in village and community affairs. Lorraine was a member of the Sands Point Garden Club and a docent at Falaise. Bill was on the Planning Board of Trustees of the Village of Sands Point, served six years on the Port Washington School Board and was board director of both the Visiting Nurses Association and Hospice Care of Long Island.

Frank Bolway and his wife Alice Ayer Bolway, who lived in Sands Point for nearly 50 years, were among the early postwar arrivals. He served with the Signal Corps in the European Theater of Operations during World War II and then became chairman of the D. H. Litter Company. He was a member of the Sands Point Village Board of Appeals, the St. Stephen's Church Vestry and the board of the Hospice of Nassau County.

Theodore M. Black, a book publisher who moved to Sands Point in the '50s with his wife Barbara, had a distinguished military career as a member of the OSS (Office of Strategic Services), predecessor of the CIA. Ted was well known and respected for his community activities and involvement with the Republican Party, and became even better known when he achieved the position of chancellor of the New York State Board of Regents—an appropriate position for a Phi Beta Kappa graduate of Princeton University. Ted and Barbara were active members of the Port Washington Yacht Club.

Kathleen Hoyt Godfrey was a war bride, though only in the timing, since she did not come from overseas. She married Ralph Leslie Godfrey, a captain in the U.S. Army Air Force, in 1942. Mrs. Godfrey had acted professionally in New York prior to her marriage and became a mainstay of the Port Washington Play Troupe for more than 25 years, acting in and directing many of its productions. She also did publicity for the Sands Point Garden Club.

Ralph Godfrey was a young NYU graduate working at an advertising agency in New York when America's entry into the war brought about a drastic career change. He served as a navigator with the Army Air Force Transport Command, where he had the job of taking men and equipment to war zones and bringing the wounded home. His was the second plane to land on Okinawa. Godfrey had achieved the rank of captain by the time he returned to his own home after the war. By the time he and his family moved to Sands Point in the '50s, he had founded his own advertising agency and became famous in marketing circles for his memorable "Fire and Ice" campaign for Revlon cosmetics. He later purchased a company that manufactured toiletries. Godfrey, too, was a Play Troupe stalwart, acting in and directing many productions.

Eugene H. Luntey, who earned a BS in chemical engineering from the University of Idaho, served as an airborne naval radar officer in the U.S. Navy during World War II. He and his late wife Beverly moved to the Village in 1959 when they built a house on land they owned in Harbor Acres, which they had purchased a few years earlier. They were living in an apartment in nearby Great Neck when Beverly saw an ad in *The New York Times* offering land for sale that had been part of an estate in Sands Point. (These were the last lots in Harbor Acres, the back part of the former Astor property.) At the time there was just one house on Astor Lane. The Lunteys liked the rural feeling of the area and the view over the IBM golf

Leonard H. Kaplan, a sergeant during World War II, and later a criminal attorney in civilian life, moved to Sands Point with his family in 1962. Shown here in 1942 with his wife Muriel. (Photo courtesy, Charlotte Muchnik)

course. After purchasing the land, they "sat on it" for a while; Beverly was busy at the time, working as social secretary for Babe Paley, wife of the Chairman and founder of CBS. Then Kirk, their son, was born and the Lunteys decided it was time to move from the apartment. They built their house and became active in community affairs about the same time they finished unpacking.

Gene Luntey has held a variety of Village posts. He figures that, as of May, 1999, he has served in Village government for 32 years: as park commissioner, Planning Board member, village trustee, police commissioner, and deputy mayor. He also served two years on the Port Washington School Board (1966-68). Outside of Sands Point, Luntey is better known for his business role, with many years as chairman, CEO and president of Brooklyn Union Gas and chairman of Long Island University's Board of Trustees. Beverly has been active with non-profit organizations and is currently on the board of the Helen Keller Center.

The move from Great Neck to Astor Lane influenced the course of young Kirk Luntey's life. The boy became a golf enthusiast and worked in the pro shop at the IBM country club during summer vacations all through Schreiber high school and college and later went to work for IBM.

Thomas Pepitone, a WW II veteran and real estate developer, moved with his wife Fay to Harbor Acres in 1956. Pepitone believed that classic styles would outlast modern—and he put that philosophy to work when he constructed many Nassau County office buildings. His red brick Georgian revival office building on Vandeventer Avenue in Port Washington is as handsome now as the day it opened in the 1970s, and the location has remained desirable as well.

Leonard H. Kaplan, who served as a sergeant in the Army-Air Force in England and France during World War II, his wife Muriel and two daughters Marla Kaplan-Freeman and Carol Prakin, moved from Port Washington to Sands Point in 1962. They were active members of the Community Synagogue and the Sands Point Bath Club. Carol defected to Greenwich, Connecticut but the other, Marla, operates a graphic design studio in Port Washington today.

Dr. Edmund Goodman, who developed and ran a naval hospital in the Galapagos Islands when he was a naval officer, and his wife Marian Goodman, a graduate of Cooper Union and professional artist, bought two acres in Sands Point in 1955 at the suggestion of Goodman's friend and patient Averill Harriman. They built a country house that became their year-round home in 1979. Goodman had met Harriman shortly before the U.S. entered WWII, when he treated a man who was the Lend Lease administrator to the U.S.S.R. at the time. To avoid publicity, the man had been flown from Russia to New York for treatment of an internal abscess. The young Dr. Goodman set up an operating room in Harriman's apartment and successfully—and confidentially—treated the problem. Goodman and Harriman became friends and later, Sands Point neighbors.

Henry and Marilyn Salomon, then living in Great Neck, built a house in the woods on Glen Road in the 1950s with a sweeping view of Long Island Sound and the nearby wetlands. Henry, the president of a chemical importing firm founded by his family in 1867, may have come by his love of the water as a result of his wartime service with the U.S. Navy. Included among his naval assignments was the job of bringing landing craft built in the Great Lakes area down the Mississippi to New Orleans, where combat

Marilyn and Henry Salomon, who have lived for many years on Glen Road, met and married in St. Louis in the middle of WWII. Henry left the Navy with the rank of Lt. J. G.
(Courtesy, Marilyn and Henry Salomon)

crews took over. Henry, who relocated his business from New York to Port Washington, devoted a good deal of energy to community service as a member of the Library's Art Advisory Committee as library trustee and board president, president of the Port Washington Senior Citizens, and a member of the Sands Point Village Landmarks Commission. Marilyn took up commuting and became a legal secretary after her older son was away at the University of Chicago and her younger son was in his last year at Schreiber High School.

After retiring from business, travel to all continents, including such infrequently visited places as the Arctic, Antarctica, Papua New Guinea, Cambodia, Easter Island and Heron Island, has been a major interest of the Salomons.

ABOVE AND BEYOND

Although most of the veterans who moved to Sands Points, as well as those already here, could rightfully be called war heroes, there were a few who had the right to boast—but seldom did—of quite remarkable accomplishments.

William A. Keyes, who lived in Sands Point from 1954 until his death in 1991, was a C-47 pilot in the 58th Troop Carrier Squadron, 9th Air Force. Captain Keyes participated in campaigns in European, African and Middle Eastern theaters, including air offensives over Italy, Germany and Northern France. He also took part in the Normandy invasion. The words in a citation to Keyes, issued by General Eisenhower, reveal just how hazardous this duty on a troop carrier was: "Despite the fact that all of the aircraft were unarmed and unarmored…and were flown at minimum altitudes and airspeeds and were flown…into the face of vigorous enemy opposition…paratroops were accurately and successfully dropped on pinpoint objectives….The courageous exploits of the 61st Troop Carrier Group reflect the highest credit on the United States Army Air Forces."

Nikolai Stevenson, a 1940 graduate of Columbia, was discharged from the United States Marine Corps in 1946 as a lieutenant colonel after five and one-half years of active service. As an infantry officer, he took part in the landings on Guadalcanal, New Britain and Peleliu and was twice decorated for gallantry with Silver and Bronze Stars. Mr. Stevenson, a retired New York sugar broker, is currently president of the Association for Macular Diseases. He is also a member of the board of *Harpers* magazine and lectures to enthusiastic audiences on subjects ranging from Balkan history to current developments in Cuba.

Stevenson and his wife Shirley, a former social worker, lived at 28 Barkers Point Road for many years in a colonial revival house (c. 1930) that was set back from the road and had a rear view out to the Bay.

On paper, the biography of Walter A. Scholl reads like a biography fabricated for a wartime movie about heroic fighter pilots—perhaps because he actually was a heroic fighter pilot in the war. He started out as a football star at his high school on Staten Island and attended Cornell University, where he studied hotel management and played baseball the year the team won its first Eastern Collegiate championship. As an Army Air Corps pilot he shot down several planes, accumulated 220 hours of combat flying and won 11 commendations, including the Distinguished Flying Cross, the Silver Star and the Air Medal with oak leaf clusters. He left the service with the rank of captain. After the war he became a member of the NY Stock Exchange and was a vice president at Merrill Lynch.

OTHER NEWCOMERS

Of course, many of the people who moved to Sands Point in the '50s were not World War II veterans. Some of them were toddlers born to the veterans and others were either too young or too old to have served.

Former Mayor Carlo F. Salvador (b. 1898) of South Road, Harbor Acres, has been a Sands Point resident since 1951. From 1956 through 1979 he held numerous Village posts including trustee, deputy mayor, mayor (1959-61) and member of the Planning Board. A devoted member of the Sands Point Golf Club, he was on its board of governors from 1965 to 1980 and served as the club's treasurer for five years. Along with all of these activities, he established his own law firm, wrote several books, and helped reorganize the New York Law School. A graduate of Fordham Law School, he married Kathleen McAloon. Their daughter Ann is a teacher in the Port Washington Public Schools.

This house on Barkers Point Road, shown in the very good dogwood spring of 1989, has been home to some of Sands Point's more distinguished residents—artist Neysa McMein, playwright-director George Abbott, and General Motors' CEO Frederick Donner. Mrs. Donner was known for the gardens she created on the wooded property. Owners in 1999 are William and Gay Schmergel. (Courtesy, Port Washington Public Library)

Frederick G. Donner, a General Motors executive, and his family moved in the mid 1950s from Bayview Colony to a handsome brick Tudor house at 34 Barkers Point Road in Sands Point. He was vice president of the corporation from 1941-56, CEO from 1958-69 and a director from 1942-86. He was also chairman of the board of the Alfred P. Sloan Foundation from 1968-85.

George Hinman, president of Pioneer Scientific Corporation, was called "an expert in the fields of optics and electronics," but was even more expert in the sport of yacht racing. As the Manhasset Bay Yacht Club Centennial Yearbook tells it, "From the 1920s on, the Hinman name appeared frequently at the top

of the competition in everything from frostbite dinghies to Twelve Meters [then used in America's Cup races]. Hinman was Commodore of MBYC from 1945-46 and later served terms as commodore of the New York Yacht Club, president of the North American Yacht Racing Association and was a member of the America's Cup Selection Committee.

Horace and Margaret Hagedorn moved their family from Luquer Road to Farmview Road in Flower Hill in 1947 and then went to Harbor Acres a decade later. He reports, not without a note of wonder, that he paid $2,500 for the third acre in Flower Hill and built a house for $26,000. The house they bought in 1957 at One South Road from Harry Downs was big enough for all six children (two sets of twins). The house was built around 1926. The Harbor acres property with house, barn (c. 1897) and pool house cost $55,000 in 1957.

By then, Harbor Acres was a well-developed area with a lot of community spirit. "We kept up the Beach House. We had to do our own painting," says Horace. At one time the Village threatened to take over the beach house for back taxes as the Harbor Acres Property Owners Association did not have enough money on hand to cover them. However, loyal Association members dug into their pockets and saved their beloved beach house and tennis courts.

OLD FAMILIES HOLD ON

While an influx of new families settled on the newly-developed streets of Sycamore Drive, Messenger Lane

Rider and horse make a flying jump at the 1954 Sands Point Horse Show. (Courtesy, Nassau County Museum Collection, Institute for Long Island Studies)

and Woodland Drive, mostly in ranch and split-level houses, pockets of old-fashioned, countrified Sands Point continued to thrive. In 1953, Robert Fraser moved his family back to Sands Point from Port Washington to a new colonial-style house near the homes of Thomas Fraser and his nephew, creating a small family compound at the end of a long single-track dirt road. His son Peter writes: "I remember great snowfalls which left us isolated, after I began living in my parents home here about 1953. The isolation was something in which we took pride. At that time the Weavers [Sylvester "Pat" Weaver, president of NBC] lived in the Old House. Tom and Peggy [Mott] lived in their 1948 house and we lived in ours. The Weavers had a caretaker living in the cottage. That was our community. My father and Tom acquired some kind of plow or 'drag' to keep the dirt surface passable. When the snow got too deep, a plow service was called on, but we were generally the last to be plowed out. Pat Weaver…offered the services of his caretaker Karl as his share of road maintenance."

The women of the family shared this pioneer spirit. After one heavy snowstorm, Anie Fraser and Peg Fraser, Tom's wife, who had matinee tickets for the next day, were determined they would not miss the performance and set out to dig a footpath to Middle Neck Road, a distance of eight-tenths of a mile. As Peter Fraser describes it, Lilian Bolton, the Fraser housekeeper, led the way, scooping up the top layer of snow, his mother Anie removed the second layer, and "Peg brought up the rear scraping the ground." They

The Laidlaw/Backus estate was Sands Point's last working farm with shrubs, saplings and vegetables sold to an eager, very local market through the 1970s. (The signs were found in a shed on the property c. 1992) (Photo by Katharine Ullman)

dug about one-fifth of the way up and found that Shorewood Drive had been plowed. The intrepid women made a right turn and shoveled across two properties to meet it. The women made their Wednesday matinee.

Dana Backus and his wife Harriet Laidlaw continued to use the old Laidlaw property as their country home. Once called Hazeldean, the estate was now know locally as Backus Farm. And for good reason. Trees and shrubs and vegetables grown on the "farm" were offered for sale at a little potting shed by the side of Sands Point Road. Many of Sands Points new homes were landscaped with very local plantings.

ENTER MAYOR BERGMAN

While the World War II veterans were settling into Sands Point, the World War I generation was still running it. John Englis, who had been a lieutenant in the Navy during World War I, was elected Mayor in 1951. A longtime resident of the Village, he had served as a Village trustee and was president of the Sands Point Bath Club for a number of years. In the business arena, he was vice president of C. Englis and Son and president of the Kill van Kull Ferry Co., Inc., the League Island Ferry Co. and the League Island Boat Corp. (His firm operated the Port Washington-New Rochelle Ferry line from 1931 to 1939, when it was put out of business after the Bronx-Whitestone Bridge opened.) In July, 1953, shortly after he was elected to a second term as Sands Point's mayor, Englis was killed in an automobile accident in Manhattan.

He was succeeded in office by George Bergman, senior Village trustee, who moved to Sands Point in 1941. Bergman became active in Village government in 1947 when Mayor Seth Thayer (1947-51) asked him to serve as building inspector (it was an unsalaried volunteer position at the time, and it is salaried now). "Village government was, at that time, very casual," said Bergman in a 1991 Port Washington Library interview; "…if you had an election, if you had fifteen people voting, it was a good turnout." Mrs. Bergman gave him a hand as building inspector because "she liked to go over blueprints and she liked to go to new housing and look at it."

Bergman was a World War I veteran who had joined the Marines when he was only 17 years of age. He owned Blair Tool and Machine Corporation, whose wartime customers included Grumman, Sikorsky and Fairchild. He brought a variety of useful business skills to his Village government duties and a forthright personality to the mayor's office. When Bergman ran unopposed for mayor the following June to serve the remaining year of Englis' term, 107 people cast votes.

ARRIVAL OF COMMUNITY SYNAGOGUE

War veterans, and other new suburbanites raised the population of Sands Point and Port Washington, creating a reason for schools and religious institutions to expand. The needs of the growing Jewish community were especially pressing.

The first Jewish congregation was established in Cow Neck in 1933 by a Conservative congregation in Port Washington. (The congregation is now housed in the modern Temple Beth Israel at the end of Haven Avenue.) By 1951, the needs of the local Reform Jewish population led to the founding of Community Synagogue (first called Temple Beth Am).

The new synagogue, which was organized by 35 families from Sands Point, Port Washington and Manhasset, held its first religious service at the American Legion Hall in Port Washington on February 8, 1952. Officers and trustees were elected at a meeting two weeks later. Sands Point's Nathaniel Hess became president and his wife Marjory was one of its four trustees. Nat Hess was a business executive and talented landscape designer by avocation, known throughout the country for his extensive rhododendron collection. Hess, said Mayor Bergman, "was the man, he was the spark-plugger."

Other Sands Point residents who were active in founding the Synagogue were Juliemarthe and Joost Jacobs, Lucille and Philip Kallenberg, Lee and Raymond Korobkin, Penny and Phillip Liflander, Barbara and Seymour Solomon, Vera and Herman Tietz and Leah and Leonard Weintraub. (Mrs. Tietz has long served as the synagogue's volunteer archivist.)

It wasn't long before the congregation was ready to move from the Legion Hall to a permanent home. By 1953 it had purchased five acres in Harbor Acres and

In April of 1953, the congregation of the Community Synagogue held a groundbreaking ceremony on five acres it owned in Harbor Acres. Before construction began, property the group deemed more suitable—the Holmes Estate on Middle Neck Road—became available. On the dais (l. to r.) are Jinx Falkenberg, Tex McCrary, Rabbi Jay Kaufman, congregation president Nathaniel Hess, Captain Video (which may account for the large number of children present) and John Daly, Port Washington school principal. (Courtesy, Community Synagogue)

was eager to begin construction. "We granted them a building permit. No questions," said George Bergman, who was mayor at the time. A groundbreaking ceremony, attended by 350 congregants, ministers from the Methodist, Episcopal and Unitarian Churches and other people took place at the end of April. And then, something happened to change those plans; The Chimneys estate, which had most recently been Bachelors Officers Quarters for the Naval Special Devices Center, came onto the real estate market. The substantial mansion, accompanied by plenty of land for parking and several outbuildings, made it the perfect place for a temple and religious school.

The synagogue applied to the Village Board of Appeals for a permit to change the permitted usage of the premises from a one-family dwelling to a house of worship and education. The Board denied the permit and stated, among other legal terms, that this use would be inconsistent with the character of the area, would not promote health, safety, convenience and welfare.

Mayor Bergman supported the Appeals Board, saying he believed that The Chimneys, which was formerly the Holmes estate and had indoor and

The Chimneys became the Community Synagogue at religious services held on June 1, 1957. Among the hundreds present at the formal dedication were (l. to r.) Seymour Udell, Rabbi Eugene Borowitz, Charles Shapiro, Nathaniel Hess, first and honorary congregation president. Not shown Carlos E. Salvador, village trustee, and George Lindig, trustee and acting mayor. (Courtesy, Community Synagogue)

outdoor swimming pools, a bowling alley, rifle range, plus a handball court, "would be a great place for social events but that wasn't what a synagogue was intended for." While some of the Village residents may have agreed with their mayor, none felt strongly enough about the subject to attend the three public hearings that were held in 1955 concerning the permit.

The synagogue continued its fight by bringing a lawsuit in New York State Supreme Court, which was turned down on December 19, 1955. Undeterred, the synagogue leaders filed a petition with the Court of Appeals, the state's highest court. That body ruled in favor of the Community Synagogue by a vote of six to one, holding that the reasons advanced by the Village Board of Appeals denying the original permit application were arbitrary and unsubstantiated. The Court's opinion stated: "We think that we should accept the fact there we are the successors of 'We the people' of the Preamble to the United States Constitution and that a court may not permit a municipal ordinance to be so construed that it would appear in any manner to interfere with the 'free exercise and enjoyment of religious profession and worship.'" The Sands Point Village Board of Zoning Appeals granted the Community Synagogue a permit to establish a house of worship and Hebrew school on the former Holmes estate on August 21, 1956. The certificate of occupancy would not be issued until required fire safety improvements could be made to The Chimneys mansion house.

Finalizing the details of the purchase fell to Charles Shapiro, Community Synagogue's second president, who was a real estate broker then living on Sycamore Drive. Writing in the congregation's 25th Anniversary Journal, he says: "I felt a special responsibility, not only as temple president, but as the one who negotiated in its behalf for the purchase of this stately property, with its glorious 24 acres and suitable buildings and residence, at a price of $215,000—a low price for its offerings but a handsome sum for a fledgling congregation."

The Chimneys became Community Synagogue at religious services held on June 1, 1957. Among the hundreds present at the formal dedication were Rabbi Eugene Borowitz, spiritual leader of the congregation; Charles Shapiro; Nathaniel Hess, first and honorary congregation president; Carlos E. Salvador, Village trustee; and George Lindig, also a trustee and acting mayor. Initial misgivings on the part of some Village residents about their new neighbor soon proved unfounded. The congregation was an excellent caretaker of the beautiful property, maintaining the Holmes mansion and its lushly landscaped grounds in their original glory.

The only other religious institution to arrive was the Methodist Church on Middle Neck Road, dedicated in 1969. While its new building was under construction, the congregation used the Comminity Synagogue for worship services. There was no appreciable increase in traffic to Sands Point due to the presence of either institution. Community Synagogue had a membership of 650 families in 1999; the Methodist Church was attended by 400 families that year. Rabbi Borowitz was succeeded by Rabbi Martin Rozenberg, who held the post for 33 years until his retirement in 1996. During that period, Community Synagogue experienced great growth in membership, expansion of adult and children's education programs and the successful inauguration of a center for pre-schoolers. His successor was Rabbi Jeffery Salkin.

By the 1950s the Hoffstot mansion, beautiful Belcaro, was falling into ruins, victim of wartime neglect and rising taxes. It was demolished soon after this picture was taken. (Photo by Harvey Weber. Courtesy, Village of Sands Point)

DECLINE AND FALL OF OLD MANSIONS

Other Gold Coast era mansions did not fare as well as The Chimneys, Hempstead House and the Solomon Guggenheim Mansion, which was to become the centerpiece of the IBM Country Club. Instead of being reused for other purposes, many Gold Coast landmarks were demolished, either by design or benign neglect, to avoid taxes. By 1950, the old Van Wart mansion was shuttered and abandoned. The Belmont/Hearst Castle had already been torn down. The Condé Nast mansion succumbed to fire before the decade was over.

Young people from Port Washington and Manhasset drove down deserted driveways and lanes, cars packed with Coca Cola, beer and blankets, to reach Sands Point beachfronts—to picnic and swim by day and build bonfires and party at night. The Sands Point police diligently chased the trespassers away when they were notified of their presence but there weren't very many watchmen or property owners around to do the notifying. Kay Ullman, a present-day resident of Sea Coast Lane, remembers being a teenager, bike riding with friends up from her home in Harbor Acres to picnic on the grounds of the deserted waterfront Hoffstot mansion and bravely exploring the house that they heard was haunted. (Nobody was quite sure whose ghost was doing the haunting.)

HARRIMAN BECOMES GOVERNOR

When it came to politics, Sands Point residents in the early '50s were interested in developments on both the local and national levels. Harry Truman had faced a momentous decision in his second term: whether to send U.S. forces to join in the United Nations "police action" in Korea. Wartime hero General Eisenhower had succeeded Truman as president in 1952, defeating Adlai E. Stevenson, the former governor of Illinois who was later appointed ambassador to the United Nations by John F. Kennedy. The Republicans were tremendously pleased to be back in control for the first time in 30 years. It was during Dwight D. Eisenhower's first year in office that an Armistice was signed between the North and South Korean governments.

If you lived in Sands Point, even more exciting than the national Republican revival was the emergence in 1954 of neighbor W. Averill Harriman as a candidate for New York state governor on the Democratic ticket. Sands Point villagers counted the 62-year-old Harriman as one of their own, even though the Harriman family compound in Orange County was, at 20,000 acres, more than 200 times the size of his Sands Point estate and logically could be considered his primary residence. Harriman owned about 150 acres in Sands Point, which Marian Goodman, his next-door neighbor, says was his "greatest relaxation place…Sands Point was real

W. Averill Harriman, multimillionaire sportsman, diplomat, one-time New York State governor and advisor to Democratic presidents, maintained a 150-acre estate in Sands Point for more than 40 years. (Courtesy, Port Washington Public Library)

country then. There were foxes, beautiful pheasants, dogs ran free." She adds, "We were great friends. Averill loved to fish and catch whitebait. We'd wade out with rod and net and bring our catch back to the Harriman cook, who would fry it right away and we would eat right away."

The *Port Washington News* described Harriman as a "multi-millionaire trouble shooter in two Democratic administrations [Roosevelt's and Truman's]." A lackluster campaigner, the somewhat shy and retiring former ambassador nevertheless managed to defeat the Republican candidate by a narrow margin of 10,000 votes. (Harriman was defeated for re-election in 1958 by the dynamic Nelson A. Rockefeller.) Living next to Averill Harriman was exciting, recounts Marian Goodman. "The world went through Averill's place and we were invited. When he was governor and we couldn't get a baby-sitter, a state police sergeant would be sent over to do the baby-sitting."

A DEMOCRATIC ERA

When Senator John F. Kennedy was elected president on the Democratic ticket in 1960, many Sands Point residents, even those who had not supported him, felt some connection to the handsome and articulate man from Massachusetts. He was, like them, from the World War II generation—the generation that would run the nation, its towns and villages for the next 30 years. The PT boat Kennedy had commanded in the Pacific could well have been built by a Long Island shipyard. His wife's family summered in Southampton, just like some of the Sands Pointers' friends.

Kennedy's influence on politics continued for years after his assassination in 1963. Locally, Republican Congressman Steve Derounian, who had represented the 5th district (which includes Sands Point) long enough to "own" it, lost his franchise in 1964 to Democratic newcomer Lester Wolff from Great Neck. Wolff was a man who had never sought political office previously, but used the expertise he had acquired as an advertising and public relations executive to mount an effective campaign.

Eugene Nickerson of Roslyn Harbor, who was elected Nassau County's first Democratic county executive in 1961, was re-elected in 1964. On the local level, the Republicans retained their grip on North

The red brick Village Hall on Tibbits Lane which opened its doors in October, 1957, was a big improvement over the Village Board's previous quarters in the Water Department pump house. Henry Titus Aspinwall of Port Washington was the architect and George Bergman was the Mayor. Additional footage was added to the original building (the center section) as Sands Point's population grew and more municipal services were needed. (Photo taken in 1999 by Will Wright)

Hempstead Town Hall. Sol Wachtler, a Republican, was elected supervisor in 1964. It wasn't until 1987, when Ben Zwirn from Port Washington was voted in, that a Democrat held the supervisor's office for the first time since the days of the popular Marcus Christ, the man who in 1907 built North Hempstead's Town Hall in Manhasset.

THE PUMP HOUSE GANG BUILDS A VILLAGE HALL

As new homes continued to go up and and new families moved in, the accompanying infrastructure grew as well, and Village government responsibilities increased. More people were needed to run the government, and a better place to house them became imperative. In 1957, the Village Board voted to build a new Village Hall—or more accurately, to build a real Village Hall. For 20 years, the Village office had shared quarters with the Water Department in a renovated pump house behind the present Village Hall. Mayor Bergman described it as a very casual setup: "it had the Water Department in there and they had their auxiliary engine in there to pump the water...we had a clerk...we had eight or nine chairs we sat around in...."

Henry Titus Aspinwall of Port Washington was the architect for the $60,000 building designed to house Village administrative offices and the Sands Point Police Department, which up until then was quartered in an old farmhouse on Lighthouse Road.

Groundbreaking for the handsome Georgian revival structure took place in January, 1957 and the flag-raising ceremony, which celebrated the official opening for business of the new Village Hall, took place in October. Tibbits Lane, which ran from Middle Neck Road only as far as far as the Village property, was extended until it intersected Sands Point Road. Pollock and Wysong, also of Port Washington, were the general contractors.

NO GIFT TO SANDS POINT

While the Village's problem with the Community Synagogue, which had a happy ending, was resolved in two years, its problems with Marie L. Fetsch, operator of the Sands Point Country Day school, and her husband Louis, began in the early '50s when Bergman was in office and lasted for years. Housed in the old Luckenback mansion, Elm Court, the stone building (similar in design to the Solomon Guggenheim mansion) purported to be a school for the gifted. "The mothers flocked there. They all had gifted children," Mayor Bergman related in 1992 in an interview. The school and its owner were suspected of violating many local laws. "We had her in court a dozen times," said Bergman, who also had suspicions about the validity of the woman's educational degrees and the school's accreditations.

Sands Point lost one of those court cases when New York State Supreme Court barred the Incorporated Village from enforcing its anti-noise ordinance. "It is a strange law indeed," the ruling judge was quoted as saying about one of the charges against the school, "that makes it criminal to play a phonograph at 2 p.m." The Appellate Court reversed the ruling and the case went back to the Village Court for final disposition of the seven noise violation charges that were pending.

Notwithstanding the shenanigans of Mrs. Fetsch that irked Mayor Bergman and his board so much, Sands Point Country Day School stayed out of the papers until 1963, when it announced the appointment of a musical director to establish vocal and orchestral music departments. Enrollment in the combined elementary and high school divisions

Donna Wenger of Woodland Drive, then living in Queens, (middle, top row) is shown with her charges at the Sands Point Country Day School summer camp in 1967. Today, Mrs. Wenger is on the Board of the Port Washington's Children Center and a past president of the Women's Division at Knickerbocker Yacht Club.
(Photo courtesy, Donna Wenger)

amounted to 100 at the time and Mrs. Fetsch hoped to bring that number up to 175 the following year. That expansion plan must have made Bergman's successor, Dr. George F. Lindig (1957-59), and the Village Board quite nervous. They became even more so in December when Fetsch announced plans for a junior college for the gifted, with additional facilities such as a junior-senior high school building, a library and a science laboratory. The prospect of several hundred college students invading Sands Point every day, no matter how high their IQ, was alarming.

The junior college never materialized. Some parents charged that the school misrepresented itself as educating "gifted" children and enrollment fell off. Fetsch retired in 1973 after selling the school property for approximately $1 million. A new board of trustees took over the school, which for a short time became Elm Court Academy. Then, in October 1974, the school was taken over by the Maimonides Institute, a nonprofit organization that operated facilities for the handicapped, which established a school for emotionally disturbed children with organic defects and learning disabilities. If any people in the neighborhood objected to this development, their views were not aired publicly. There were just three students in attendance when it opened, with a projected enrollment of 70. Ironically, Myra and

Gene Gamell moved to Sands Point in 1977 so that their severely retarded daughter could attend the Maimonides School. It closed six months later and the Luckenback Mansion was demolished shortly afterwards.

The only schools in Sands Point today are the Hebrew school at the Community Synagogue and the Sunday school at the Methodist Church, and the non-sectarian Child's World Nursery School sponsored by the Church, using its grounds and parish hall. The largest school in Sands Point is the public Guggenheim Elementary school, with a student body of around 620 in 1999.

And this is where the help lived? Former carriage house on the Solomon Guggenheim estate (IBM Country Club) had living quarters on the second floor. (Photo, Joan G. Kent)

IBM COUNTRY CLUB

One large piece of property that escaped the subdividers was the Solomon Guggenheim estate. Although efforts were made to develop the land in 1953, they fell through and the estate was purchased by IBM to serve as an employee country club and conference center. Even though few Village residents ever set foot on its golf course or tennis courts, they were delighted with their new neighbor, which produced no children to crowd the schools, very little traffic and offered a pleasant green vista to those driving by on Middle Neck Road.

The corporation made a few alterations to the interior of the main house to provide space for seminars and meetings, but the mansion remained essentially the same as it was when the Guggenheims were in residence. The grounds, gardens and golf course were equally well maintained. If a Village Historic Landmarks Preservation Commission had existed at the time, its members would have been

extremely pleased. When the Village acquired the IBM Country Club in 1994, it bought a property that was quite easy to convert to a Village country club and recreation center.

This white colonial on Cornwells Beach Road was the home for several years of singer and TV personality Perry Como. (Photo by Will Wright)

Mob boss Frank Costello kept a low and benign profile during the years he lived on Barkers Point Road. (Courtesy, Port Washington Public Library)

COMO AND COSTELLO

Sands Point's favorite celebrity resident in the '60s was singer Perry Como. Como, a recording artist and TV performer, and his wife Roselle were popular members of the community, active in Our Lady of Fatima Roman Catholic Church, and lent both their names and energy to local charities.

Crime boss Frank Costello was Sands Point's most notorious celebrity. In the '50s and '60s he lived quietly in a colonial on Barkers Point Road. Port Washington resident Marla Kaplan-Freeman, whose childhood home in Sands Point was behind Costello's, says that Costello would often go for walks and pass out lollipops to the neighborhood children.

Evelyn Fitzsimmons, a Cow Neck Historical Society Trustee and parishioner at St. Peter of Alcantara Roman Catholic Church, talks of a young priest who proudly told her about a generous contribution the church had received from a Mr. Costello in Sands Point. Then he asked, "Do you know who he is?" After Miss Fitzsimmons explained Mr. Costello's sources of income, the priest asked if she thought he should return the donation. "No," she replied, "but perhaps it would be better not to solicit him for funds in the future."

DOG ORDINANCE

As the human population increased, so did the pet community. By 1958 the problems caused by free-roaming dogs had become the Village hot-button issue. Dogs tore up lawns, frightened former city dwellers unused to animals, scared little children, got into fights, bit each other and sometimes bit people, claimed those who sought a dog control ordinance.

More than 100 villagers crowded into the Village Hall on Tuesday evening, April 22, 1958, to voice their opinions, pro and con, about the proposed ordinance to "prohibit dangerous dogs from running loose." Those with large properties felt their dogs should be allowed to run free. Their neighbors with smaller properties were tired of having their newly planted lawns torn up. There were more "fors" than "againsts." The law passed and the Village Justice, then Robert Forman, was given the power to fine owners of a dangerous dog $25 for the first offense and $100 for the second.

THE WRATH OF HURRICANES

Sands Point had its usual share of disasters. On September 9, 1954, Hurricane Carol felled hundreds of trees, ripped boats from their moorings and dashed them onto the shores of Manhasset Bay. A 54-foot schooner was flung up onto Bar Beach. High tides inundated Shore Road and the Plandome Bridge, washed over beachfront swimming pools and set Manorhaven Park benches afloat. In Sands Point, private beaches on the Sound were obliterated, water covered the airplane runway at the hanger near the Nadler home at 63 Cornwells Beach Road and reached the top of the sea wall at the home of publisher Walter J. Black, who lived at 12 Sands Light Road. The waterfront Sands Point Police headquarters had to be vacated.

Harvey Levine recalls that, "Hurricane Carol's high tide flooded our basement [Plum Beach Road] to

Colonial revival architecture was popular in the later '20s and early '30s. Publisher Condé Nast's home on Sands Point Road was a splendid example. Unfortunately, it was destroyed by fire in the early '50s. The elaborate two-story detached garage was untouched. (Courtesy, Port Washington Public Library)

within inches of the ground floor. The house next door wasn't so lucky. Their first floor was about 12 inches lower than ours and the salt water ruined the entire first floor carpet which had just been installed prior to new owners moving in."

Hurricane Donna hit on September 12, 1960, causing extensive damage throughout the Cow Neck peninsula. Trees went down on nearly every block in Port Washington, and one unfortunate man inching along Middle Neck Road suffered a concussion when a tree fell on his car. Homes in Manorhaven and Sands Point were the worst hit, and they had no electric power for up to three days. Trees crashed through the roof of Mrs. George P. King at 29 Woodland Drive and C.J. Sarzin on Shorewood Drive. The residents of Old Lighthouse Road and Sands Light Road were trapped for hours by fallen live wires.

FIRES DAMAGE AND DESTROY

As in earlier decades, water shortage was to blame when the Fire Department was unable to contain the flames of a large fire that consumed the 12-room caretaker's cottage on the former Hoffstot estate in July, 1953. The PWFD laid more than 5,000 feet of hose and desperately pumped salt water from Long Island Sound to bolster the hydrant supply. The 51-acre estate had recently been purchased by the Sands Point Realty Corp., which planned to subdivide the land and build new houses. (It was not until the '60s that the Hoffstots Lane-Lands End area was actually developed.)

A home that had passed through several pairs of famous hands was destroyed when Sandy Cay at 231

Sands Point Road was all but leveled in a $200,000 fire in July, 1954. The home of New York real estate developer Percy Uris at the time, it had previously been owned by author Clarence Buddington Kelland and magazine publisher Condé Nast. Kelland, who was living at 23 Cedar Lane by then, was a very prolific and very popular author of romance and adventure stories who also dabbled in politics. He once served as the Republican national committeeman for Arizona.

Only the chimney remained after a spectacular fire in August of 1957 destroyed the two-story frame house, valued at $65,000, that belonged to Harry B. Anderson of 40 Cornwall Lane. Several years later, it was difficulty of access that led to major devastation in April of 1963 when a brush fire spread to the boarded-up Van Wart mansion, an old Mott house that once belonged to Washingtin Irving. Although its pumper trucks arrived promptly, the Port Washington Fire Department had to cut its way through heavily locked gates and then twist and turn down an overgrown dirt road to reach the fire, which was so intense that all three Port Washington Fire Companies plus the Manhasset-Lakeville Fire Department were called into action. It was to no avail; by the time the fire was under control, there was nothing left but a chimney and a flight of stone steps leading to a basement…and stories about the Van Warts.

The Van Warts were a family of two brothers and two sisters who shared a country home in Sands Point. Edwin, who was close to 80 when he passed away, was the only one of them who married. The siblings' funds came from Manhattan real estate holdings (at one time they owned the Flatiron Building), and some of them were used to acquire their 200-acre Sands Point property prior to 1928. Edwin died shortly after his marriage (the 1923 Belcher & Hyde map shows Mrs. Edwin Van Wart as the owner of a large parcel to the north of the Daniel Guggenheim estate). His widow Maud soon boarded up the house and made New York her full-time home. She left everything in the home as she found it, and after the fire such items as a 1928 Lloyd's Register, a set of 1943 auto license tags, a horse-drawn carriage and an old black Packard were found on the grounds and in the garage.

While she might not have known the value of vintage cars and old yacht registers, Mrs. Edwin Van

The Sands Point Golf Club's "new" clubhouse, shown in 1996, went up in the 1960s after the original had been destroyed in a local epidemic of country club fires. (Photo by Joan G. Kent)

Wart proved herself a shrewd business woman. From her suite at the Biltmore Hotel she sold off the acreage and dictated stiff brokerage agreements. She rented the caretaker's cottage (which had no electricity) during World War II to Air Force officers stationed at Mitchel Field.

Fortunately, there was no water shortage at Sands Point Golf Club when a rash of club fires broke out along the North Shore in the late l960s. The Club had put in its own well at a cost of $40,000 in 1967, eliminating the necessity of obtaining sufficient water from the Village. However, water from the new well was not enough to dampen a fire of undetermined origin that destroyed the cottage behind the 18th hole in 1968. Arnold E. Monetti, who wrote the history of the Sands Point Golf Club in 1979, commented, "while this was disconcerting, it had little effect on the Club's operation as the building was insured and a new and better one was quickly erected."

More devastating was the March 29, 1970 blaze, again of "undetermined origin," which completely destroyed the clubhouse. While insurance covered most of the costs of replacement, the club "faced the prospect of maintaining membership in a time of economic recession and without a clubhouse," said Menotti. The barn provided temporary quarters and the building committee, consisting of Roy Olson, chairman, Joe Wheeler, Charles Trunz, Louis Schott, Carlos Salvador, Richard Dirkes and Elliot McCormack, presided over construction of the amiable clubhouse that members enjoy today.

The people who made the laws in Sands Point and the people who enforced them posed for this group shot in the late '60s. Shown (l. to r.) in the first row are: Village Clerk Philip G. Lewert; Trustee Stanley Hyde; Police Chief John Bailey; Mayor David Kane; Treasurer Kenneth Fraser; Trustee Jerome Weinstein, who was to serve as Mayor in 1970. On the far right in the second row is Police Officer Michael Connolly, who was appointed chief upon Bailey's retirement.

A CONTESTED ELECTION

The two-party system came to the little Village of Sands Point in a big way with its first contested election, held in June, 1958. Incumbent trustees Roy C. Olson, 78 Barkers Point Road, and Benjamin C. Milner III, 66 Barkers Point Road, sought reelection under the banner of the Citizens Party, which claimed a "record of accomplishment, improvements and progress." And indeed, their administration had codified traffic regulations, improved traffic law enforcement, expanded the Village water system and did so, as far as the written record shows, with few complaints from villagers.

The opposing Taxpayers Party, maintaining that the two-party system is essential to good government, presented two trustee candidates of its own: Dr. Solis Resnick, an anesthesiologist, and Ernest J. Thompson of Tibbits Lane, a Port Washington contractor. If there was a basis for the Taxpayers' discontent, it wasn't shared by the majority. The incumbents were returned to office and Olson, an executive with Otis Elevator, went on to serve as mayor from 1961-65.

PIPELINE THREATENS SANDS POINT

It seems that every Sands Point mayor had to wrestle with at least one major quality-of-life issue. For Carlo Salvador, it was the startling proposal to erect an oil tanker facility in the Sound off of Sands Point. The Lewken Corporation (Harvey Lewis and William F. Kenny, Jr., proposed that pipeline be laid under Sands Point Road and lead to a petroleum products storage facility that would be con-structed in Port Washington North, next to the existing Lewis Oil storage tanks. The pipeline would be underground for its entire length, from the moorings to the storage tanks.

Despite the assertions of Kenny, Lewken's president, that tankers would off-load infrequently, the moorings would be practically invisible, the storage tanks would be hidden and barge traffic on the Sound would actually be reduced, residents had visions of oil leaks above ground and under water dancing in their heads, and they vigorously objected to the proposal. The Harbor Acres Property Owners Association issued a statement opposing the $5 million dollar project. The thorough and thoughtful League of Women Voters came out against it. The strongest protest of all came at a meeting on March 29, 1960 sponsored by the Greater Port Washington Civic Council that was attended by 200 people who met at Paul D. Schreiber High School. The 13 member associations of the Civic Council voted to condemn the plan, which they called, "monstrously nightmarish," as did the representatives of 14 other local organizations including the Sands Point Association, Sands Point Bath Club and four local yacht clubs. All of them were concerned about the possibly of pollution in the Bay from pipeline leaks.

The strong opposition from his neighbors proved too much for Port Washington-based Lewis, who pulled out of the pipeline scheme forthwith, stating: "We have decided to withdraw our interest in the

Owners of water front property such as Land's End on Long Island were justifiably concerned for the future of Sands Point's beaches when plans for an oil tanker facility immediately off shore, and companion pipelines, were announced by the Lewken Corp. in 1960. Local yachtsmen, no matter where they lived, weren't happy about the proposal either. (Photo by Harvey Weber. Courtesy, Inc. Village of Sands Point)

The First Methodist Church moved from its old site on lower Main Street in Port Washington to larger property on Middle Neck Road in 1968. This photo shows construction of the new church (left) and fellowship hall (right). (Courtesy, United Methodist Church)

Dr. William Bruce Reed, pastor, watches as 60-foot steel spire is hoisted into place at the new United Methodist Church on Middle Neck Road, Sands Point, in May, 1968. The church was open for services in 1969. (Photo, Everitt J. Henn. Courtesy, United Methodist Church)

laying of a pipeline through the village of Sands Point. This decision has been made because many of our friends and customers have voiced their objections to the project...."

After Lewis' defection, Kenny said, "I still feel that it is a worthwhile project for the people of Long Island," and added that he "intends to continue with the project." Whatever Mr. Kenny (who was president of Meenan Oil Co. as well) did to pursue his plans was not recorded in the local press. And it didn't work. Tankers are not anchored off Sands Point and dozens of storage tanks did not sprout up in the middle of Port Washington North.

ANOTHER HOUSE OF WORSHIP

In contrast to the early objections to its zoning requests that Community Synagogue encountered, no one was opposed when the First Methodist Church bought eight acres of the old Fraser property along Middle Neck Road in July of 1963. It purchased the property, which was adjacent to the IBM Country Club, from the Ed Donner Lumber Corp., its most recent owner, at what current Pastor Rev. Edward Horne says, "was a very good price." The Church, which was located at the time on lower Main Street, had felt the pressure of the community population explosion and needed room for expansion, especially for parking. (The Port Washington Library purchased the site vacated by the Methodists.)

The easy-to-find location was ideal, and the building permits and variances necessary to build a new church were granted at an April meeting of the Sands Point Board of Zoning Appeals. No one even complained that property was coming off the tax rolls. Stanley Hyde of Harbor Acres, a Sands Point Village trustee, was vice chairman of the Building Committee. At the groundbreaking ceremony on March 19th, 1967, more than 325 people attended, including the local clergy and Town officials. The doors to the handsome new church officially opened on April 13, 1969, with the Rev. William B. Reed, who had overseen its construction, officiating.

It should be noted that as time went by, Sands Point—official and unofficial—found that its religious institutions offered several special advantages. When overflow crowds threatened to overwhelm the Village Hall at a public hearing, the spacious community rooms at the church and synagogue have provided much-needed extra space. Both institutions offer cultural programs open to the public regardless of religious beliefs and make their facilities available to community groups.

BUILDING THE "NEW" LIBRARY

Building a new library required more than simply buying the property the Methodists had vacated—it required an enormous volunteer effort to convince the voters to approve the necessary construction bonds. It was Sands Point's Caroline Hicks and the Woman's Club she organized that founded the Port Washington Public Library in 1891. Decades later, in 1965, a group of Port Washington and Sands Point women, including Joyce Fieldsteel of Cornwells Beach Road, established "The Friends of the New Library" to advocate construction of a new building. The facility was designed to house an expanded book and media collection and to offer meeting space for its community programs.

The Friends, which rapidly became a unisex organization, pushed, publicized, cajoled and gained approval for the bond in a vote on October, 19, 1965. Out of the 2,047 votes cast, there were 1,621 in favor and 476 in opposition. That accomplished, The Friends of the New Library did not fade away, considering their work was done. Instead, they dropped the "new" from their name and, to the present day, continue to play an active role supporting the library. Both Mrs. Fieldsteel and her husband

Robert have served on the board of The Friends. (In 1999, The Friends were tapped to promote a new library bond issue to add 10,000 square feet to the existing building, which was passed with a near 75% approval.)

This elegant Georgian revival house was designed by architect J. A. R. Carpenter in 1931 for his personal use. He died in 1932 before the mansion on 4.8 acres at 155 Middle Neck Road was completed. However, his widow moved in and lived in Sands Point for many years. Egyptian Prime Minister Gamel Abdel Nasser chose it for his residence in the fall of 1960 while attending United Nations General Assembly sessions. (Courtesy, Port Washington Public Library)

A PRIME MINISTER'S TEMPORARY HOME

One of Sands Point's most imposing houses, the Georgian revival mansion at 155 Middle Neck Road situated on 4.8 acres, became the temporary home of one of the most influential Middle Eastern leaders. In the fall of 1960, Egyptian Prime Minister Gamel Abdel Nasser chose the house as his residence while he attended United Nations General Assembly sessions. The house was designed by the award-winning architect J. A. R. Carpenter in 1931 for his personal use. Unfortunately, Carpenter died in 1932 before the mansion was completed. However, his widow did move in, and she lived in Sands Point for many years before selling it. Situated across the street from the Community Synagogue, the mansion's location as well as its availability for rental may have appealed to the Prime Minister's sense of humor.

His presence required a multitude of security measures, including extra duty for the Sands Point Police Department. One time, Mrs. Edward Levine was returning from Kennedy Airport in the family limousine when, according to her son Harvey, she spotted a procession of limos with a police escort heading out to Long Island. She told her driver to join the line, hoping that would enable her to avoid the anticipated traffic tie-up on the Long Island Expressway. She was surprised to find that the parade kept going her way, even taking the Searingtown Road exit and driving north to Sands Point. When it arrived at the Nasser domicile, the Sands Point policeman on duty tried to wave Mrs. Levine into the driveway— until he recognized her and realized she was not part of the entourage and signaled her to proceed.

Major Harrington Gillespie, who was apparently attached to the Naval Training Devices Center, is shown receiving a commendation ribbon for meritorious service while advisor to the Korean Army School. Captain Edward Callahan, USN, Commanding officer at USNTD, is shown on the right.
(Courtesy, Nassau Country Museum System)

WHAT WAS TO BECOME OF THE SPECIAL DEVICES CENTER?

The year 1967 brought something new to worry the Village Board and residents. The Navy Special Devices Center, which had occupied the former Daniel Guggenheim estate since 1947, packed up and moved to Orlando, Florida. (The Navy, which first had leased the property, purchased it from the Institute of Aeronautical Sciences in 1951.) Area Congressman

Philanthropist, publisher and aviation pioneer Harry Guggenheim made a gift of 17 Sands Point acres to the Port Washington School District in 1970. Still undeveloped in 1999, it provides a welcome vista of open space to passersby. (Courtesy, Port Washington Public Library)

Lester Wolff fought hard to keep the Special Devices Center in Sands Point, citing its benefits to the local economy and the waste of taxpayers dollars in a move to Florida. He was unsuccessful, however, and now the General Services Administration had to dispose of the 168 acres owned by the U.S. government. According to law, the federal government and its agencies had preference. At one point, the Defense Department caused shudders in the local populace by suggesting it as a possible Nike Missile site, to be part of a defensive ring around New York City. (This was during the Cold War.) The state caused additional dismay with a study that considered turning the property into a drug rehabilitation center. Much more appealing was County Executive Eugene Nickerson's request that it become a county park. (Harry Guggenheim had already promised the county his adjacent house and 80 acres.) Other groups suggested a community college, camp grounds and a home for the aged. The School Board announced that it was seeking 50 acres of the former Special Devices property as a site on which to locate a high school for 3,000 students.

In November, the General Services Administration sliced the Special Devices pie in ways that have proved most fruitful over the years. Nassau County received the biggest piece—128 acres—for a park, thereby preserving such wonderful treasures from Sands Point's past as Hempstead House, the Castlegould stables, and a number of charming outbuildings, all for the education and pleasure of the public. Twenty-five acres were granted to the Industrial Home of the Blind, which built the Helen Keller Center for the Deaf Blind. Five acres went to the Port Washington School District for non-spectator sports and four acres to the Village of Sands Point for construction of a well, pumping facilities and underground water storage tanks.

The Village Board, fearing that streams of cars carrying families on outings would tie up traffic on Middle Neck Road, was apprehensive about the prospect of a park even though the Nassau County parks commissioner promised that the park and preserve would be used only for conservation, education, hiking, salt water studies and "limited" camping. The County and the Village worked out manageable restrictions; most events, such as exhibits, take place throughout the day.

The in-ground swimming pool was the status symbol of the '50s and '60s. This 20' x 40' gunite "boomerang" shaped pool with slide was installed in 1962. (Courtesy, Marla Kaplan-Freeman)

A SWIMMING POOL IN EVERY YARD (ALMOST)

Postwar improvements in swimming pool construction made them more affordable and easier to maintain, so they were no longer an amenity only for the very rich. Installing a pool of their own was in the realm of possibility for nearly all Sands Point homeowners. Some saw the backyard pool as a status symbol; some as a center of family fun and recreation;

others as a big, fat nuisance that needed to be skimmed, cleaned, back-washed and dosed with chlorine on a daily basis. Still other residents regarded pools as potentially dangerous. Those who felt positive about pools predominated in the '50s and early '60s. A multitude of different models, from well-engineered gunite (sprayed concrete over steel) installations, complete with diving boards, to above ground ovals with step ladders, appeared outside homes throughout the Village.

Stephen R. Kent of 9 Sycamore Drive, then director of advertising for American Aviation Publications and an engineer by training, put in the first in-ground gunite swimming pool on his block in 1953. Located in the side yard, it was screened from the street with a six-foot high stockade fence and the fence, in turn, was hidden by newly-planted trees so no one could see it. It was enjoyed by the family, including Kent's daughter Pamela (who swam up to a mile at a time in 45-foot laps) and the people they invited over for a swim.

Not all the local pools were so unobtrusive. Some sat beckoning and unfenced in plain view—and were accidents waiting to happen. One occurred in the winter of 1967, when a three-year-old boy, who had wandered from his home in Manorhaven, fell through the ice of an uncovered pool on property at the corner of Sands Point and Barkers Point Roads and drowned. At the time no village, town or state ordinances existed requiring pools to be fenced and/or alarmed—a situation the Village set out to correct (there were about 100 pools in the Village at that time). An ordinance requiring pools to be fenced in was drawn up and met with contention and the customary rights-of-property-owners argument. Seventy residents squeezed into the Village Hall and, at a vocal public hearing, heard Sands Point Mayor David Kane describe the proposed law as "a fair and reasonable ordinance" that "would go some way toward preventing accidents." The ordinance was passed by the board and fences went up.

BATH CLUB DAY AND NIGHTS

Some pool users preferred to pay private club dues and join the Sands Point Bath Club or a nearby yacht or country club and let somebody else worry about algae and safeguarding children. From the 1920s into the 1980s, the Bath Club was a happy family playground by day and a glittering Mecca by evening for many. Sands Point children learned to swim in its pool and splashed their feet the edge of the bay. Their parents enjoyed being on land, playing tennis or bronzing in the sun, and on the water in sail and motor boats. Most country club presidents and yacht club commodores today count themselves lucky if they can get their membership to dress well for the annual New Year's Eve Dance...but at the Bath Club, a full and formal entertainment schedule was the norm.

A story in the *Port Washington News* about the Gala Opening Dinner Dance at the Bath Club on May 23, 1959, neatly describes the scene there, which was typical for most summers between 1930 and 1970—the war years, of course, excepted. Black tie dinner dances were held every Saturday evening from Memorial Day through the closing dance, which was September 12 that year. Buffet dinner dances were on Sunday nights, and fashion shows and bridge luncheons during the week were planned for "the ladies." The club, which was situated on a sand spit sticking out into Manhasset Bay (Plum Point), was subject to considerable winter wear and tear and had been refurbished. The *Port News* says: "New concrete steps and a black-and-white vinyl tile entrance match the new paint on the Club's

Sands Point Bath and Racquet Club shown from the water in an undated photo--probably 1960s. (Courtesy, Institute for Long Island Studies, Hofstra University)

facade. Brand new wrought iron deck furniture will surround the repainted pool...and the Bay beach play area bulldozed level." Louis F. Lauck of Sands Point Road was club president that year. Jack Miller, a songwriter and arranger for singer Kate Smith, was entertainment chairman. Fred Schroeter probably had the most onerous job of the lot; he was the maintenance chairman. Miller had endeared himself to members earlier (around 1939) by composing words and music for "Sands Point is Nearer to Heaven," a composition that was frequently rendered at Saturday night Bath Club parties.

People loved the Bath Club for many reasons, some difficult to understand. Its clubhouse, on five acres leased from the Pell family, was not imposing. There was always the threat that the short-term lease would not be renewed. The four nearby yacht clubs could beat it hands down for docking and sailing facilities. The swimming pool was filled with eye-smarting chlorinated saltwater. And it usually took half the season for the dining room to get organized. Perhaps members loved it because it seemed the essence of the Gatsby era to them—and they wished they'd been part of that period. Or maybe it was because the Bath Club was just a very pleasant place to be on a summery Saturday night or a sunny Sunday afternoon. You could see many of your friends there.

The Bath Club was the scene of much good fun in the '50s. This is just one of the many groups that enjoyed the place for the celebration of special occasions—or simply seeing one another.
(Courtesy, Port Washington Public Library)

Your kids learned to swim and play tennis there. For those who met the then-restricted membership qualifications and chose to join, it was the nearest the Village came to having a community center.

Hedley Donovan, onetime editor-in-chief, Time Inc., lived with his wife Dorothy in the historic Tristram Dodge House in Harbor Acres. Both were active in local civic affairs. (Courtesy, Time-Life Syndication)

EDITORS AND PUBLISHERS

Just as prominent figures from the world of entertainment made Sands Point their home in the '20s, '30s and '40s, leaders in the field of book and magazine publishing and broadcasting chose Sands Point in the '50s, '60s and '70s. One of the most visible and well-liked was Hedley Donovan, editor-in-chief of Time Inc., who purchased the 18th century Tristram Dodge House on Hempstead Harbor in 1957 and lived there until his death in the 1990s. He and his wife Dorothy remodeled the house in an architecturally sympathetic manner and proudly displayed a sign proclaiming their home was a historic landmark. Located at the end of Harbor Road, it remains in private hands today.

Mr. Donovan enjoyed several perks not available to the average Sands Point resident. When he needed to get to the office in a hurry, the Time-Life helicopter swooped down on his front lawn and carried him into Manhattan (as it did regularly for Time Inc. President James Shipley, who lived nearby for a number of years).

A representative of electronic journalism was Jessie Zousmer, a New Yorker who met his Ohio-born wife Ruth at the renowned Medill School of Journalism at Northwestern University. He worked with radio and TV legend Fred Friendly on the production of the *See It Now* television series, which was hosted by an even greater legend, Edward R. Morrow. Later, Zousmer became director of news for ABC. The couple died with their journalistic boots on when the plane carrying them to Japan blew up over Tokyo, for reasons never determined, in the mid-1960s.

Book publisher Max Schuster of Simon and Schuster lived in one of the old Mott houses during the '60s, not far from where publisher William Lippincott had lived in the '20s. *Sports Illustrated* executive John Tibby and his wife lived in the Cornwall House for a number of years. And one of the best known of the publishing figures, Harry Guggenheim, continued to watch the growth of *Newsday,* the little Long Island tabloid he helped his late wife Alicia Patterson found in the '40s, now one of the largest dailies in the country with a circulation of close to half a million.

MAGAZINE SWEEPSTAKES ARE BORN

Somebody had to sell all the periodicals American publishers were churning out. Most magazines had their own circulation promotion departments, which spent a great deal of money trying to get citizens to spend a little bit on magazine subscriptions. In 1953 Harold Mertz, publishing executive who lived with his wife LuEsther on Round Hill Road in Sands Point, came up with a subscription promotion idea—to include multiple solicitations in one envelope. LuEsther and their daughter Joyce ran the business they called Publishers Clearing House from home while Mertz continued to work in New York. They thought up the now famous sweepstakes, offering prizes of up to $1 million, in 1967. (According to *Newsday,* the company says it has given away about $159 million in prizes.)

The privately held company began making a great deal of money and giving a good portion of it away as well. LuEsther founded Choice Magazine Listing, an audio recording service for the blind and donated heavily to New York City arts groups through the Joyce Mertz-Gilmore Foundation. The LuEsther T. Mertz Charitable Trust, established upon her death in 1991, is valued at $86 million. And with PCH located on Port Washington's Channel Drive, Mrs. Mertz indirectly provided full and part-time jobs for a number of the community's residents.

THE WAR THAT WENT ON...
AND ON...AND ON

It can be said that the war in Vietnam lasted from 1950, when President Truman sent a 35-man advisory force to aid the French (who were fighting to hold onto what was then called French Indo-China), until 1975 and the fall of Saigon. At the height of U.S. involvement in 1968, there were 525,000 Americans in Vietnam. The separation between those who thought the war was stupid, probably illegal, and ill-advised (believing that the U.S. should not be involved in what was essentially an internal war), versus those who supported our country's leadership, increased as the years passed. Draft-dodging became almost socially acceptable.

While the duration of the Korean War was short enough not to impact the lives of the majority of Americans, the long drawn-out Vietnam conflict was of considerable concern to many people, even in historically patriotic Cow Neck. In March of 1966, the editor of *The Port Mail* wrote: "The military draft hangs like a dark cloud over the heads of legions of young men these days. Large numbers of them who, only a very short time ago, seemed safely ensconced in deferred classifications, now are receiving their 'Greetings,' or soon will. The quotas rise steadily and sharply and this, it is expected, is only the beginning."

"The cause, of course, is the war in Vietnam, with its enormous drain on available military manpower. And no one can now say with certainty just how great the Vietnam demands will ultimately become."

Relatively few of America's young men actually went to war, but many of those who did were killed or wounded. At home there were massive student protests and suspicions that the government wasn't telling the truth. Regardless of their politics, most of the population was very involved with the conflict in Asia because of the unprecedented television coverage. The long, drawn-out no-win war with its mounting casualties made President Lyndon Johnson so unpopular that he declined to run for a second term in 1968. It was up to his successor, Richard M. Nixon, to bring the war to its somewhat ignominious conclusion—something that didn't help Nixon's popularity rating because Americans were accustomed to winning wars.

Bobby Salomon's sixth grade birthday party in 1957 was celebrated on the shores of Hempstead Harbor with his entire class in attendance. The teacher standing in the back row is Lee Aschenbrenner, who went on to become the principal of the Manorhaven School. (Courtesy, Marilyn and Henry Salomon)

HOMETOWN POPULATION EXPLOSION

As the '60s came to a close, pressure on the school district from a rising population once more threatened the waning, but still treasured, rural serenity of Sands Point. The Port Washington school system was running out of classrooms and longing glances were cast towards empty spaces in Sands Point. Though the school district had not been able to obtain the 50 acres it wanted from the split of the former Naval Special Devices Center property—only a four-acre piece—it received a gift of 17 acres on Middle Neck Road from Harry Guggenheim and the Guggenheim Foundation in 1969, on which a school has yet to be built.

There was no question in the minds of most taxpayers that new schools were needed. You only had to look at simple population statistics to learn the answer to the question, "Where were all the children coming from?" In 1950, the population of the Village of Sands Point was 860. Ten years later it was 2,161; and a decade later, more people moved in or were born, increasing the total population to the peak of 2,916 in 1970. In the Town of North Hempstead, the population grew from 142,613 to 235,007. In Nassau County there were 1,321,582 people, and at rush hour many of them filled the cars crowding the highways. The prewar county of small villages, commuter enclaves, country estates and genuine working farms had become what Nassau County Historian Ed Smits called "Suburbia, U.S.A."

CHAPTER 13

1970-1990
IS BIGGER BETTER?
REAL ESTATE BOOM IMPACTS VILLAGE

As the population of Sands Point grew (an increase of 2,000 in 20 years), running the village and its institutions became more complex. The Village had to provide more services and hire additional personnel to serve the 2,916 residents in 1970. The composition of the population created another challenge; the influx of young professional families brought in more people who wished to have a say in who ran the Village and how they did it. The traditional, comfortable system of letting a willing few do the job undisturbed was soon put to the test.

BRIDGE SCARE THE IMPETUS FOR A CIVIC ASSOCIATION

The Sands Point Civic Association (SPCA), which replaced the near-dormant Sands Point Association, became a potent force for change in the Village. While civic associations generally prosper primarily in communities with weak or inaccessible governments, in Sands Point, where residents have direct access to generally responsive officials, the Sands Point Civic Association has thrived for nearly 30 years.

The present Civic Association came into existence because a group of people were unhappy with the way the Village was run. On the night of June 20, 1971, close to 300 Sands Point residents crowded into the Sousa School cafeteria to attend a meeting to consider forming a new association. News of the meeting had been publicized in a mailing signed by 15 residents. Among the signers of the letter were Charles Shapiro, James Lundquist, Norman Blankman, Michael Salomone, Aaron Scharf and Earl Kirmser. The letter writers were upset about a number of issues, including the possibility that Sands Point might disband its police force and turn to Nassau County for protection.

Visitors have a view of live horses when the Nassau County Police sends its mounts to the former Guggenheim pastures at the Sands Point Preserve for a bit of R & R. (Photo by Will Wright)

Furthermore, the signers objected to a recent tax increase. They were worried about the park that was to be created by Nassau County from the former Navy Special Devices Center. And they objected to the way candidates for office were selected.

However, what scared Sand Pointers most was a recommendation by the Regional Planning Association to build a new bridge from Sands Point to New Rochelle, across Long Island Sound. The projected daily traffic flow over the proposed 3.3 mile long bridge was 85,200 vehicles—enough to cause anxiety attacks up and down the length of Cow Neck!

The tone of the letter, which *Port Washington News* Editor Amy Pett said, "implied that the village might be going to hell in a hand basket," did the trick and motivated people to attend the meeting. It also got some of them mad. Thomas Pepitone of the Harbor Acres Property Owners Association wrote, "At this time the writer does not know if the Sands Point Civic Association 'in formation' is a true civic association or a political entity in the guise of civic association."

Bruce Shroyer, Sands Point Civic Association president at the time, and his wife Pat, organized the Association's first annual community-wide fall party in 1979. (Courtesy, Pat Shroyer)

POLITICAL UNREST AT THE LOCAL LEVEL

Whether or not the people who started the new civic association also wanted to start a new political party is debatable, but some of them undoubtedly supported the formation of the Beacon Party. The Beacon Party put up a slate in the June, 1971, election for Village offices to run against the incumbents, who were members of the Citizens' Party.

The election challenge of 1971 saw a contest between sitting Mayor Roy C. Olson of Sands Light Road, the retired vice president of Otis Elevator Co., and John Bauer, 120 Sands Point Road, an attorney with a New York firm. Olson had served as a village trustee from 1956-61, mayor from 1961-65 and trustee from 1969 to January, 1981, when he was appointed mayor after Jerome Weinstein stepped down from the position to serve as a North Hempstead Town Councilman. Bauer was no stranger to mayoralty. Before moving to Sands Point, he was a trustee and later mayor of Port Washington North. In running for the Sands Point position, he proposed "a program of increased public information to involve more residents in activities and major decisions of local government." The only person with a demonstrated Civic Association connection running for office at that time was Aaron Scharf of Sea Coat Lane.

The voters who turned out in unusually large numbers (774 votes at the polls plus 10 absentee ballots) apparently thought they'd been receiving all the information they needed and that the "old guard" was doing a good job of running the Village. Olson

received 562 votes and Bauer 220. Other challengers were defeated by similar margins, though they may have found it ironic when Olson stated, "We believe in an active Sands Point Association and shall help in reorganizing it."

The next election challenge came in June, 1977, when incumbent Village board members once again faced an opposition slate. The Homeowners Party sought the seats of incumbent Trustees Edward Madison, Eugene Luntey and Richard Dirkes, and both the challenged and the challengers ran vigorous campaigns, exchanging insults and writing letters to the editor. The challengers were Dr. Jules Lane, owner of the American Medical Insurance Company, Betty Lou Kelliher, a Sands Point Civic Association trustee, and Anthony Bottitta. Those who supported the status quo pointed out that challenger Lane supplied the Police Department with dental insurance and therefore had a possible conflict of interest. They claimed that Bottitta had a conflict as well; he was in the process of suing the village in a case involving an automobile accident suffered by his wife. Village mailboxes were stuffed with campaign literature and village cocktail parties were livelier than usual. The result was another large voter turnout that kept the incumbents in office. Mayor Olson received 671 voters; other results were Dirkes - 650, Luntey - 648, Madison - 615, Kelliher - 200, Lane - 186 and Bottitta - 153.

ACHIEVEMENTS OF THE CIVIC ASSOCIATION

The Civic Association's first president was attorney Clarence Fried, followed by Earl Kirmser, then Bruce Shroyer. Under Shroyer's leadership, the association built its membership, enlarged its newsletter, inaugurated an annual community-wide fall party and, in 1979, published an illustrated and enthusiastically-received brochure about the history and government of Sands Point. Shroyer, a graduate of the United States Military Academy, and his wife Pat, who grew up in Port Washington, moved to Sands Point in 1970. He later served on the Board of Zoning and Appeals before moving to Manhasset in the '90s. Subsequent SPCA presidents were Alan Ades, Eleanor Kurz, Edward Adler, Richard Sirow, Mark Silbert, Alyson Adler Green and Phillip Wachtler.

Sands Point Civic Association President Ellie Kurz and her husband Martin welcomed guests to an SPCA brunch at the IBM Country Club in October, 1982. It may have been a harbinger of the many parties that followed, when the property became The Village Club in 1994. (Courtesy, Eleanor Kurz)

Mayor Roy Olson presents Police Chief John Bailey with the keys to the shiny new patrol cars parked in front on Village Hall in the winter of 1971. The young officer behind the mayor is present chief John Montalto, who joined the Sands Point Force in 1969. (Mason Studio Photo. Courtesy, Sands Point Police Department)

The Civic Association's annual party in 1980 drew close to 500 members and guests to the spacious rooms of Hempstead House. The total cost of the party was defrayed in part by the one-time sale of etchings of the Sands Point Light, commissioned by the Association. Daniel Scheyer, editor of the bimonthly *Civic Report,* wrote, "It was for many the first chance to meet the people behind the names on the mail boxes, and provided a communal opportunity to exchange the proverbial cup of sugar without intruding behind a neighbor's hedges."

By 1981, more than half the families of the Village had joined the SPCA. For a payment of $7.50 in family dues, members received a VSP bumper sticker, an invitation to the annual party and a subscription to the *Sands Point Civic Report.* (The Sands Point Association, founded sometime prior to 1958, offered membership to one member of each property owning family and required sponsorship by a current member. The by-laws provided that "no person shall be elected to membership if five or more trustees disapprove his election." The new Civic Association was open to all members. The only requirement for membership, the payment of its modest dues.)

The Civic Association has always considered communication its primary mission and worked to keep village residents apprised about the activities of their Village government. To that end, SPCA representatives regularly attend Village board meetings

and meet with officials. Newsletters carry information about Village board activities and police news as well as historical vignettes. Said Shroyer in 1999, "Growth of the Civic Association reflects the growth pattern of the Village. The Civic Association opened the door of the Village Government. The Board gradually saw the Association as constructive and Mayor Roy Olson and Deputy Mayor Gene Luntey enthusiastically supported it."

ABOLISH THE POLICE DEPARTMENT?

By 1975, the Village police force numbered 19. Paying for salaries and equipment took a major portion of the Village funds, and the Police Department felt that its members were entitled to salaries and benefits comparable to those of the Nassau County Police Department. In February they presented a list of 64 demands—with salary increases, cost of living increases, death benefits, additional pay for working on holidays—as the basis for their negotiations of a new contract, which would begin that June. When the Village released their demands to the local press, the Sands Point PBA (Police Benevolent Association) responded by calling publication an "unfair labor practice."

After Village Mayor Roy Olson and Trustees Stanley Hyde, Harry Thornbury, Jr., Sydney Tessler and Charles Powers searched for ways to contain costs, they concluded that the best course might be to

Mayor Edward Madison (left) and challenger Adam Hanft (right).

September, Sands Point voted on the proposal; the tally was 444 against disbanding and 333 in favor. Mayor Olson estimated that Sands Point's tax rate of $4.10 per $100 assessed valuation would increase by a minimum of 70¢ when the new police contract was signed. It turned out that fears they would need to vastly increase the force were unfounded. There were only two more police officers in the department in 1999 than in 1975.

dissolve the SPPD and turn to Nassau County for protection. The Board expected that residents would save up to $100,000 in police costs the first year. The PBA stuck by its police-issue guns. Negotiations came to a halt and the irate Village Board voted in July to disband its local police department. The Board hoped to reassure residents by arranging for all Village policemen to be offered jobs on the Nassau County police force.

The police officers themselves seemed satisfied with the plans, and PBA president Patrolman John Melillo said, "after all, all we're fighting for is parity with the Nassau Police." He added, however, that "it is the Sands Point residents who are losing because they will be losing the personalized service that the Sands Point Police Department provides."

Most of Sands Point seemed to agree with Melillo. Peppered with arguments and questions from homeowners, the Village Board held a public hearing in August at the United Methodist Church Fellowship Hall, a space considerably larger than the Village Hall. At least 300 residents turned out. The Board struggled mightily to convince the raucous crowd that giving the Sands Point Police Department the time off and benefits it sought would require an increase in the size of the force and, a resulting rise in the size of the budget.

The prevailing sentiment among the residents seemed to be "costs be damned, let's keep our own force." The activists went to work collecting signatures on a petition for a referendum to put the abolishment of the police department to a vote. They needed the signatures of 270 residents to force the referendum—and got them. In fact, a total of 416 people signed. In

Sands Point Historic Landmarks Preservation Commission members Grace Frank (left) and Joan G. Kent attend a luncheon at George Washington Manor celebrating the 350th anniversary of the arrival of English settlers in Manhasset Bay (c. 1640). (Courtesy, Gordon Frank)

PRESERVING SANDS POINT HISTORY

An expanded population also brought a dire threat to some of Sands Point's most visible assets—its splendid collection of pre-Revolutionary houses and spectacular mansions from the estate era. Unfortunately, not everyone viewed an old white farmhouse on waterfront property as an historic treasure; some saw a desirable site with exciting knock-down possibility. By the 1980s, the demand for buildable land was so strong that many of these old homes were threatened and a few were destroyed. An 18th century Mott house was demolished while another was altered beyond recognition. Mansions from 1910 were torn down to make way for new homes. Extensions and alterations changed the appearance of classic structures.

Members of the Cow Neck Historical Society had already succeeded in persuading the Town of North Hempstead to adopt a historic landmarks preservation ordinance in 1983. Encouraged by the Town's action,

The Sands-Nostrand House, then owned by John Fernbach, on Sands Point Road as it looked in 1986 when it became the first house designated a landmark by the Village after establishment of the Sands Point Historic Landmarks Preservation Commission. (The air conditioning units weren't "historic," but as they did not permanently alter the facade, were accepted.)
(Photo by Harvey Weber. Courtesy, Inc. Village of Sands Point.)

Mayor Leonard Wurzel presented homeowner Ann Mai with a bronze plaque designating her house a Sands Point historic landmark. The marker reads, "Cornwall House, circa 1676, main section rebuilt 1840, Historic Landmark, designated August, 1988, Village of Sands Point." (Inc. Village of Sands Point)

Sands Point residents Joan Kent and Grace Frank approached the Village Board. The Board recognized the mounting threats to Sands Point's historic sites and was sympathetic. In 1985, the Board passed a preservation ordinance patterned after a model law drawn up by the New York State Department of Historic Preservation. The law is designed to protect designated structures and sites from unseemly alteration and arbitrary demolition. A landmark designation is made by the Village Board on the recommendation of the Landmarks Commission.

Mayor Edward Madison announced the appointment of five Landmarks Commission members in May of 1986: Edward (Ted) N. Lapham, Jr., trustee of the Cow Neck Historical Society and trustee emeritus of Friends Academy; Alvina Wiles, retiring village historian and former president of the Sands Point Garden Club; Henry Salomon, a past president of the Port Washington Public Library; Mrs. Kent, a marketing consultant and president of the Port Washington Public Library at the time; and Bernard Rumphorst, president of a firm that specialized in interior architecture. Mrs. Kent was named chairman of the Commission. The Commission's life began productively when John Fernbach applied for Village landmark status for his home, the old Sands house at 195 Sands Point Road. It was the first of a number of historic buildings in Sands Point that were subsequently protected.

A reprint of the sheet music for "Sands Point is Nearer to Heaven" was distributed as a 75th Anniversary souvenir. The song was written around 1939 by resident Jack Miller, who was an arranger for Kate Smith, then America's leading radio and recording singing star. The song was introduced at a Bath Club Saturday Night party and became a "hit" with the Club members. It was used as background music for the 75th Anniversary multi-image production, Echoes on the Sound.

CELEBRATING AN ANNIVERSARY

Ed Madison, mayor during most of the 1980s, liked to point out that Village government was "a government of volunteers." He was a dedicated volunteer himself, and also had a talent for recruiting other volunteers. At his suggestion, plans for the 1985 celebration of the 75th Anniversary of the Incorporation of the Village got under way in 1983. Madison appointed an Anniversary Steering Committee consisting of Alvina Wiles and Thomas Flynn, co-chairmen; Bruce Shroyer, treasurer; Robert Forman, Village attorney; Eleanor H. Kurz, president of the Sands Point Civic Association; and the mayor himself.

Some of the proposals from this group required both hard work and attention to detail. Nevertheless,

The schedule of events for Sands Point's 75th Anniversary Celebration

This arresting shot of the Sands Point Lighthouse taken by Newsday photo editor Harvey Weber was used on the cover for the brochure describing the Anniversary Committee's multimedia presentation, Echoes on the Sound. (Courtesy, Inc. Village of Sands Point)

quite a few willing volunteers stepped forward to make possible a series of events designed to showcase Village history and some of the cultural aspects of the complex and varied community. The projects planned were a residents' art exhibition, a historic photo exhibit, a book of newspaper clippings, a house tour, and a multimedia production, plus opening and closing receptions.

The celebration was designed for residents only, but news of the colorful events quickly circulated beyond the Village borders. Village historians and students from outside Sands Point asked their friends to invite them along on the house tour, where history came alive at the Sands-Nostrand House (John Fernbach), the Tristram Dodge House (Hedley and Dorothy Donovan), the Cornwall House (Ann and Vincent Mai), and Howard Bayard Swope's former home, Lands End (Virginia Kraft Payson).

The anniversary's multimedia presentation was an audio/slide show on several projectors produced by George Pickow Associates of Port Washington, and written and narrated by folk singer Oscar Brand of Great Neck. One of the tunes used for the background music was "Sands Point is Nearer to Heaven," the song Jack Miller composed around the '40s that was played at many Bath Club parties. The anniversary

committee issued replica sheet music for the song, based on an original in the collection of Ellie Kurz, and distributed the sheets as souvenirs. Villagers at the celebration's opening reception, and later at the Port Washington Public Library, were totally enthralled by the multimedia presentation. Scrapbooks were also produced, as planned, and displayed at the opening and closing receptions. They contain microfilm printouts of the *Port Washington News* stories about Sands Point and its residents from 1903-1985. The scrapbooks are now in the collection of the Library, where they are readily accessible to the public.

THE HELEN KELLER CENTER IS ESTABLISHED

The Industrial Home for the Blind (IHB) received 25 acres of the former Navy Special Devices Center property in 1971. That land, plus $7.5 million in government grants, gave it the resources needed to build the Helen Keller National Center for Deaf-Blind Youths and Adults on property which fronts on Middle Neck Road opposite the Sands Point Golf Club. Construction took place from 1974 to 1976, and Governor Hugh Carey attended the opening. There was space for up to 50 clients with a staff of about 80.

The basic mission of the Helen Keller Center, according to longtime IHB board member Beverly Luntey, is to train deaf-blind people to function on their own in the outside world. Clients usually live and train there for six to twelve months, learning essential skills for daily living such as how to keep house and

financial panic that could have ensued was, fortunately, averted, though many a Long Islander rued his or her belief in grandpa's infallibility.

War was endemic; although Ford's successor Jimmy Carter (1976-80) made valiant efforts at peacekeeping, crisis after crisis in the Middle East made hostilities almost routine news. Americans continued to support Israel and many raised funds for educational and social purposes in the young nation.

The successful conclusion of the war in the Falkland Islands in 1982 showed that Britain was still capable of swift and decisive action. Democracy appeared to be winning the ideological war with communism, indicated by mass demonstrations in China (1989), the reunification of Germany (1990) and the increasing unrest in the Soviet Union.

The 1980s was the era of the Yuppies, as the business-oriented administration of President Reagan (1980-88) brought a healthy national economy and an increase in the number of people who could be accurately called Young Upwardly-mobile Professionals. Yuppies saw Long Island as an excellent place to live and show off their success. They found Sands Point attractive for their primary homes, just as New Yorkers of past years had found it attractive for their country homes. And their children loved President George Bush (1988-1992), who threw political correctness to the winds and candidly told the electorate that he hated broccoli.

REAL ESTATE BOOM

The Yuppies were partly responsible for creating a real estate boom. They and other people who moved into the Village of Sands Point in the '70s, '80s and '90s produced a larger population and built many more

Relatives from all over the United States gathered in the summer of 1985 to celebrate the 50th wedding anniversary of Mr. and Mrs. Clifford Marbut of Harbor Acres. Shown with their cousins at the Harbor Acres Beach Club, where a party took place, are the Marbut's grandchildren Frank Ullman (striped shirt), and on the far right, Valerie Ullman (Taylor), Susan Ullman, and Laura Ullman (Schwartz), children of Kay and Leo Ullman of Sea Coast Lane. (Courtesy, Katharine Ullman)

houses, albeit on less than estate-size properties. Still, Sands Point remained highly attractive for many reasons: proximity to Long Island Sound, tree-lined streets in a sought-after community, ready access to an excellent school and library system, and plenty of recreational facilities, including four yacht clubs, three golf clubs plus a fast commute to NYC.

The demand for Sands Point property was so robust beginning in the middle 1980s that homeowners who had bought an ordinary ranch house in Sands Point 30 years before, generally paying between $35,000 and $45,000, could now sell at prices as high as $650,000 to $700,000.

At the end of 1980 it could still be said that Sands Point was one of the most desirable places to live on the North Shore, and the Villagers were making a strong effort to keep it that way.

Infrared aerial photo of Sands Point and Port Washington c. 1994. Namesake Point is at top left, Hempstead Harbor at right. (U.S. Geological Survey)

CHAPTER 14

1990-2000
SANDS POINT TODAY
LIFESTYLES CHANGE;
THE VILLAGE CLUB OPENS

 rior to 1900, the homeowners and farmers of Sands Point were primarily of Northern European descent, mostly English and Dutch. Between 1900 and the first World War, however, some very wealthy industrialists from other regions and backgrounds established country homes in Sands Point. Among them were several Jewish families, including the Guggenheims and Fleischmans. While this immensely rich minority was influential, the old-line WASPS continued to dominate Village life. Servants were at the other end of the economic scale. At the turn of the century they were a diverse group of immigrants from Ireland, Wales, Scotland, Italy, Poland and Nova Scotia, plus a few members of Port Washington's long-established black community.

The post-World War II building boom of 1950-70 brought about a population explosion. Suddenly, the Village was no longer a "second-home" community. Sands Point had become an upper income suburb of year-round residents. Many of the old WASP families prominent in the 19th century remained, but lost their dominant position as a significant number of Jewish, Irish, Italian and German-American city dwellers moved out to the suburbs. The mix became more diverse during the '70s and '80s when newcomers from Asia and the Middle East, as well as black professionals, became Sands Point homeowners.

A GENERATIONAL SHIFT

In the last decade of the 20th century there seemed to be more young families moving into the Village than ever before. Trustee and Village Building Commissioner Edward A. K. Adler recalled his impression of the neighborhood when he and his wife arrived in 1976: "Karen could walk a mile pushing a stroller and never see another mother. Now you see play sets in front yards."

Substantial wrought iron gates operate electronically and serve as the main exit from The Village Club of Sands Point. The 200-plus-acre property was formerly owned by Solomon Guggenheim, followed by IBM. The Village purchased the IBM Country Club in 1994. (Photo by Joan G. Kent)

What brought all these young children to Sands Point? More couples had more income at an earlier age...more parents had more money and were helping their young married children buy homes...the excellent Port Washington school system attracted parents with school age children...and the older population was decreasing, the result of large-scale moves to other areas along with death in the WWII generation.

A real estate market favorable to buyers also facilitated home sales in Sands Point to the younger

During the latter years of the 20th century, the juvenile population in Sands Point jumped as more young families moved into the Village. Here, mother and daughter share a summer event at The Village Club in 1998. (Courtesy, The Village Club of Sands Point)

generation. "House prices took quite a dip in the early '90s and recovered later than some areas, particularly New York City," Adler explained. "So, for a number of years—until about 1997 or 1998—homes in Sands Point were a relative bargain compared with, say, a co-op or condo in the city. This also gave a window of opportunity to many families already living in the Port area to move to Sands Point."

THE VILLAGE CLUB

Certainly some of the newcomers were drawn to the Village by the much-heralded purchase of the IBM Country Club. When IBM's 25-year scenic easement agreement with Nassau County ran out in 1994, the corporation was no longer prohibited from selling to developers. IBM decided it was time to sell its 208-acre property in Sands Point as part of a cost reduction program. Mayor Leonard Wurzel believes that the opening of The Village Club in 1995 produced further diversity in the population. The prospect of an active club life with golf, tennis and swimming practically in the residents' front yards appealed to home seekers from many backgrounds.

On a clear day you can see almost forever! One of the many pleasures of The Village Club is the far-reaching view of New York City to the west. Those dim shapes on the horizon are the towers of Manhattan. (Courtesy, The Village Club of Sands Point)

When the IBM Country Club first came on the market, both Village trustees and residents were apprehensive about the future of this highly desirable property—how would it be used, and by whom? If it were to become a school or religious institution, or purchased by some other non-profit organization, the Village would lose $106,000 in taxes. If the land were to be sold for private development, there might be as many as 80 houses built on the property, which was zoned for two acres. This would add 100 or more children to the school system, 200 or more cars to the daily traffic stream, and diminish the water resources. The other side of the coin was that development would produce a welcome increase in the Village tax base.

Laura Sibigtroth (right) and a friend enjoy lunch at The Village Club pool. (Courtesy, The Village Club of Sands Point)

Mulling over the pros and cons, Mayor Wurzel, assisted by Robert Berens, came to the conclusion that a park or club for Village residents would be the best use of the property. It already had a nine-hole golf course, tennis courts, beach, and a well-cared for mansion. He viewed it as a wonderful amenity for the Village: a place for community interaction and a way to preserve open spaces in a Village that really wanted to retain some vestiges of its rustic origins. He had little difficulty obtaining agreement from fellow Board members William Perdue, Daniel Scheyer, Eugene Luntey and Adler. (Because he was moving away from the Village, Arthur Turner Soule resigned his trusteeship in April, 1994, and Daniel Scheyer was appointed in his place.) Then came the task of selling the country club to the residents and agreeing on the purchase price with IBM.

APPROVAL BY A WHOPPING MAJORITY

Before diving into the project, Mayor Wurzel called a Village meeting to hear what residents thought of the idea. On May 12, 1994, a record crowd of 700 people packed the Community Synagogue to learn about the proposal. There were plenty of questions, of course, but it soon became evident that a clear majority of

The Village Board convinced residents of the many benefits they would enjoy from the acquisition of the IBM Country Club. Board members who negotiated the favorable deal with the corporation were: (standing) Edward A. K. Adler, William Perdue, Daniel Scheyer; (seated) Mayor Leonard Wurzel and Deputy Mayor Eugene Luntey. (Courtesy, Inc. Village of Sands Point)

An interesting feature of the The Village Club's mansion is that it has no "bad side" from an architectural viewpoint. All four sides of the Mediterranean-style building are equally attractive. This photo shows the west side of the building in 1999. (Photo by Joan G. Kent)

those present favored the idea. The meeting lasted over three hours and over 35 spoke. Two Sands Pointers who disagreed, Patrick J. and Suzanne Matthews Foye, wrote to the *Port Washington News* that while they felt the Village was well run, "We strongly feel the village should forego this opportunity to buy the club and allow a private investor to assume the risk that the market will support another north shore golf course." At the time of this writing, Foye says, "We're members of the club. I was totally wrong about that and I'll even eat crow."

On June 6, more people came out to vote on the IBM property bond referendum than had ever gone to the polls in Sands Point. Of the 1,859 registered voters in the Village, a record 63% cast ballots, voting 1,006 to 166 in favor of the purchase—a whopping 86%. The vote authorized the sale of $15 million in bonds.

The time had come to negotiate the deal. According to the *Port Washington News*, IBM attorneys stated that they had early offers of between $18 and $20 million from developers, but would sell the property to Sands Point for $17 million. The Village Board raised the zoning on the property from two acres to five acres. According to Adler, "We had to change zoning. It was a very complex situation."

Although the negotiations were difficult, it was well worth the time and effort spent. The contract, signed on Tuesday, October 25, 1994, formalized a

price of $12.7 million. Despite some strong-minded dissenters, most Village residents were pleased with the purchase and their Port Washington neighbors were, too. The closing transaction took place at the club "mansion" on November 30, 1994. In an editorial headed "The Wizardry of Wurzel," the editor of the *Port Washington News* wrote: "His administration has left a legacy that benefits not only his village residents, but all of Port Washington." To celebrate the Club's opening, a tented affair described by Wurzel as "the gigantic, fantastic party at the new Village Club of Sands Point" was held on May 13, 1995. The gala evening, originally planned for 200 guests, attracted a spirited group of 750. A high point for the Mayor undoubtedly was the unveiling of a plaque at the Club's beach, naming the spot "Wurzel Cove."

PLANNING AND DEVELOPMENT

Looking back, Dick Bernhard, chairman of the Club Development Committee, explained in a 1999 interview that "the golf course was not in great condition" when the Village took it over; it was "pleasant but not challenging." Furthermore, the course did not compare well with other clubs in the area, such as the private Sands Point Golf Club or North Hempstead Country Club. The Village Board appointed a Residents' Club Commission to develop a master plan for future development. Robert Berens, who had been active in the Hoffstots Lane Civic Association, was named chairman of the Commission; Robert Bernhard served as co-chairman during the first year. They quickly established sub-committees to make recommendations and plan programs: Mansion, Land Use, Golf, Tennis, Beach, Youth Activities, and Social and Community Affairs, among others. The intial Commission members were: Thomas Flynn, Lynn Najman, Don Stein, Richard Bernhard, and Fred Jaroslow.

Dick Bernhard, Chairman of The Village Club Development Committee, might have been explaining nuances of the master plan to Village Trustee Dan Scheyer at the 1999 Village Club Holiday Party. (Courtesy, The Village Club of Sands Point)

Sandra Cardiello, a member of The Village Club's Land Use Committee, subsequently became deputy chairperson of the Residents' Club Commission. (Courtesy, The Village Club of Sands Point)

The response to this call for help produced a gratifying response from 160 residents who agreed to serve on the 12 proposed committees. The Golf Committee was the most popular choice (30) and Food Service (4) the least. Finding itself in the enviable position of having too many volunteers for some committees, the Residents' Club Commission decided that Committee members would be appointed for three-year terms, with rotation of membership to give everyone who volunteered a chance to serve.

THE MASTER PLAN MEETS OPPOSITION

On two evenings in August of 1995, the Committees presented their findings at public meetings. A headline in the *Port Washington News* proclaimed there was

One of the nine holes added to The Village Club course in 1999 is this waterfront hole on Hempstead Harbor. (Courtesy, The Village Club of Sands Point)

"Trouble and Discord in Paradise." Commissioner Berens related, "The golfers were upset with the Land Use Committee recommendations on Tuesday night and the Land Use people were upset on Wednesday Night." The latter were unhappy that the golf plans included clearing a wooded area, which threatened some favorite views and the established landscapes. Golf-playing residents who had been content with just nine holes were concerned that expansion of the course to 18 holes would bring an increase in annual family membership fees from about $4,000 to $7,500.

The frustrated Land Use Committee, which was afraid its hard work and recommendations would be cast aside, sent a letter to all Sands Point residents urging them to support slower development and environmental preservation. Its chairperson, Eleanor Kurz, stated, "The Land Use Committee stands for the rights and needs of all the residents and balanced allocation of Club land assets."

Bernhard, who was responsible for the plan's implementation, explained that the proposal had evolved from public meetings, focus groups, and various interest groups encompassing many facets, from golfers, tennis players and pool swimmers, to proponents of quiet recreation and "tree huggers." "We threw all that in the pot," he added, "and hired Richard Webel, a prominent land planner, to draw up a master plan based on the information we had gathered. Tom Doak, a nationally-known golf course architect, drew up dozens of routing plans. Another dozen variations on the master plan have been done since we started in 1995. We have a golf plan in place but the master plan is still a work in progress."

The organizers of the Village Independent Party, which ran two candidates for open seats in the 1996 Village Board election, included Willard and Roberta Block and Myra and Gene Gamell. The couples are shown here on a New Hampshire vacation trip. (Courtesy, Myra Gamell)

CONTESTED ELECTION

Agreeing with the Land Use Committee, some residents gathered signatures for a petition asking to save the allée, to allot more time for planning, and to have financing in place before undertaking any development. They collected 550 signatures and presented the petitions to the Village Board. But Myra Gamell of Barkers Point Road felt that it didn't seem "to make much difference" in the Board's attitude, and she asked the trustees, "Doesn't 550 signatures mean anything?"

The dissenters formalized their protest by organizing the Village Independent Party (VIP) and registering it with the Village on New York State Board of Election forms. The party leaders included Gamell and her husband Gene, Willard and Roberta Block, Ken Gorman and Judith Clark. The group sought representation on the Village Board to ensure that the former IBM property would be treated as a neighborhood park rather than be developed into an 18-hole golf course and that environmental concerns be further addressed. The VIP raised "quite a bit of money from about 300 contributors," Gamell related, and the party endorsed Clark, of Harbor Acres, and Daniel Scheyer for the two Village Trustee openings in June of 1996. The Citizens Party (the incumbents) nominated Ed Adler and Scheyer,

unaware that Scheyer was considering the VIP endorsement (which he later accepted). Both sides ran vigorous campaigns; harsh (and sometimes inaccurate) accusations were exchanged in campaign literature and letters to the editors of the local papers.

The Village Independent Party did not win the election, but it did motivate many residents to cast their ballots. There was a grand total of 1,139 voters—close to the number that had voted on the bond referendum in 1994. Village Justice Edward V. Alfieri, Jr., who was running unopposed, was re-elected with 725 votes. For the two trustee spots, Adler received 774 votes; Scheyer, 553; and Clark, 385.

Looking back on that period, Myra says, "I really feel we accomplished something—saved the allée and managed to stall the golf course development four or five years so that more thought was given to planning." Though the Village Independent Party has been dormant for several years, it maintains its registration and bank account in case "a burning issue comes along."

ONGOING OPPOSITION TO THE MASTER PLAN

Defeat at the polls did not squelch the opposition, which continued to fight to obtain what it wanted. During the election campaign, a Committee for Fiscal Responsibility was organized by Norman Blankman, a substantial property owner who was concerned about financial aspects of The Village Club. Blankman publicly endorsed the VIP slate—a move, Gamell believes, that cost the VIP candidates votes. "Rightly, or wrongly, Blankman was seen by some as a bogey

The lovely tree-lined allée can be seen from The Village Club terrace, looking to the west. It served as the entrance drive for the original house on the property. (Photo by Will Wright)

man," she observed. In a letter to the editors of the local papers dated October 31, 1996, Blankman stated: "The fact is that no one knows how much has been spent and how club deficits have been met...." The mayor's response was, "there is no decifit." The Committee claimed some victories; the *Sands Point Monitor*, a publication first issued in November of 1996, reported that its supporters had blocked the use of the allée as an entrance road to the club mansion.

SUING THE VILLAGE

A lawsuit was brought against the Village in December, 1997, by Evelyn Blankman (Mrs. Norman Blankman), owner of a home on over ten Sands Point waterfront acres, and Elaine Langone, wife of investor Kenneth Langone and a substantial property owner as well. (Kenneth Langone, co-founder of Home Depot, was recently added to the Forbes 400 list of billionaires.) They charged that the Village had spent more than the $15 million authorized by the bond issue for the purchase and improvement of the IBM property. (This was not the first suit the two families had brought against the Village; earlier, they had unsuccessfully sued the Village to prevent sale of the land donated to the Village by Averill Harriman.)

Blankman and Langone, as members of the Sands Point Committee for Fiscal Responsibility, sent letters to Sands Point homeowners asking each family to contribute $100 towards the fight to prevent the Village from making further expenditures. They felt that the Club should solve its financial problems itself. Blankman wrote, "I and others like me are paying taxes so that people in Port Washington and other places can be members of a world-class golf club."

Poolside socializing has brought Sands Point residents new friends of all ages. (Courtesy, The Village Club of Sands Point)

The Village Club pool and pool house overlooking Hempstead Harbor opened on July 4, 1996. (The slide at left front was a temporary attraction.) (Courtesy, Village Club of Sands Point)

Mayor Wurzel pointed out that only $13.5 million had been spent to date and declared: "We maintain that this suit is completely without merit." The New York State Supreme Court agreed and on January 15, 1999, granted the Village's motion for summary judgment with costs against the plaintiffs, dismissing the suit against the Village and the mayor and trustees individually. Four other lawsuits brought against the Village in this matter were also decided in its favor.

EXPANSION PLANS APPROVED

With a major victory behind them and a master plan more or less in place, the Village asked the voters in October, 1998, for approval to build the 18-hole course. The funding would come from the $4.1 million sale of Village property (nine shorefront acres donated without restriction to the Village in 1980 by Harriman) and $1.5 million from bonds authorized in 1994 but not yet sold. According to *The Village Club Voice*, no tax increase was required.

An opposition group calling itself The Sands Point Committee of Concerned Citizens (which included some members who had supported the Village Independent Party) sent out flyers voicing its objections and urging "no" votes. The anonymous writer explained, "Before any Village funds from taxes, asset sales or exorbitant club fees are spent, we must know not only the cost of club expansions, but the revenue expectations as well. We all need to know if we are building a course for an increasingly nonresident membership." The writer also questioned the benefits that would be derived from these improvements by the "more than three-quarters of the Village that are not golf members of the club." Despite active opposition, the 1998 referendum passed easily by a vote of 779 to 239.

SELF-SUPPORTING CLUB

As of January 2000, there are 14 tennis courts along with a standard competition size pool and a new, modern playground near the waterfront. A new one-and-a-half acre pond has been dug to hold 3.5 million gallons of water for the irrigation system; the golf course is doubling its holes to 18; and a new golf club house is in the planning stage. Membership is increasing.

All that development did not come about easily, and Village Trustee Ed Adler says, "The Village Club is a huge burden." The Board is responsible for the management and financial health of the Club (the Residents' Club Commission reports directly to the Village Board), and must also explain and justify its actions to the residents, most of whom have little expertise in country club management.

The Village trustees require that the Club operate self-sufficiently. "Village responsibilities have grown since we acquired the Club," says the Mayor. "This has become a real business operation. We have a $3.5 million Club budget." The April, 2000, Sands Point Budget Report stated: "The Club completed its fifth year in December, 1999. The budget prepared with Granite Golf Management Services shows an excess of receipts over expenditures for the fiscal year to May 31, 2001, in the same manner as will be achieved in the current year to May 31, 2000. The Club currently pays $106,000 to the General Fund in lieu of taxes

New York State Governor George Pataki (center) was the guest of honor at a reception hosted by Michael Siris of Manhasset at The Village Club on July 11, 1998. Mayor Wurzel is at left. (Courtesy, Village Club of Sands Point)

that IBM paid yearly and its water bill to the water fund in the current year was $70,000. The Club is self-supporting and operating expenses are not supported by taxes." In fact, when presented, the final May report showed the Club had made a net profit of $161,000. Part of the budget goes to pay the wages of 107 employees in the summer (33 full time, 74 part time) and 35 during the winter months (25 full time).

Non-resident member Fredric Kramer of Roslyn Estates, a longtime Port Washington resident with many Sands Point friends, has been a golf member at The Village Club for three years. Enthusiastic in his praise, he declared: "In my opinion the residents of Sands Point, and the trustees in particular, have created a wonderful asset for the community. Golf

The children's carnival in the summer of 1998 drew a big crowd of little people to The Village Club. (Courtesy, Village Club of Sands Point)

playing members and I truly appreciate being able to be part of this beautiful Club. I enjoy the wonderful dining facilities and the camaraderie of all my friends." Dick Bernhard agrees, saying: "Len Wurzel should get adequate recognition. The Village owes him a big hug for getting the balloon off the ground."

ATTRACTING OUTSIDERS

The principal way the Club can be self supporting is to permit nonresidents to join, and to charge them higher fees. Preference for outside members is given to parents and children of residents, former residents, and residents of Port Washington. From the very beginning, Mayor Wurzel strongly believed that The Village Club golf course could not operate in the black without nonresident members. The Village of Lake Success and the City of Glen Cove have nonresident members, he pointed out; the course in Lawrence has approximately 75% nonresidents.

Only about 35% of the homeowners in Sands Point play golf. If all of them joined the Club for golf, there still would not be enough members to support the Club at the relatively modest fees charged by The Village Club. It needs the transfusion of nonresident dollars to stay healthy. There were 340 golf memberships (family and individual) at The Village Club in 2000; of those, 36% were nonresident. Dues will go up for both residents and nonresidents when the 18-hole course opens, said Dick Bernhard; "It costs more money to maintain 18 holes." But Village Club dues should continue to be lower for residents than those at other Long Island clubs.

Barbara and Robert Barker and Audrey Scheyer were among many resident members who attended the annual Village Club Holiday Party in 1999. (Courtesy, The Village Club of Sands Point)

IT AIN'T JUST GOLF

The Village Club offers a great deal more than golf. The pool, constructed at the urging of the younger residents, has been a tremendous success. It was built in record time under the direction of resident Anthony Denisco and opened on July 4, 1996. It provides three things you don't have with a home pool—life guards, professional instruction and competitive swimming. It also brings people together. One pool member told the Mayor that she lived in Sands Point for six years without getting to know anyone. Now that she frequents the pool, she has made a number of friends. Bernhard agrees and observes: "Sands Point real estate prices have risen since advent of the Club. Many more young families are moving in because of the recreation facilities. The pool gives families a place to socialize."

Longtime residents Marcia and Jay Forman do not belong to the Club but believe it helps create a feeling of community. Marcia says that younger people, especially those with small children, appreciate the pool because it is a source of playmates (without the effort of bringing them to one's own home). Her daughter Karli Hagedorn and son-in-law Jim are members and their son Chris enjoys the golf course.

RESIDENTS HAVE THEIR SAY

The members want a voice in running the Club—and they have it through the Residents' Club Commission, which in 1999 consisted of Chairperson Fred Jaroslow, Deputy Chairperson Sandra Cardiello, Richard Bernhard, David Deutsch, Michael Elzay, Marie Jacaruso, Candi Rossetti, William Sherman and Harold Spielman. The Club employs a management company which, in turn, employs a general manager, golf professionals, tennis professionals, a food and beverage manager, chef and a pool and recreation manager. The general manager for four years, until his resignation, was Carlos Duarte, succeeded in 2000 by Ed Ronan. Volunteer Elaine Wurzel, wife of the mayor, presides over the First Lady's Gallery, a display space in the mansion devoted to interesting, unusual artifacts and antiques borrowed from residents.

Assisting The Village Club can be a very satisfying experience. Sandy Cardiello says that her stint on the Land Use Committee was a "very nice experience," where she met "really nice people such as Tom Flynn, Vincent West, George Frank and Fred Jaroslow."

Sands Point resident Cyrus McCalla, who lives on Forest Drive, had questions about the use of Thayer Lane as a Village Club exit. A public hearing for discussion was held in February, 2000 at the Community Synagogue. (Photo by Will Wright)

STILL STIRRING UP CONTROVERSY

The Village Club continues to evolve, and plans for the future continue to produce controversy. Three families who own properties on Astor Lane (sub-divided from the original Guggenheim property back in 1951), fearing they might have to play host to golfers in their front yards, sued the Village to challenge the proposed location of some of the new golf holes. The official Village newsletter, *The Sands Point Report*, stated in May, 1999, that "We feel that there is no basis for the challenge and that we will, again, prevail in the courts, albeit with more costs. Construction however, is proceeding." That case has been settled by compromise.

The major controversy at the end of the 20th century concerned proposals to use an existing gate on Astor Lane as a Club exit and Thayer Lane as both entrance and exit to Middle Neck Road to serve the expanded golf course. Infrequently used in recent years, Thayer Lane began life as an entrance drive to a large, shingled center hall colonial revival house built

Residents Annette Oestreich, of Astor Lane, and Dr. Barry Jason, of Forest Drive, listened attentively at a Village Board meeting. (Photo by Will Wright)

around 1906 on a bluff overlooking Hempstead Harbor as a country home for Francis K. Thayer.

Proponents for connecting the lane to the Club argued that an added entrance to and exit from the Club would improve traffic flow within Club grounds as well as on Middle Neck Road, the main public road. Vocal opponents Annette Oestreich, Barry Jason and Adam Hanft of Harbor Acres (a former candidate for mayor), and others felt that a change in the traffic pattern would cause more accidents. In May of 2000, after the required environmental review, the Village Board voted unanimously to amend the Master Plan and include the Astor Lane east gate as an exit and Thayer Lane as an entrance and exit to the club. (Oestreich and Jason ran unsuccessfully for the two vacant seats on the Village Board in June, 2000, failing to defeat incumbents Adler and Scheyer. Jerome Boros was elected Village Justice.)

The former Harriman property is now the site of new homes. One of the first dwellings, photographed here in 1998, reflects the traditional colonial style favored by many earlier Sands Point home builders. (Photo by Joan G. Kent)

TOO MANY MANSIONS?

There were other significant developments in Sands Point, in addition to the acquisition of The Village Club, during the last decade of the 20th century. Several mansions (using the American Heritage Dictionary definition of "mansion" as "a large stately house") made splashy returns to the local real estate scene. Although many mansions had been built from 1880 to 1930, and a number are still standing, most growth in Sands Point in the '50s, '60s and '70s came from relatively modest ranch houses that were affordable for upwardly mobile WWII veterans and their families.

One of the larger properties subdivided in the '90s was the 14-acre Backus Estate, once the home of James Lees Laidlaw, Sands Point's first mayor. Fortunately for history buffs, the original house, slightly enlarged, remains intact. This 1996 photo was taken after renovations were complete. (Photo by Joan G. Kent)

The landmark, "Pheasant Hill," constructed on Middle Neck Road c. 1873, was in a deteriorating state in 1992. Subsequently, it was demolished to make way for new house construction in the 1990s. (Photo by Katharine Ullman)

Then came the prosperous '80s and '90s when a booming economy made it possible for more people to own bigger homes at an earlier age. The development of the 86-acre Harriman tract began slowly in the early 1990s, but by 1999 most of the 35 buildable lots were approved, more than 18 homes completed, and nine more under construction. The remaining eight lots were sold, but applications to commence construction had not been submitted as of April 1, 2000. In addition, five large new homes have been built on the subdivided Backus estate. For the most part, the new houses on Sterling Lane and Ariel Court in the so-called Harriman Development follow traditional architectural styles, echoing Sands Point favorites of earlier eras. They range from 6,000 to 7,500 square feet and are worth well over $2 million, says Sands Point Village Clerk Linda Mitchell.

Developers sought permission to subdivide smaller properties and, once they received it, constructed two or three new houses where a single dwelling had previously stood. Numerous times, older houses— even those of landmark caliber—were demolished to make way for new. Since most Sands Point properties already had houses on them, many homes from earlier eras met their demise by bulldozer. The price premium on Sands Point land was so high that it was difficult for some longtime owners to resist the lure of the developers' cash, especially when they were considering retirement to warmer climates.

Frank and Suzanne Arnold purchased Pheasant Hill (c. 1873), a gambrel-roofed colonial revival house on Middle Neck Road once owned by Alvina Wiles and later by Jim and Eleanor Stulburger, and replaced it with new construction. However, unlike many who chose to replace the old with the new, the Arnolds took great care to ensure that their impressive new home complemented the tiled-roofed Mediterranean style of the adjacent Alker Mansion. The Langones' graceful Normandy-style country house (c. 1992), perched on a hilltop for views of Long Island Sound, replaced a smaller French farmhouse that had been on the site and was owned for many years by Mrs. Stella Ketchum.

An even more spectacular housing statement was made at the end of the 1990s when Eileen and Donald Vultaggio (chairman of Arizona Iced Tea), purchased the former property of S. Heagan Bayles, complete

Near the spot where the Belmont-Hearst towers once stood, this 21st century castle rises on the tip of Sands Point. The Sands Point Light is directly to the right. (Photo by Will Wright)

with the Sands Point Light. The lighthouse and the keeper's house are Village Landmarks and therefore protected against alteration. But the Bayles house, a 1930s colonial that was not designated, was replaced by a mansion that some say is a close reproduction of the old Belmont/Hearst Castle that stood nearby from 1916 to 1942. The Vultaggios included all of the requisite touches—stone construction, turrets, tall chimneys and balconies.

Harvey Levine, a longtime Sands Point resident as well as chairman of the Historic Landmarks Preservation Commission in 1999, is not pleased with what he sees in Sands Point today and regrets the fact that "very young, very wealthy people are buying lovely old houses and tearing them down to build new ones." Lifelong resident Jay Forman is equally distressed and says ruefully, "As old residents, we're not happy to see new ones," especially the builders of oversize houses, but "you can't do anything about it."

The building boom and desire for larger homes that brought about the destruction of numerous old houses was accompanied by another trend: putting up houses too large for their plots or neighborhood. Some very large homes went up on relatively small sites, dominating the streetscape or spoiling the neighbors' view. In cases where the new owner installed a

The property of Don and Eileen Vultaggio (front row, second and third from left) encompasses Sands Point's beloved lighthouse. The venerable structure was named an official Sands Point Landmark by the Village Board in 1992. Shown here: (front row) Grace Frank, Village historian; the Vultaggios; Mayor Leonard Wurzel with commemorative plaque; and Katharine Ullman, chairman of the Historic Landmarks Preservation Commission; (back row) Erdem Tuncsiper, Landmarks Commission; Edward A. K. Adler, William Perdue and Arthur T. Soule, Village trustees; Harvey Levine, Landmarks Commission. (Courtesy Katharine Ullman)

The Sands Point Golf Club is just that, a golf-only club. Its challenging course has been a favorite with serious golfers since the 1920s. (Photo by Joan G. Kent)

swimming pool and/or tennis court, the plot was nearly fully-covered with concrete and asphalt, thus hampering drainage and water recharge.

Something had to be done, and that something was to tighten building and zoning codes. Though its proposals were met with resistance on the part of developers and potential homeowners with big dreams, Sands Point amended its zoning codes in 1989 and 1994. The revised code set ratios of habitable floor area to lot size, limited the area coverage (including pools, tennis courts and accessory buildings) and established height-to-setback ratios (the higher the house, the further back from the road it must be).

CLUBS AND BEACH ASSOCIATIONS

The Village Club is not the only club in the village and the Sands Point Civic Association is not the only association. The private Sands Point Golf Club continues to attract a devoted coterie of serious golfers from Sands Point and neighboring communities. The Golf Club is currently in the midst of restoring the course, redesigned in 1963, to its original configuration. Dr. Edmund Goodman, a longtime member, said, "it is the first club I know of where the charter says it has to be non-sectarian." The Harbor Acres Property Owners Association and several beach associations continue to maintain their neighborhood groups.

On a more intimate scale, the Sands Point Garden Club celebrates its 50th anniversary in the year 2000. The Club continues to offer an opportunity to

Past Garden Club President Edie Katz, new member Kat Wasserman and incoming president, Ginny Hoynes, celebrate the Sands Point Garden Club's 50th Anniversary at a luncheon held at the Manhasset Bay Yacht Club in 2000. (Photo by Jackie Pierangelo, Port Washington News)

Groundbreaking ceremonies for the sensory garden at the Helen Keller Center, sponsored by the Sands Point Garden Club, took place in May of 1982. Pictured here are the late Mike Van Owen, a onetime client and then intern of the Center, with his guide dog Amos; and Garden Club members Virginia Klump, Terry Creem and Alvina Wiles, all former Club presidents. (Courtesy, Helen Keller Center for the Deaf-Blind)

sharpen gardening skills and show the members' expertise through flower shows and special projects. The membership, which is by invitation, usually runs to about 40 women. Says immediate past president Edie Katz, "I enjoy the intergenerational aspects of the club as older members share their knowledge with newcomers." According to longtime member Lorraine Sulkes, the Club was founded by a group of eight friends in 1950: Mrs. George (Mary) Schirer, who became the first president, Mrs. Henry A. (Charity) Alker, Mrs. Walter Hipp, Mrs. Louis Rabinowitz, Mrs. John P. (Marietta) Wilde, Mrs. Glen (Hazel) MacNary, Mrs. Chester H. Toomer and Jeannette Campbell.

Some present members are the children of earlier ones. Katherine Wasserman is the daughter of Van McDonald; Ann Louise Buerger is the daughter of Johanna Buerger, who started the wildflower garden at the Sands Point Preserve; incoming Garden Club president Ginny Hoynes is the daughter-in-law of the late Terry Creem, a club president in the early 70s.

Matthew Sven Katz, age 10, son of Garden Club then-President Edie Katz and Dr. Stanley Katz, was the official photographer at the Helen Keller Sensory Garden cocktail party in the summer of 1998. (Courtesy, Edie Katz)

One special project of the Club was the creation of a Sensory Garden at the Helen Keller National Center for the Deaf-Blind. When the $50,000 project was completed in 1983, the Helen Keller Center was extremely pleased with its new garden, which was filled with shrubs and plants chosen for their texture and fragrance. Guide rails and Braille identification plaques help clients make their way around the garden and enjoy its many pleasures. The Garden Club renovated the garden, which had proved quite popular with the Center's deaf-blind population, in the fall of 1999.

HARBOR ACRES ASSOCIATION… STILL GOING STRONG

One of the primary functions of the Harbor Acres Property Owners Association is to foster communication between residents and maintain Association-owned recreational areas. According to 1999-2000 President Judith Clark, about two-thirds of the families in Harbor Acres belong to the group (112 of 170). With annual dues of $350, its income is close to $40,000. Over half that amount, about $22,000, goes for payment of property taxes, for the tennis courts and beach house. The balance is spent on operating expenses and maintenance—although members do a lot of the work themselves. Judy's husband Bruce, for example, mans the roller to

Sands Point Civic Association President 1999-2000, Philip Wachtler (left), confers with board member Eric Brown prior to a meeting held at the Village Hall. (Photo by Will Wright)

smooth the venerable red clay tennis courts. Volunteers come out for the annual beach clean-up at the end of April.

While some Harbor Acre residents prefer to spend their recreational dollars on The Village Club, which has a swimming pool and a greater number of tennis courts, the Harbor Acres courts and beach house are still heavily used. Older people like the resilient clay courts, says Clark, and men can play singles on Saturday mornings. The beach house gets good use as well; 15-20 private parties were held there last summer, including a wedding reception for Mina and Stephen Weiner's son and daughter-in-law. The beach has children's play equipment and the Association has a dock and mooring rights, albeit no launch facilities.

The Association puts out three newsletters per year, publishes a residents' directory and holds an annual dinner at The Village Club. It also acts as an advocate for residents' concerns. When the new owner of the old Tristram Dodge House, directly to the north of Harbor Acres beach, built a dock with a hoist in front of his property that obstructed views from the Harbor Acres beach house, the Association sued the Village of Sands Point, claiming there was inadequate environmental review before permission was given to build the dock. The Association lost and had salt rubbed into its wounds when the owner counter-sued.

The only drawback of life in Harbor Acres, according to Clark, is that, "you can't walk to town."

However, "One of the pleasures of living in Harbor Acres is that you can walk from our beach along the shore past the Park and Preserve all the way to the beach in front of the Payson house [Lands End at Prospect Point]."

CIVIC BETTERMENT

There are others beaches in Sands Point, with the rights to use them often included in the deeds of adjacent and nearby property owners. The Village Hall tries to maintain a voluntary list of such associations. The current list includes the Half Moon Beach Association, which also set up a nature conservancy to protect adjacent wetlands; the Sousa Beach Association; Cornwell's Beach and Cedar Lane Association; and the Harbor Acres Property Owners Association.

The Sands Point Civic Association is still working for the betterment of the village. Some people thought, with good reason, that constructing 24 additional parking spaces in front of the Village Hall would leave that handsome building surrounded by a sea of ugly asphalt. But fortunately, these parking spaces, added in the early '90s to accommodate increased attendance at meetings and other events, were carved from the hillside site without creating an eyesore. Landscaping financed by the Sands Point Civic Association, plus artful lighting, produced an almost park-like appearance. The Association also contributed to the Village ambiance by improving road signage, planting trees and providing a "host of golden daffodils" along village roads.

Horace and Amy Hagedorn are two of Sands Point's best-known philanthropists, admired and appreciated for their generosity and concern. (Courtesy, Horace Hagedorn)

CHARITABLE SUPPORT

Despite the growing number of working mothers, Sands Point residents in the '90s were as heavily involved in community affairs as their counterparts of 50 years ago, with many active in local churches and synagogues and serving on boards and committees of the schools and library. And many have been generous contributors to charity. Some Sands Pointers might have disagreed about The Village Club, zoning, roads and leash laws, but most found common ground in other areas, such as the importance of the Community Chest, the Landmark on Main Street, the Historical Society and other worthy community service endeavors.

LEADERSHIP GIVERS

One couple, Horace and Amy Hagedorn, made community service and philanthropy into nearly full-time jobs. In his business career, Horace parlayed a $1,000 investment in a liquid plant fertilizer into Miracle-Gro, a major garden products company. In 1995, he sold the well-known company to Scotts Lawn Products for $200 million in convertible preferred stock. With his wife Amy, Hagedorn gave his shares of Scotts Lawn Products to the New York Community Trust, which issues grants to non-profit organizations. Since then, The Horace and Amy Hagedorn Fund has made about 275 grants totaling about $1 million annually, many of them to Long

Island recipients. The Hagedorns are especially interested in assisting organizations with headquarters in the area, which makes it easy for them to visit and see their gifts at work. The recipients of their donations have included North Shore University Hospital, Helen Keller National Center, The Family and Children's Association, and the Port Washington Public Library.

Horace Hagedorn's first acquaintance with his present home on Old House Lane occurred when he was married to his first wife, Margaret, and the second floor of their frame house in Harbor Acres was set on fire accidentally and nearly destroyed. With the house unlivable, Horace and Margaret packed up themselves and their children and moved into the Garden City Hotel. Horace recalled: "Six kids in a hotel was just terrible." When he learned that Tom Fraser's waterfront house (c. 1947), at the foot of what is now Old House Lane (just a private dirt road then), would be vacant for the winter, he rented it for six months. Insurance paid for the refurbishing of his fire-blighted home and the family eventually returned to Harbor Acres. Three years later, when the Fraser house was for sale, the Hagedorns bought it and moved back. According to Horace, "Peg didn't like all the trees" around the Harbor Acres house; the home on Old House Lane is more open and has views across Hempstead Harbor and Long Island Sound. Horace married Amy several years after Margaret Hagedorn's death in 1984.

Other members of the Hagedorn family also support charitable endeavors, and all of them are proud of Miracle-Gro Kids, a program they started in 1991 that offers special tutoring, enrichment and guidance to 50 low-income children, and promises full college tuition if they graduate from high school. The family also sponsors a program at a Vermont farm providing farm vacations for underprivileged kids.

Ed and Jeanette Pratt have also done a superb job of giving money away to worthy causes. Ed, the former chairman and chief executive officer of Pfizer, Inc., the pharmaceutical company, and his wife Jeanette, donated $12 million to Long Island University in 1998 to fund new academic, computer and library facilities. The money was split evenly between LIU's three campuses: Southampton, C.W. Post and Brooklyn. (The Pratts' oldest son, Randy, graduated from Post in 1977.) The Pratts have lived in Port Washington and Sands Point for more than 40 years and are strong supporters of local organizations. The couple donated generously to the development of the Landmark on Main Street.

Janet Walsh, founder and chairman of the board of the Long Island Alzheimers Foundation.

Janet Walsh, whose father died of Alzheimer's disease, is Chairman of the Board of the Long Island Alzheimer's Foundation, an organization she founded in 1988. Walsh established the foundation to foster medical research and provide a resource for the community. Her husband Stephen, an investor, is a staunch supporter of Janet's crusade and serves as a member of the LIAF board. Sands Point's Robert Leopold is another board member. The organization, which is headquartered in Port Washington, sponsors educational workshops, a hotline and symposiums for professionals and the public. The Foundation's first fund-raiser was a brunch at Walsh's sprawling French Norman house. Congressman Robert Mrazek was guest of honor.

COMMUNITY DEVELOPMENT

Village board members are involved as private citizens in the greater Port Washington community, as well as serving in official roles. The mayor is an active supporter of the Community Synagogue, Cow Neck Historical Society and Residents for a More Beautiful Port Washington; Kay Ullman, a one-time school board member, is presently an active member of the League of Women Voters since 1968; Ed Adler is a member of the Port Washington Library Foundation. Gene Luntey, former chairman of the board of trustees of Long Island University, was also a Port Washington school board member.

Hundreds of other residents, many more than can be mentioned, devote tremendous time and effort serving on school and library boards, supporting

Sands Point's Patty Anderson (left) and husband Harry (not shown) served for many years on the board of the Family and Children's Association. She is shown in this photo taken in the mid '90s with George W. Frank, Jr., Irma and George Frank, Sr., also of Sands Point. Irma is a past president of the organization. The late George Frank made Hospice Care of Long Island a full-time job after retiring from Gallo Wine and is credited with much of its growth and development. (Courtesy Family and Children's Association)

religious institutions, and assisting non-profit organizations as well as youth activity groups.

For example, Barbara Claire Barker, wife of tennis great Robert Barker, is a singer and dancer who appeared on Broadway and in such "golden age of TV" shows as the Jackie Gleason Show and the Jimmy Durante Show. She has taught tap and jazz dancing in her own school and in adult education courses in Port Washington and Manhasset. A member of the Music Study Club, she sings in the Congregational Church Choir in Manhasset.

The late Beverly Luntey and her husband Eugene have a strong history of community involvement. Bev was past president of the North Shore chapter of the American Association of University Women, a member of the Sands Point Garden Club and a trustee of the Helen Keller Center for the Deaf-Blind. Gene, a member of the Board of Long Island University, can claim 32 years of service to the Village in one capacity or another including, Deputy Mayor. (Courtesy, Village Club of Sands Point)

Sands Point residents are involved in a myriad of community activities. Ruth Feingold of Shorewood Drive (left) and Jacqueline Wood of Port Washington, co-chairpersons of the Music Advisory Council, were honored in 1998 by the Friends of the Port Washington Public Library for their 25 years of service to the Library. Friends' President Nancy Wright is at center. (Courtesy, Port Washington Public Library)

Ruth Feingold, a clarinet player and performer, is also a member of the Music Study Club. She has co-chaired the Port Washington Public Library's Music Advisory Committee, bringing major musical events to the institution for more than 25 years, and scheduled musical programs for the Community Synagogue. Her sons Richard and David are both teachers of music.

Several Sands Point residents have been actively involved in the Family and Children's Association (formerly the Family Services Association) including longtime board members Harry and Patty Anderson, Irma Frank and Carol Wessel, who was most recently chairman of its Board of Trustees.

All of this participation beyond the borders of Sands Point can be explained, perhaps, by Mayor Wurzel's comment, "Port Washington is what makes Sands Point. We live next to a wonderful community, which has so much to offer. I tell real estate agents who are showing Sands Point houses to take people around Port Washington first."

PERENNIAL VULNERABILITY

While forecasters today can better predict storms today than they did 100 ago, it doesn't follow that we can fend off the furies of nature any better, as the weekend of December 11, 1992, amply demonstrated. Howling winds, driving rains and high tides took their toll. A vivid recap, published in a special storm supplement to its newsletter a few days later by The

Sands Point Civic Association, provided details of the events, reporting that "swimming pools, sea walls and patios were wrecked or disappeared." Waterfront properties were hardest hit, and Lighthouse Road, which skirts the shore on Half Moon Bay, was partially washed out by wave action. Half Moon Lane was under four inches of water. Trees toppled, blocking roads. One resident was bruised when a large tree fell on her car as she drove along Middle Neck Road.

Chaos threatened to take over Village Police Headquarters as the phones rang with an overload of questions about power outages and requests for help. False burglar and fire signals went off due to storm-caused electrical failures. Officers on duty were held over when their tours ended and off-duty personnel were called in. Problems were attended to as quickly as storm damage conditions permitted. When normal conditions resumed, the Village found itself with a $48,000 repair bill for Lighthouse Road, which had just been repaved, and sufficient damage to Village property elsewhere to put in a claim for $125,000 to the Federal Emergency Management Association. Damages suffered by individual property owners totaled considerably more.

In October of 1996, Half Moon Lane was hit again when a storm that Sands Point Police Chief John Montalto described as worse than the "nor'easter of 1992, as far as coastal damage," put that road under three feet of water. The Rangi family on Sea Coast Lane found something even more astonishing than sea water in their back yard: the 44-foot racing yacht *Gold Digger*. This veteran of the Newport to Bermuda race had broken loose from its mooring in Rye, New York, sailed itself across Long Island Sound, and beached itself under the Rangi's deck. Fortunately, the frantic owner spotted his $800,000 boat on the property near Sloanes Beach when he was cruising the Sound searching for his missing boat. Mrs. Rangi was glad to see it depart and relieved that her property had escaped more severe hardship. "If the water was a little higher, the boat could have sailed into my house—and it weighs 22,000 pounds," she told the *Port Washington News.*

POLITICAL TURMOIL

Politics—both national and local—affected Sands Pointers in the '90s and was a prime topic of

The October, 1996, hurricane surprised a Sea Coast Lane family by blowing a 44-foot racing sailboat across the sound and up on its beach. The boat's Rhode Island owners were just as astonished to find that it survived the storm in good condition. (Courtesy, the Rangi family)

conversation. Despite the triumph of the short Gulf War with Iraq, the Republican administration of President George Bush gave way to a Democratic administration when Bill Clinton defeated the incumbent in 1992. Although Clinton proved adept at foreign policy, he nearly lost his office over a purely domestic scandal with a White House intern. The House of Representatives voted to impeach him for lying under oath, an offense serious enough to warrant a trial in the Senate. The affair, and the legal and political maneuvering, provoked live television viewing and stimulated cocktail party conversation throughout the winter and spring of 1998. The Senate did not muster the two-thirds majority vote required for removal from office and Clinton continued to lead the nation.

Local political activity wasn't as salacious, but it was of great concern. Nassau County citizens were shocked in 1999 when they learned that Standard and Poor's bond rating of their county—the highest taxed and richest in New York State—had dropped to just above junk bond status. How the long-entrenched Republican administration had managed to do this in a period of unprecedented prosperity was a mystery to most, and residents feared repercussions in the form of higher taxes as the county's power to borrow money dwindled. The voters struck back in November of 1999 by electing enough Democrats to give that party a majority in the county legislature. The state later established a board to oversee the county's fiscal affairs. In contrast to that dreary picture,

Town of North Hempstead Supervisor May Newburger was pleased to announce that the the Town of North Hempstead's bond rating was raised from A3 to A2 in 1999—the first upgrade of the Town's rating in 29 years. Newburger attributed the rating rise to debt reduction and balancing of the budget.

POLICE PROTECTION: LUCK AND ALARMS

Residents who had voted to retain the Sands Point police in 1975, rather than transfer this service to Nassau County, must have congratulated themselves on their good judgment in 1992 when they heard the latest Police Department statistics. The December issue of the *Sands Point Civic Report* announced that the Department handled 2,500 complaints that year, with only two burglaries. The reporter, Sgt. Anthony J. Bordinko, attributed that record to "observant police patrol, excellent alarm systems and some luck, but then luck is often the residue of design." Calls from residents regarding suspicious circumstance "often give us a head start," he remarked.

The man responsible for those good statistics was most likely Chief Michael J. Connolly, who retired in 1995 after 31 years on the Sands Point Police Force. He is credited with expanding police headquarters, implementing the use of new weapons and installing the Law Enforcement Training Network. (He was also first vice president of the Nassau County Municipal Chiefs of Police Association.) The new chief, John Montalto, joined the Sands Point Police in 1968 and was promoted to lieutenant in 1992. Montalto inherited a force of 14 patrol officers, four sergeants and one lieutenant. He holds a masters degree in criminal justice.

The Police Department statistics for 1999 were much the same as 1992. Despite a slight population increase, there were 2,539 complaints filed, with one burglary and 10 attempted burglaries. The total value of property lost or stolen was $96,809. Modern alarm systems and the presence of more patrol cars on the road—two or three at all times—helped reduce crime in Sands Point over the past few years. Ironically, however, Police Commissioner Luntey had three burglaries at his Astor Lane house. "The only time a gun has been fired in anger in Sands Point was at my house. A burglar set off a silent alarm. The police arrived and a youth ran out across the back yard. An officer ordered him to halt and later fired a bullet which creased his back as he ran off." The burglar, who apparently wasn't very smart, went to St. Francis Hospital to have his wound dressed, and was reported to the authorities. When apprehended, he claimed he'd been in the Luntey back yard looking for fishing worms. The only thing taken was a medallion the Luntey's son had won. The culprit was sent up for five years.

"The major crime today is taking automobile radios," Luntey said. "Our police are pledged to enforce Village ordinances, something they don't always like to do. Beach parties pose a problem, especially in Harbor Acres, where youths often claim they have permission of a resident, who is sometimes conveniently out of town on the night of the party." And, he added, "every once in a while someone decides to take a four-wheel drive vehicle and knock down mail boxes."

Enforcing tree ordinances and building codes is a challenge; the police watch to see if any construction is going on and check their permit list to see if the property is on the list. However, they can't be everywhere, and illegal construction does take place. "Some people have so much money they don't care about fines," Luntey observed.

IS THERE ANY SPACE LEFT?

Is there any empty property in Sands Point available for building? In 1992, the Village commissioned Frederick P. Clark Associates, planning, environmental and traffic consultants, to study current conditions. The results, presented to the Village Board in May of 1993, revealed that 23% of the Village's 2,688 acres could be classified as "recreational" or open space. While the number of housing units had remained about the same, the population had increased 7% from 1980 to 1990. About 20% of the residents were senior citizens, some of whom could be expected to sell and relocate.

According to a study by Village Clerk Linda Mitchell and Building Inspector Dennis Davison,

The Sands Point Police Department in 1994: Mayor Wurzel (bottom row third from left); Chief Michael J. Connolly; Deputy Mayor and Police Commissioner Eugene Luntey; and Lt. John Montalto, who replaced Connolly as Chief on the latter's retirement in 1995. (Courtesy, Village Club of Sands Point)

conducted at the behest of the Planning Board chaired by Michael Puntillo, as of March 1, 1999: "89 new homes could possibly be built in Sands Point under current zoning" (one or two acres) on various properties now in private hands. However, it is unlikely that the maximum of 89 new houses would go up in the near future on the land because the sub-dividable acreage is held by 34 separate property owners.

The study did not include the larger property holders: The Village Club, Nassau County, The Industrial Home for the Blind, Sands Point Golf Club,

Snow may have delayed construction, but it didn't stop growth in Sands Point. This new house on Ariel Court went up in the winter of 1999. (Photo by Will Wright)

Union Free School District No. 4, the Village of Sands Point, the Methodist Church and the Community Synagogue. Those properties total 656 acres. Given the worst case scenario—all going bottoms-up at once and forced to sell—no more than 130 houses could be constructed. With admirable foresight, all those properties were zoned for five-acre lots in 1993.

THREATS, RUMORS AND CONTROVERSIES

The potential development of Davids Island, located off New Rochelle in Westchester County directly opposite Sands Point's Half Moon Beach, aroused the concern of residents in the mid-1980s. When the plan for high-rise buildings was defeated, the future of Davids Island slipped from local notice. The Sands Pointers' fears were revived in 1995 by Donald Trump; environmental advocate Marcia Forman announced in the *Sands Point Civic Report*: "Mr. Trump proposes a 45-story Trump Tower plus three 22-story buildings, a heliport, a 1,200 boat marina and, probably in time, a large bridge connecting Davids Island to the mainland." Trump dropped the plan the following year, but Sands Point residents still wonder when another will come along and receive a thumbs-up from Westchester authorities.

Although religious institutions in Sands Point proved themselves good neighbors, dwellers in the vicinity were upset when Won Buddhism of America sought to purchase a residence on Tibbits Lane for a retreat. Where would congregation members and visitors park their cars? Would religious services bring traffic and clog the short but busy street? As Dan Kurshan, who lived nearby, wrote, "The Board should require a complete record of the retreats now maintained by the petitioner in this country and abroad so that affected parties might study their impact on the various communities and help the Board determine whether or not the proposed occupancy would be detrimental to the neighborhood, alter its essential character or tend to depreciate property value." Perhaps sensing that Sands Point was not putting out the welcome mat, the property owners withdrew their application for a zoning change and the Buddhists decided to look elsewhere.

Across Hempstead Harbor from Sands Point, residents of the Village of Sea Cliff were likewise

Four generations, representing two Sands Point families, posed for this photo in 1982. Shown are (from left): Katherine Forman, who married a distant cousin (her parents, Mr. and Mrs. Alexander Forman, moved to Sands Point around 1922); her granddaughter Karli Forman Hagedorn (Mrs. James); Karli's mother Marcia Forman (Mrs. Jay); and fourth generation Alexandra and Christopher. Their father, James Hagedorn, who grew up in the Village (as did his wife), is the son of Horace Hagedorn, a longtime Sands Point resident, and his first wife Margaret. (Photo by Jay Forman)

disturbed when they heard the announcement that a new ferry service, aimed specifically at taking passengers across Long Island Sound to Foxwoods Casino Resort near New London, Connecticut, was starting operations in May, 2000. The passenger ferries were scheduled to depart from a Glen Cove marina (located just south of Sea Cliff, across the bay from Sands Point). Many residents on Sands Point's eastern shore were concerned as well. While they couldn't complain, as Sea Cliff residents did, of the threat of traffic tie-ups caused by gamblers and travelers on excursions, they objected on a different basis. Several small boat sailors and rowers, such as Monika Dorman and Amy Hagedorn, argued that the big, fast boats would create large wakes and endanger smaller vessels. A different view was stated by veteran yachtsman Ed du Moulin, a former Knickerbocker Yacht Club Commodore, who pointed out that the schedule of early morning and early evening ferry sailings would not interfere with small boat sailing and racing.

Another change, long urged by the local fire department, is the pending assignment of house numbers to Sands Point residences. For years, letters addressed only to a street name had found their way to the right house without too much difficulty. But that wasn't always the case with some first-time guests who would wander about, looking for the homes of their hosts. More serious were situations when the police, fire and emergency services attempted to locate people who needed help and had trouble finding the correct home. In 1997, the Board of Trustees adopted Local Law No. 11 mandating the assignment of address numbers for every property in the Village. The Village Police Department will be able to enroll in the Enhanced 911 program, a system that enables law enforcement personnel to read the exact address of the caller and thus deliver assistance in an expedient manner.

Schreiber High School senior Lucas Hanft of Harbor Acres was honored to be named a finalist in the highly prestigious Intel Science Talent Search (formerly Westinghouse). He conducted research in the area of social science. (Photo by Jackie Pierangelo, Port Washington News)

Original mathematics research on a superior level earned Kristin Kovner, a Schreiber High School senior, the coveted award of finalist in the Intel Science Talent Search. She is the daughter of Amy and Jeffrey Kovner, a former Village Planning Board member. (Photo by Jackie Pierangelo, Port Washington News)

SANDS POINT STUDENTS SHINE!

Most Sands Point residents tout the excellence of the Port Washington public school system. In 1999 they had substantial proof to back their pride when nine seniors were named semifinalists in the Intel Science Talent Search (formerly the Westinghouse). This remarkable achievement was unparalleled, for Port Washington not only had a large number of winners, but the total of nine was the greatest number of students from one school—more than any other in the country. Two of the winners from Sands Point, Kristin Kovner, daughter of Jeffrey and Amy Kovner, and Lucas Hanft, son of Flora and Adam Hanft, were later named as finalists. Kristin was recognized for her math research program and Lucas for his investigation in the area of social science. (Both were bound for Yale University.) All semifinalists won a $1,000 prize; the finalists received a $5,000 scholarship, laptop computer and an expense-paid trip to Washington, DC, for the awards ceremony. Schreiber High School received $1,000 awards for each semifinalists. The elated high school principal, Dr. Sidney Barish, pronounced, "Every one of the semifinalists, as well as the other students in the research program, deserve our highest esteem and admiration...it puts Schreiber High School on the national map and spills over to all of us." Not long after, Schreiber had even more to be proud about; Port Washington teen, Viviana Risca, was named an Intel National Finalist.

OUR OWN OLYMPIAN

The Intel scholars weren't the first young Sands Pointers to achieve national recognition. Twenty-one year-old Carrie Sheinberg made it all the way to Norway as a member of the U.S. Women's Olympic Ski Team. Since skiing began to be taken seriously by Long Islanders in the late 1930s, athletic residents have been trekking to the mountains. Carrie's parents, Jill and Richard Sheinberg, took skiing more seriously than most and sent her off to the Stratton Mountain, Vermont, ski school when she was in 10th grade. She qualified for the 1994 winter Olympics with a 15th place finish in a World Cup slalom in Spain and succeeded in keeping most of Port Washington glued to the TV screen for the women's slalom event in Lillehammer. She finished 18th of the 55 who started the race (and the 28 who finished it) and was pleased with her accomplishment. "The Olympics are everybody's dream," Sheinberg was quoted by *Newsday* as saying. "They aren't everybody's goal." Carrie had achieved her goal and seemed to have enjoyed getting there. Today, she lives in Salt Lake City where she writes and skis in the Rockies.

An even younger Sands Point athelete, Sarah Levine, 10-year-old daughter of Laurie and Dennis Levine, a fifth-grader at the Manorhaven School,

Sands Point's Carrie Sheinberg, wearing her cow print baseball cap, was a member of the U.S. Women's Olympic Ski Team in 1994. (Courtesy, Port Washington News)

won the 1997 All-Around Individual Gymnastic Championship of the Long Island Independent Gymnastics League. The League includes girls from 27 Long Island towns, with the All-Around Individuial Championship awarded to the gymnast earning the highest cummulative point score for the four individual events. Her parents told the *Port Washington News*, "Sarah is extremely dedicated and trains very hard."

SANDS POINT ON THE EDGE OF THE NEW MILLENNIUM

There is a significant difference in the number of Sands Point children attending public school today compared with 20 years ago, according to Eleanor Grogan, who has three children in the Port Washington schools and takes advantage of the many programs and services the system offers. Parents who can well afford to send their children to private schools have chosen the public ones because of the fine reputation of the Port Washington school district, especially in the elementary grades. "Our elementary schools are outstanding," Grogan proudly announced. Parents have also recognized that their children enjoy interacting with the neighborhood kids, playing with one another as well as attending school together. And they appreciate the fact that attending the public schools presents opportunities for their children to broaden their circle of friends within the local district boundary.

Grogan and her husband Bob, residents since 1989, chose Sands Point because he liked the fast train

commute. And both of them desired the Village's tranquility. However, Eleanor says she does not appreciate the factor that creates this serenity, which is Sands Point's distance from schools, the library and major recreational facilities. "'Hauling' is the bane of the Sands Point mother's existence," she commented. Last year, she put 16,000 miles on her car, mostly taking care of household errands and making sure her children got where they were supposed to go. One day alone she clocked 177 miles. She found some relief as each child reached about age 12, the point when she felt comfortable using taxi cabs as needed, thanks to Port Washington's reliable taxi service. Other merchants and local services are equally helpful and reliable. "Where else could you call up the movie theater or a pizza parlor and ask, 'Is Robbie Grogan there?'" (Most times, she has received an informed response.) Local merchants also support many community endeavors, which is another reason why Grogan makes it a practice to support local merchants by doing her shopping in Port Washington when possible.

Recent transitions in lifestyle go beyond the trends of a greater percentage of children in the public schools and the construction of larger homes on the properties. Mayor Wurzel is worried that "fewer people respect the history of the Village and its rural atmosphere. They tear down perfectly good houses to put up huge houses, some of them unattractive." He also expressed concern about the Village environment: "There's more littering and people don't clean up in front of their fences. I'd like to see the Civic

Remembrance of things past. Though showing some wear, the medieval towers and fence built in 1916 to guard the long-demolished Belmont Towers (later called the Hearst Castle), still stand watch along the edge of Lighthouse Road, as shown in this 1999 picture. (Photo by Will Wright)

Association spearhead a clean-up campaign."

Formal home entertaining is rapidly vanishing as Sands Point residents generally take guests to The Village Club or serve an informal buffet or barbecue at home. Wally Bellman, a cook and waitress who has spent close to 40 years assisting at Sands Point parties, has observed the changes, most of which she doesn't like. "All our old customers have moved away. There is a completely different crowd of people in Sands Point—young people who don't know how to cook." Earlier generations had sit-down dinners, according to Mrs. Bellman; this generation it's all catered buffets. It's a far cry from what it was like with customers such as Stella Ketchum, whose "pots and pans…were so clean they looked like they had just come from the store," and who owned a vast collection of silver. "A museum didn't have the silver she did, and she used every piece," Bellman recalled, at the same time admitting that pressures on two-career households, greater parenting obligations and the need to drive kids to so many lessons necessitates a less formal lifestyle.

The Village hosted a 100th birthday party in 1997 for former Mayor George Bergman, and one at another time for former Mayor Carlo Salvador. Shown (left to right) are former Board Member Marjorie Weinstein and her husband Jerry, a former mayor; Elaine and Leonard Wurzel; Bergman; "Skip" and Dick Wall; and Helen and Bill Porth. (Courtesy, Elaine Wurzel)

Village Clerk Linda Mitchell shows longtime resident Herman Tietz plans for Village Club improvements at a 1999 Board Meeting. (Photo by Will Wright)

Population growth and a shift in demographics have forced changes in Village government as well. Dan Scheyer, who has spent a great deal of time serving the Village (nine years on the Zoning Board and six on the Village Board) contended, "The Village maintains its status because it is hard-nosed [with] tough zoning, fairly administered. If you don't have sound zoning you're going to have a place that looks like Great Neck." (Some areas of Great Neck are unincorporated, and not within the jurisdiction of any village. This has led to spot zoning and "mansionization" in several sections of that peninsula.)

Scheyer also warned of potential water problems, such as saltwater intrusion, which can be avoided if action is taken. "We have an aging infrastructure," he explained; "we have to keep a balance between water in the ground and saltwater." It is a safe bet to say that Sands Point residents would object vigorously to the proposed addition of a water tower in their backyard. However, the Village will have to add more storage if people continue to use much more water, Scheyer predicted, especially if there is a repeat of the summer of 1999 when there was "more non-compliance with watering restrictions" than ever before. An additional facility to store water is under study.

Trustee Adler, who has spent nine years as Building Commissioner, supervised the rewriting and simplification of Building Department documents. He started in 1991 by sending a personal letter and questionnaire to every resident who completed a building project asking, "Could you tell me about

The Sands Point Village Board in 1999: (standing) Daniel Scheyer, Katharine Ullman, Edward A. K. Adler; (seated) Mayor Leonard Wurzel and Deputy Mayor Eugene Luntey. Luntey, also the Police Commissioner, noted that the burglary rate in Sands Point went down. (Courtesy, Inc. Village of Sands Point)

your experiences?" Acting on their responses, in 1996 he announced: "We went to a full-time building inspector instead of several part-time inspectors. We wanted to make the (permit) process as easy as possible to get through…Little by little, we turned around the perception of the Building Department." The Village also put a violation system into place that is, according to Adler, "making a more active attempt to pay attention to what's going on, to ride around and look."

There are many positive elements in the transformation of the Village over the last decade or so. Dan Scheyer, who has lived here with his wife Audrey since 1975, complimented the Village for being "much more open than it used to be. We have a more diverse population. People from many different ethnic groups have been welcomed." Eleanor Grogan credited

Saul Ferdman and singer Virginia Steibel look like they enjoyed themselves as they leave the 1998 Village Club holiday party. (Courtesy, Village Club of Sands Point)

increased attendance at public schools for enriching the lives of Sands Point's children and The Village Club for acting as a magnet, providing excellent facilities and drawing Sands Points residents together. Fred Jaroslow, Chairman of the Residents' Club Commission, also praised The Village Club, naming it the decade's major agent for change and maintaining that the Club has "brought neighbors together who never knew each other, provided a valuable recreation facility for minimal cost and improved the resale value of Sands Point houses."

Elaine and Mayor Leonard Wurzel welcomed the 21st Century on December 31, 1999 at, as might be expected, The Village Club party. They are standing in front of the stairway leading to the second-floor guest rooms. (Courtesy, Village Club of Sands Point)

Yes, The Village Club has brought change to Sands Point. So have many factors over the past centuries—wars and alliances, prosperity and depression, developments in transportation and communication, industrial progress, cultural diversity. The peninsula that once upon a time was a summer camp for native Americans evolved from cow pasture to farm country, from an area of relatively modest country homes for city dwellers to great estates, from a Gatsby-era playground to a post-World War II bulwark of business managers and professionals. At the edge of the new millennium, it is home to a diverse cross-section of American achievers in business, the arts and professions of the 21st century. While old money doesn't always approve of new money—an old story—and jet skiers off Plum Point have brought shudders to the hearts of yachtsmen, Sands Point

The Methodist Church on Middle Neck Road is a 20th Century Sands Point Landmark. After many years in Port Washington, the congregation moved to Sands Point, erecting a new and larger building which was dedicated in 1969. The current pastor is Edward C. Horne. (Photo by Will Wright)

to please the eye in the verdant landscape of woods, sea and sand.

Whether longtime residents or newcomers, preservationists or renovationists, community activists or evaders of the limelight, most Sands Pointers today value their elegantly rustic way of life as passionately as their counterparts of earlier times did, and most applaud the Village government's efforts to preserve that lifestyle for future generations.

continues to be a community of exceptional vigor, considerable charm, strong opinions and active participation in community affairs, both within Sands Point's borders and beyond. The architecturally new often reflects traditions of the past, and despite the disappearance of much open space, there is still plenty

Windsurfing is a popular sport with Sands Point youth. Max Hazan, son of Mr. and Mrs. Ira Hazan, is shown surfing off the beach at the family home on Plum Point. (Photo by Jerry Morea)

BIBLIOGRAPHY

Abramsom, Rudy, *Spanning the Century: The Life of W. Averill Harriman,* New York: William Morrow & Co., 1992.

The American Heritage Dictionary of American History, New York: Henry Holt & Co., 1998.

American National Biography, American Council of Learning Societies, New York: Oxford University Press, 1999.

Amory, Cleveland, *Who Killed Society?,* New York: Harper & Brothers, 1960.

Atlas of Long Island, New York: Beers & Comstock, 1879.

Atlas of Long Island, New York: Beers & Comstock, 1906.

Atlas of Long Island, New York: Belcher and Hyde, 1914.

Auchincloss, Louis, *The Vanderbilt Era,* New York: Charles Scribner and Sons, 1989.

Austin, David B., "The Austin Brothers Went West," *Long Island Forum,* 1941.

Backus, Dana Converse and his daughters, *Christmas 1973: Memories of Louise Laidlaw Backus,* self-published.

Bahn, Jacqueline, and Williams, George L., *Sketchbook of Historic Houses,* Cow Neck Peninsula Historical Society, 1982.

Bahn, Jacqueline K., "'Gentleman' Samuel Sands," *Cow Neck Peninsula Historical Society Journal,* 1984.

Bahn, Jacqueline K., "The World of Cato Sands," *Cow Neck Peninsula Historical Society Journal,* 1980.

Bailey, Paul, ed., *Long Island: Nassau & Suffolk,* Lewis Historical Publishing Co., 3 Vols., 1949.

Barber, John W. and Howe, Henry, *Historical Collections State of New York,* S. Tuttle, NY 1892

Berg, A. Scott, *Lindbergh,* New York: G. P. Putnam and Sons, 1998.

Bernstein, Lawrence, *As Thousands Cheer: The Life of Irving Berlin,* New York: Viking, 1990.

Bolte, Lora O'Reilly, *A Family History,* Jacksonville: self-published, 1996.

Bowen, Constance Gerrodette, "Soldiers of the American Revolution, Patriots and Founders of Our Country Interred in the Sands Family Burying Ground," unpublished paper, 1962; revised 1967. Copy at Cow Neck Peninsula Historical Society.

Brands, H. W., *The Reckless Decade: America in the 1890s,* New York: St. Martins Press, 1995.

Brown, Sr., Albert, "Memories of Port Washington," *Cow Neck Peninsula Historical Society Journal,* 1988.

Cagney, W. Oakley, *Long Island, Long Ago,* New York: Long Island Press, 1970.

Chapman, A. Wright, *Aron and Mary Wright,* New York: Charles Francis Press, 1942.

Christ Church, The First 150 Years, Manhasset: Christ Church, 1952.

"The Christmas Blizzard of 1811," *Long Island Forum,* 1942.

Coffey, Frank, and Layden, Joseph, *America on Wheels,* Los Angeles: R. R. Donnelley & Sons, 1996.

The Columbia Encyclopedia, Fifth Edition, New York: Columbia University Press, 1993.

Community Synagogue, *25th Anniversary Journal,* Sands Point, 1977.

Cornell, Thomas C., *Adam and Anne Mott: Their Ancestors and their Descendants,* Yonkers: privately printed, 1890.

Cornwall, Kenneth, "Cornwallton," *Cow Neck Peninsula Historical Society Journal,* October, 1976.

Davis, John H., *The Guggenheims: An American Epic,* New York: SPI Books/Shapolsky Publishers, Inc., l994.

Davis, Kenneth C., *Don't Know Much About History,* New York: Crown Publishers, 1990.

Davis, Kenneth C., *Don't Know Much About the Civil War,* New York: Morrow, 1996.

Dayton, Fred Irving, *Steamboat Days,* New York: Frederick A. Stokes Co., 1925.

Dearing, Mary R., *Veterans in Politics,* Louisiana State University Press, 1952.

Dictionary of American Biography, New York: Scribners, 1936.

Dietz, Howard, *Dancing in the Dark: An Autobiography,* New York: New York Times Book Co., 1974.

"Disasters on Long Island Sound," *Magazine of American History,* February, 1893.

Faragher, John Mack, general editor, *The American Heritage Dictionary of American History,* New York: Henry Holt & Co., 1998.

Felsenthal, Carol, *Alice Roosevelt Longworth,* New York: G. P. Putnam's Sons, 1988.

"The Flower Hill Canning Company," *Cow Neck Historical Society Journal,* 1976.

Fraser, Peter, "The Most Exclusive Yacht Club on Cow Neck," *Cow Neck Peninsula Historical Society Journal,* 1984.

Gandt, Robert L., *China Clipper: The Age of the Great Flying Boats,* Annapolis: Naval Institute Press, 1991.

Garraty, John A., *The American Nation,* Fifth Edition, New York: Harper & Row, 1983.

Gates, Arnold, "Nassau County and the Civil War," *Nassau County Historical Society Journal*, Winter, 1966.

Gates, John D., *The Astor Family*, Garden City: Doubleday and Co., 1981.

Graf, Jr., George, *A Centennial History of the Manhasset Bay Yacht Club*, Manhasset Bay Yacht Club, Port Washington, 1991.

Haller, Margaret, "Main Street, Port Washington-1914," *Journal of Long Island History*, Vol. 5., No 2. Spring, 1965.

Hanaford, Phebe A., *Daughters of America or Women of the Century*, Augusta, Me.: True and Company, c. 1900.

Hicks, Henry C., ed., *Records of the Towns of North and South Hempstead*, Vols. I-VIII, Long Island, NY, 1896.

History of New York State, New York Historical Society, Vol. I, 1935.

History of Sachem Tackapusha and Long Island Indians, Town of North Hempstead, 1976.

Holbrook, Stewart H., *The Age of the Moguls*, Garden City: Doubleday, 1956.

Homan, John Gilbert, "Civil War Recollections," *Long Island Forum*, May, 1978.

Kent, Joan Gay, "Cow Neck History Series," *Port Washington News*, 1995, 1996, 1997, 1998.

Lassner, Robert George, "Noah Mason and Sands Point Lighthouse," *Long Island Forum*, January, 1982.

Lewis, Alfred Allan, *Man of the World*, New York: Bobbs-Merrill, 1978.

Luke, Dr. Myron H., and Venables, Rover W., *Long Island in the American Revolution*, Albany: NYS American Revolution Bicentennial Commission, 1976.

Luke, Dr. Myron H., *Vignettes of Hempstead Town: 1643-1800*, Hempstead: Long Island Studies Institute, Hofstra University, 1993.

Mackay, Robert B.; Baker, Anthony; and Traynor, Carol A., *Long Island Country Houses and Their Architects, l860-1940*, New York: Society for the Preservation of Long Island Antiquities, 1997.

Manetti, Arnold E., *History of Sands Point Golf Club*, Sands Point, c. 1970.

Manhasset Bay Yacht Club Yearbooks, Port Washington, 1903, 1911, 1928-29.

Manhasset Community Liaison Committee, *The First 300 Years*, Manhasset, 1980.

McFetridge, Ellen, "The Barn," *Cow Neck Peninsula Historical Society Journal*, October, 1978.

McGurrin, James, *Bourke Cockran: A Free Lance in American Politics*, New York: Charles Scribner's Sons, 1948.

Meinig, D. W., *The Shaping of America, Vol. 1*, New Haven: Yale University Press, 1988.

Memories of Dana Converse Backus, 1907-1989, by his daughters, self-published.

Merriman, Charlotte, *Tales of Sint Sink*, Port Washington: Port Washington Junior High School, 1935.

Meyer, Sylvia, "Travel To and From Port Washington," *Nassau County Historical Society Journal*, Fall-Winter 1964-5.

Milburn, Frank, *Polo, The Emperor of Games*, New York: Alfred A. Knopf, 1994.

Milton Hopkins, "The Cornwall Cemetery," *Cow Neck Peninsula Historical Society Journal*, Port Washington, 1967.

Moger, Roy W., *Roslyn, Then and Now*, Roslyn: The Bryant Library, 1992.

Morrison, Samuel Eliot, and Commager, Henry Steele, *The Growth of the American Republic*, Vol. 2, New York: Oxford University Press, 1942.

Munsell, W.W., *History of Queens County*, New York, 1882.

Newsday, *Long Island Our Story*, Melville, NY, Newsday, 1999.

O'Shea, John, *History of the Town of North Hempstead*, Manhasset: Town of North Hempstead, 1982.

Onderdonk, Jr., Henry, *Queens County in Olden Times*, Jamaica: Charles Welling, 1865.

Onderdonk, Jr., Henry, *Revolutionary Incidents in Queens County*, New York: Levitt, Trow and Co., 1846.

Overton, Jacqueline, *Long Island's Story*, Garden City: Doubleday Doran & Co., 1932.

Paine, Ralph D., *The First Yale Unit: A Story of Naval Aviation 1916-1919, Vol. I*, New York: The Riverside Press, 1925.

Pegram, Thomas, *Battling Demon Rum*, Chicago: Ivan R. Dee, 1998.

Pennypacker, Morton, *General Washington's Spies*, The Long Island Historical Society, 1939.

Portrait and Biographical Record of Queens County, New York: Chapman Publishing Co., 1896.

Renehan, Jr., Edward J., *The Lion's Pride: Theodore Roosevelt and His Family in Peace and War*, New York: Oxford University Press, 1998.

Sands Point Civic Association, *Sands Point Civic Association Newsletter*, 1980-1999.

Sands Point Civic Association, *Sands Point*, 1979.

Schneider, Dorothy and Carl J., *American Women in the Progressive Era*, New York: Facts on File, 1993.

Schroeder, Rita, "A Cultural Geography of Long Island's 'Gold Coast,'" *Long Island Forum*, Summer, 1993.

Schultz, Bernice, "Colonial Hempstead," *The Review-Star Press*, 1937.

Seyfried, Vincent F., *Long Island Rail Road: A Comprehensive History, Part II*, New York: Expert Printing Co., 1979.

Shodell, Elly, *Cross Currents*, Port Washington Public Library, 1993.

Shodell, Elly, *In the Service*, Port Washington Public Library, 1991.

Shodell, Elly, *Particles of the Past*, Port Washington Public Library 1985.

Smith, Sally Bedell, *Reflected Glory: The Life of Pamela Churchill Harriman*, New York: Simon & Schuster, 1996.

Smits, Edward J., *Nassau, Suburbia, USA: The First Seventy-Five Years of Nassau County*, Friends of Nassau County Museum, 1974.

Strong, John A., *The Algonquian People of Long Island from Earliest Times to 1700*, Interlaken: Empire State Books, 1997.

Thompson, Benjamin F., *History of Long Island, Third Edition* (c. 1849), reprinted Port Washington: Ira. J. Friedman, Inc., 1962.

Vahey, Mary Feeney, *A Hidden History: Slavery, Abolition, and the Underground Railroad in Cow Neck and on Long Island*, Port Washington: Cow Neck Peninsula Historical Society, 1998.

Wanzor, Jr., Leonard, *Patriots of the North Shore*, self-published, 1906.

Warren, Mary V., "The Gates Rights Map," *Cow Neck Peninsula Historical Society Journal*, Port Washington, October, 1976.

Webster's American Biographies, Springfield: G. C. Merriam, 1974.

Williams, George L., *The Mill Pond*, Port Washington: Cow Neck Peninsula Historical Society, 1979.

Williams, George L., *Old Mitchell Farms*, Port Washington: Cow Neck Peninsula Historical Society, 1986.

Williams, George L., "Bayview Colony," *Cow Neck Peninsula Historical Society Journal*, Port Washington, NY, 1999.

Wilson, Rufus Rockwell, *Historic Long Island*, Bekeley: The Berkeley Press, 1902.

World War II and the Homefront [collected letters], Port Washington: Cow Neck Peninsula Historical Society, 1995.

"A Working Farm in North Hempstead in the 18th Century," *Cow Neck Peninsula Historical Society Journal*, NY, 1976.

INTERVIEWS BY JOAN GAY KENT, 1999-2000

Edward A. K. Adler
Wally Bellman
Robert Bernhard
Sandra Cardiello
Judith Clark
Marcia and Jay Forman
Fay and Richard Fraser
Peter Fraser
Marla Kaplan-Freeman
Myra Gamell
Marian and Edmund Goodman
Eleanor Grogan
Amy and Horace Hagedorn
Rev. Edward Horne
Fred Jaroslow
Edie Katz
Harvey Levine
Beverly Luntey
Gene Luntey
Dan Scheyer
Bruce Shroyer
Vera Tietz
Katharine Ullman
Elaine Wurzel
Leonard Wurzel

ORAL HISTORY TRANSCRIPTIONS

George Bergman - Port Washington Public Library, 1994

Gertrude Crampton Nicoll - Port Washington Public Library, 1983

Jack and Margaret Floherty - Cow Neck Peninsula Historical Society, 1964

Theodore Lapham - Port Washington Public Library, 1982

Mahoney brothers - Port Washington Public Library, 1983

Pansy Schenck- Village of Sands Point, 1985

Emily Ullman - Port Washington Public Library, 1991

Richard Zausner - Port Washington Public Library, 1996

INTERNET

Newsday Internet Library - www.newsday.com

Netscape Internet Encyclopedia

New York Times - www.nytimes.com

Pan Am Flying Boat Photo Archive, Daniel J. Grossman, Atlanta, 1999

Sands Family, Larry & Kathy McCurdy, East Lansing, Michigan, 1998

NEWSPAPER FILES ON MICROFILM OR PAPER

Brooklyn Eagle, New York State Library, Albany

The Port Washington Mail, Port Washington Public Library

Port Washington News, Port Washington Public Library

Port Washington Sentinel, Port Washington Public Library

Plain Talk, Port Washington Public Library

Roslyn News, Bryant Library

VILLAGE OF SANDS POINT FILES

Code of the Village of Sands Point, 1999

Draft Environmental Impact Statement, Village Club of Sands Point, Proposed Master Plan - 1998

Intensive Level Survey, Revised Edition, Historic Landmarks Preservation Commission, Inc., Village of Sands Point, 1998

Landmark Designation applications

Minutes of Sands Point Village Board

Sands Point Report, 1989 to 1999

Sands Point Police Blotter, 1928-1930

75th Anniversary album of newsclips, 1903-1985

DOCUMENT FILES

Civil War Draft Lists, Town of North Hempstead, Bryant Library, Roslyn

Cornwall family papers, Cow Neck Peninsula Historical Society

Cornwall family genealogy, Cow Neck Peninsula Historical Society

Elijah Ward Post, GAR [Grand Army of the Republic] Minutes, Bryant Library, Roslyn

Home Guard Enrollment Papers, Port Washington Public Library

Mott family genealogy, Cow Neck Peninsula Historical Society

Sands family genealogy, Cow Neck Peninsula Historical Society

Sands family papers, Cow Neck Peninsula Historical Society

Village Welfare Society, Port Washington Public Library

Willets family genealogy, Cow Neck Peninsula Historical Society

Wysong Document Collection, Port Washington Public Library

WHO WAS WHO

MAYORS
INC. VILLAGE OF SANDS POINT (1910-2000)

1910	James Lees Laidlaw*
1919	Howard Thayer Kingsbury*
1927	Alfred Valentine Fraser
1941	Henry Eagle
1940	Clifton Thompson
1947	Seth Thayer
1951	John Englis
1953	George S. Bergman
1957	Dr. George F. Lindig
1959	Carlo F. Salvador
1961	Roy C. Olson
1965	David S. Kane
1968	Alfred Smits
1971	Jerome J. Weinstein
1971	Roy C. Olson
1982	Edward N. Madison
1986	Leonard Wurzel

* President designation was subsequently changed to Mayor.

CHIEFS OF POLICE
INC. VILLAGE OF SANDS POINT (1928-2000)

1928	William Francis Borer**
1941	Robert E. Rumens
1959	Peter M. Horr
1965	John P. Laskewsky
1966	John B. Bailey
1977	Eric G. Jude
1983	Michael J. Connolly
1995	John M. Montalto

** Although the Village employed its own policeman as early as 1923, the position of Chief was not established until 1928, when there were enough patrolmen to warrant the position.

VILLAGE CLERKS

Harry Thornbury, Jr. * . . .	— 1963
Phillip G. Lewert	1963 - 1974
Evan Stephens	1974 - 1986
Margaret C.Timm	1986 - 1993
Linda H. Mitchell	1993 - present
Sarah S. Cocks	
Acting Deputy Clerk	1942 - 1952
Deputy Clerk	1953 - 1972

* Volunteer

(Note: At one time, the position of Village Clerk was held by volunteers, often Village Board Members, or the work fell under other job titles. As Sands Point grew and responsibilities mounted, professionals were employed as full-time village clerks.)

PRESIDENTS
SANDS POINT CIVIC ASSOCIATION (1971-2000)

1971	Clarence Fried
1972	Earl Kirmser, Sr.
1976	Bruce Shroyer
1980	Alan Ades
1982	Eleanor Kurz
1986	Edward Adler
1990	Richard Sirow
1994	Marc Silbert
1997	Alyson Adler Green
2000	Phillip Wachtler

PRESIDENTS
SANDS POINT GARDEN CLUB (1950-2000)

Mrs. George (Mary) Schirer
Mrs. Henry A. (Charity) Alker
Mrs. Louis (Hannah) Rabinowitz
Mrs. John B. (Marietta)Wilde
Mrs. Glen (Hazel) MacNary
Mrs. William J. (Betty) Haude
Mrs. M. Mark (Lorraine) Sulkes
Mrs. Thomas B. (Collie) McLaughlin
Mrs. Joseph (Madelaine) Bellavia
Mrs. George (Irma) Frank
Mrs. Gloyd M. (Alvina) Wiles
Mrs. William (Carol) Stoddard
Mrs. Nicholas (Helen) Bachko
Mrs. Theodore (Virginia) Klump
Mrs. John (Terry) Creem
Mrs. Harry B. (Patty) Anderson, Jr.
Mrs. Thomas (Margaret) Stacey
Mrs. Frank (Mella) Ioppolo
Mrs. John (Annette) Stokvis
Mrs. Eugene (Estelle) Farro
Mrs. George (Joanne) Bundschuh
Mrs. Stanley (Edie) Katz
Mrs. Louis (Virginia) Hoynes

PRESIDENTS
HARBOR ACRES PROPERTY OWNERS ASSOCIATION (1952-2000)

1952	Paul MacMillan
1954	Edward Smith
1955	Harry Downs
1956	Walter G. Schalitz
1958	Henry Harder
1959	Frank Keller
1960	Stanley Hyde
1962	Reginald Snyder
1963	Robert Coors & Reginald Snyder
1964	Norton Leslie
1965	Norman McCarthy
1966	Tom Pepitone
1967	Bill Maloney
1968	Tom Buonascra
1969	Gerard Tully
1970	William Tavoulareas
1971	Jack Bond
1972	Stephen Weiner
1973	Felix Zaremba
1974	Donald Capobianco

1975   Jack Van Name
1976   Alan Sackman
1977   Beverly Tuttleman
1978   Janesta Marlin
1979   Gerard Tully
1980   David Deutsch
1981   Richard Albert
1983   Ed Conte
1984   Leo Ullman
1985   Michael Zenobio
1987   Alan Sibigtroth
1988   Steven Zalben
1990   Diane Kasselman
1992   Michael Zenobio
1993   Lynn Najman
1996   Steven Zalben
1997   Earl Kirmser, Jr.
1998   Judith Clark

SANDS POINT LIGHTHOUSE

Sketch by Anne Marie Colton. (Courtesy, Cow Neck Historical Society)

DESIGNATED HISTORIC LANDMARKS, INC. VILLAGE OF SANDS POINT

Name	Address	Date Constructed	Year Listed
Sands-Nostrand House	185 Sands Point Road	c. 1729	1988
Cornwall House	50 Cornwall Lane	c. 1691	1988
Cockran Gatehouse	Port Washington Boulevard	1907	1988
Sands Burying Ground	off Sands Point Road	c. 1700	1988
John Philip Sousa House	14 Hicks Lane	1907	1991
Sands-Hewlett-Tibbits House	210 Sands Point Road	c. 1695	1992
Sands Point Light House	Sands Light Road	1809	1992
Hazeldean Manor (Laidlaw)	Sands Point & Middle Neck Roads	1905	1995

INDEX

ABOUT THE AUTHOR

Joan Gay Kent is the historian for the Town of North Hempstead, a member of the Town Landmarks Preservation Commission, president of the Cow Neck Peninsula Historical Society, past president of the Board of the Port Washington Public Library, and past chairman of the Historic Landmarks Preservation Commission of the Incorporated Village of Sands Point.

A former weekly newspaper and business magazine editor and an award-winning advertising copywriter, Mrs. Kent has written many articles on local history. She is a lifelong resident of the North Shore (30 years in Sands Point), a member of an old Long Island family and a direct descendant of the first woman driver in Roslyn. She currently lives in Port Washington, NY.

Designed by Smallkaps Associates, Inc., Port Washington, NY
Printed by Finer Touch Printing Corp., Port Washington, NY